CiTY·SMaRT™
GUIDEBOOK

Minneapolis
St. Paul

by Rick Nelson

*SURE IT'S COLD, BUT
AT LEAST THERE'S A LOT
OF SNOW.
~~THIS~~ THESE ARE GREAT
CITIES. PERHAPS
THIS CAN HELP
YOU DIG THEM
MORE.*

*Kyle &
Dawn
Christmas
'97*

John Muir Publications
Santa Fe, New Mexico

Acknowledgments

Thanks to my parents, Judy and Don, for encouraging and facilitating my curiosity of—and affection for—the Twin Cities. And a special thanks to David Carr and Terry Fiedler, two gifted editors who each took a leap of faith with an inexperienced writer.

ABOUT THE AUTHOR

Rick Nelson was born and raised in suburban Minneapolis and lives in the city's Uptown neighborhood. A graduate of the University of Minnesota, he is a contributing writer to the *Twin Cities Reader*, a frequent contributor to *Corporate Report Minnesota*, and the editor of *Q Monthly*.

John Muir Publications, P. O. Box 613, Santa Fe, New Mexico 87504

Copyright © 1997 by John Muir Publications
Cover and maps © 1997 by John Muir Publications
All rights reserved.

First edition. First printing March 1997.
Printed in the United States of America.

ISBN 1-56261-301-4
ISSN 1088-9310

Editors: Kristin Shahane, Dianna Delling, Elizabeth Wolf
Design: Janine Lehmann
Graphics Coordinators: Joanne Jakub, Jane Susan MacCarter
Production: Janine Lehmann, Nikki Rooker
Cover Design: Suzanne Rush
Cover photo: Capitol Quadriga Statuary by Marc Caryl
Back cover photo: Both images courtesy of GMCVA
Maps: White Hart Design
Typesetter: Paula Eastwood Design
Printer: Publishers Press

Images credited GMCA are provided courtesy of the Greater Minneapolis
Convention and Visitors Association.
Images credited SPCVB are provided courtesy of the St. Paul Convention and
Visitors Bureau.

Distributed to the book trade by
Publishers Group West
Emeryville, California

CONTENTS

Appendix: City•Smart Basics   215

MAP CONTENTS

HOW TO USE THIS BOOK

Whether you're a visitor, a new resident, or a native of the Twin Cities, you'll find the *City•Smart™ Guidebook: Minneapolis/St. Paul* indispensable. Author Rick Nelson brings you an insider's view of the best the Twin Cities have to offer.

This book presents the cities in five geographic zones. The zone divisions are listed at the bottom of this page and shown on the map on the following pages. Look for a zone designation in each listing and use it to help you locate the listing on one of the zone-specific maps included in each chapter.

Example:

MINNESOTA HISTORY CENTER
345 Kellogg Blvd. W., St. Paul
612/296-6126   **DSP**

Zone abbreviation = DSP
The Minnesota History Center location will be shown on the
Downtown St. Paul map unless otherwise noted.

Minneapolis/St. Paul Zones

DMP—Downtown Minneapolis

DSP—Downtown St. Paul

MP—Minneapolis, including portions of north and south suburbs

SP—St. Paul, including portions of north and south suburbs

GTC—Greater Twin Cities, including outlying areas

GREATER TWIN CITIES

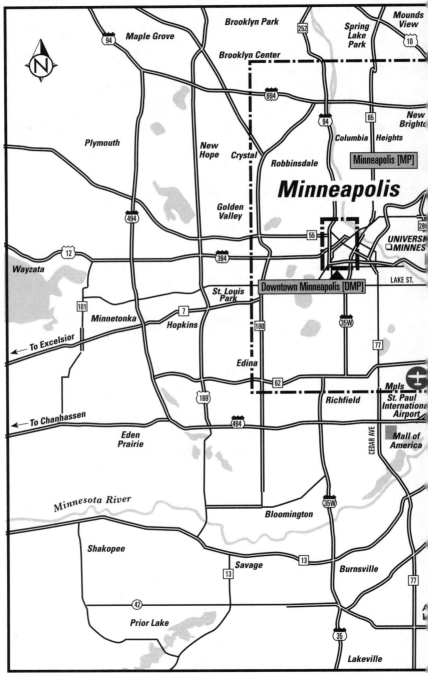

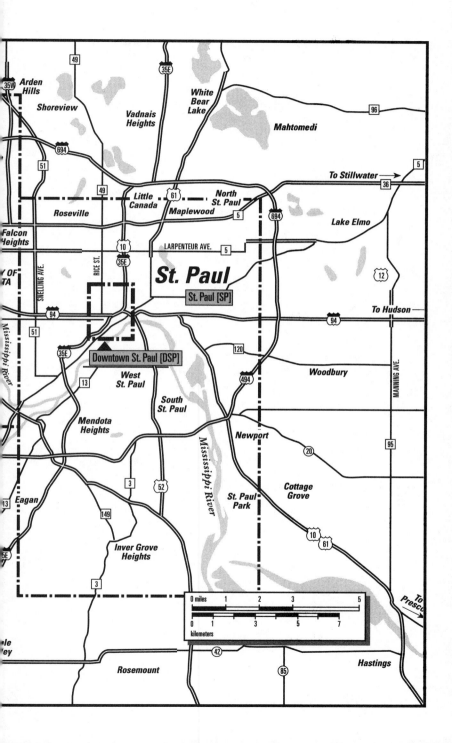

1

WELCOME TO
THE TWIN CITIES

Although their nickname implies a pair of clones, the cities of Minneapolis and St. Paul are really more fraternal than identical siblings. Both have distinctive histories, topography, and identities, as well as a rivalry that goes back almost 150 years.

St. Paul's roots are in transportation; outside of Fort Snelling, the city's landing marked the northernmost navigable destination on the Mississippi River, and this choice location later drew the railroads as well as the state capitol. From its very early years, Minneapolis' fortunes were centered almost entirely upon the power of St. Anthony Falls, the only falls along the entire length of the Father of Waters. Within two decades of the city's initial settlement, more than two dozen lumber and flour mills were clustered around the falls, harnessing its considerable power, and by the end of the nineteenth century, boomtown Minneapolis was the flour-milling capital of the world.

Early settlers of both cities were determined to make their hometowns centers of commerce, education, and culture, and their built-in Yankee work ethic and dedication to philanthropy set a civic example that continues today and has made the Twin Cities one of the nation's most livable and lively urban areas.

The Pioneers

Marc Caryl

A Brief History of the Twin Cities

Geologists estimate that the last glaciers inched their way across the area that is now Minnesota more than 12,000 years ago, leaving in their wake a landscape dotted with lakes and ponds. Minnesota's nickname is "the land of 10,000 lakes," but accuracy was replaced with ad-agency finesse, since it's actually the land of about 18,000 lakes.

Water plays a major role in the Twin Cities. Both cities hug the banks of the Mississippi River, the source of their births and growth, and the white settlement grew up around the American Army outpost at Fort Snelling, which guarded over the strategic junction of the Minnesota and Mississippi Rivers, about 8 miles downstream from St. Anthony Falls. Minneapolis isn't called the "City of Lakes" for nothing; there are 22 within the city limits.

The area was first settled by a number of New England Yankees who moved west in the 1850s and 1860s to seek their fortunes in the rustic Minnesota territory. Pioneers like Hill, Pillsbury, Crosby, Steele, Lowry, and Washburn all made their mark on the region, founding major companies, creating civic institutions, and establishing government posts that remain integral components of contemporary Minneapolis and St. Paul.

Those early settlers were followed by waves of German, Swedish, Norwegian and Irish immigrants, and by the turn of the century, nearly a half-million people lived in the Minneapolis/St. Paul area. Tremendous growth occurred from 1900 to the end of World War I, as both cities began to mature and develop infrastructures, create cultural institutions, and build schools and parks. The advent of the streetcar in the late nineteenth century pushed the borders of both cities far beyond their original boundaries, and whole neighborhoods sprang up as workers migrated to the cities to work in the area's busy flour mills, grain elevators, and factories including the mighty Minneapolis Moline plant, the world's largest farm-implement manufacturer.

The prosperity of the 1920s led to a building boom in both cities that came to a screeching halt with the Great Depression. Little growth occurred during the 1930s, and most of the construction that took place was done under the auspices of government relief programs. As the crippling years of the Depression wore on, the Twin Cities became a center for the nation's organized labor movement and the Communist and Socialist Parties.

The postwar period—and its attendant prosperity—brought great change to the Twin Cities. An explosion in suburban development began in the early 1950s and has gone on, unabated, for nearly half a century, transforming the two relatively compact cities into two central cores surrounded by a sprawling, seven-county metropolitan area. Today, two-thirds of the area's 2.5 million residents reside in the suburban areas ringing the two cities.

Such unchecked growth led to problems, which in turn led to the creation of a unique government body to provide guidance and direction for the booming seven-county metropolitan area. Founded by the state legislature in 1967, the Metropolitan Council's job is to solve disputes among municipalities and deal with urban management problems on a regional basis. Today the council has jurisdiction over rapid transit, parks, water and sewer service, and airports. To date, the council has been successful in many areas that are of a regional concern, but the encroachment of suburban sprawl on once-rural areas—unchecked by any natural barriers such as mountains or large bodies of water—continues to be a vexing situation and will quickly turn the already spread-out seven-county area into an 11-county metropolitan region.

The Twin Cities gained national prominence after World War II as a leader in progressive government, business, and the arts. An example is the Five Percent Club, founded by the Dayton Company. When the company founded the group in 1946, it pledged to donate 5 percent of its annual pre-tax profits to charity and asked other businesses to follow suit. Since that time, more than 200 companies have signed on to the program (now known as the Keystone Program), and billions of dollars have been donated over the past half-century to support the area's rich array of cultural, social, and educational institutions.

The People of the Twin Cities

Although the Minneapolis/St. Paul metropolitan area has traditionally been almost overwhelmingly white, an influx of new residents over the past several decades has greatly improved the racial diversity of the area. Still, the

Love Is All Around

To most Americans, Minneapolis will always be the home of Mary Richards, the quintessentially spunky all-American career gal of the 1970s. The variations of the opening credits of the Mary Tyler Moore Show put Miss Moore all over Minneapolis, and it's a fun adventure to retrace her steps today.

Phyllis Lindstrom's rambling Victorian house—where Mary lived on the second floor and Rhoda Morgenstern rented a studio on the third floor—is two blocks west of Lake of the Isles Parkway at 2104 Kenwood Parkway, in Minneapolis' fashionable Kenwood neighborhood. The house is now owned by the director of the Minneapolis Institute of Arts and his family.

When Mary moved to her fashionable high-rise apartment later in the series, she took up residence in Chase House, the luxury building of Cedar Square West (now Riverside Plaza, at Cedar and Riverside Avenues, near the West Bank campus of the University of Minnesota).

WJM-TV, the ratings-basement station where Mary worked as a news producer, was located in the Midwest Plaza Building in downtown Minneapolis (801 Nicollet Mall).

Three shots of the brand-new IDS Center were incorporated into older versions of the opening credits. One has Mary riding the escalator in the Crystal Court, holding a potted chrysanthemum; the second shows her lunching on the balcony of the Gallery Restaurant (now Basil's); and the third depicts her window-shopping at Mary Jane Shoes (now Badiner Jewelers) at the base of the IDS Tower at Eighth Street and Nicollet Mall. Several shots of the center under construction can be seen in early MTM episodes.

Mary's grocery-shopping scene was shot at the Red Owl store (a now-defunct chain) at Hennepin Avenue South and 25th Street in south Minneapolis. She's exasperated because she's buying a meat product called Juicy Burger II, a low-priced hamburger-like product the store introduced when beef prices skyrocketed.

> *The opening credits' most memorable moment—and the show's signature—was when Mary is so overcome with the sheer thrill of being young, single, and in downtown Minneapolis that she twirls on her heel and hurls her tam into the air. It was shot on the corner of Seventh Street and Nicollet Mall.*
>
> *In the show's closing credits (just before the "meow" of the MTM kitten), Mary and a male friend are seen strolling hand in hand down the Nicollet Mall between Third and Fourth Streets in front of the Sheraton-Ritz Hotel. The Mall has since suffered an unpleasant facelift, and the hotel was replaced by a parking lot in the early 1990s.*

area is almost relentlessly homogeneous. According to the U.S. Census Bureau, nearly 91 percent of the area's population is Caucasian, 4 percent is African American, almost 4 percent is Asian, and 1 percent is Native American. German-Americans are the largest single ethnic group, followed by Scandinavians, Irish, and Hispanics.

Minneapolis has the nation's largest urban concentration of Native Americans in a community centered primarily in the neighborhood around the Minneapolis Regional Native American Center (the nation's first community center designed especially for Native Americans) on East Franklin Avenue in south Minneapolis. Hmong, Vietnamese, and Laotian refugees began arriving in the Twin Cities in the late 1970s, and today have thriving communities, particularly around Nicollet Avenue South in Minneapolis and along University Avenue East in St. Paul. Traditionally, the local Hispanic community has been anchored on the east side of St. Paul.

*Spoonbridge and Cherry
Minneapolis Sculpture Garden*

GMCVA

The African American community is making great strides in the Twin Cities. For example, Minneapolis is the first major American city to elect an African American female to the office of mayor; the Honorable Sharon Sayles Belton has held the top title in the City of Lakes since

Twin Cities Time Line

The area's original residents were members of the rival Dakota (Sioux) and the Ojibwa (Chippewa) Indian tribes. Their first contact with Europeans came in the late seventeenth century, and they were driven from the area almost entirely by the 1860s.

1680 Father Louis Hennepin, a Franciscan missionary, is widely believed to be the first European to see the 25-foot falls of the Mississippi River, which he names for his patron saint, Anthony of Padua.

1763 France relinquishes its claim to territory that includes much of the future state of Minnesota.

1767 Explorer and cartographer Jonathan Carver surveys the region for the English crown.

1803 The United States purchases the Louisiana Territory, and the remaining area around the Twin Cities is placed under American domain.

1805 U.S. Colonel Zebulon Pike signs a treaty with the Dakota Indians that establishes a military post at the confluence of the Mississippi and Minnesota Rivers

1820 Fort St. Anthony is founded by Captain Josiah Snelling; five years later it is renamed in his honor.

1823 The first steamboat arrives at Fort Snelling from St. Louis.

1837 Saloonkeeper Pierre "Pigs Eye" Parrant builds a cabin a few miles downstream from Fort Snelling; it becomes the first building in what is now St. Paul.

1841 Father Lucien Galtier builds a chapel in Pigs Eye and dedicates it to Saint Paul, and the hamlet takes on the same name.

1849 St. Paul becomes the capital of the Minnesota Territory.

1850 The town of St. Anthony is founded on the east bank of the Mississippi at the Falls of St. Anthony, and John Stevens builds the first house on the west bank of the river on what eventually becomes the city of Minneapolis.

1854 The first bridge spanning the Mississippi is built, connecting Minneapolis with Nicollet Island.

1855 Minneapolis (a combination of Sioux and Greek to create "city of waters") is founded on the west bank of the river, opposite St. Anthony.

1858 The University of Minnesota is founded.

1862 The area's first railroad opens.

1872 Minneapolis annexes the city of St. Anthony.

1881 The world's largest flour mill, the Pillsbury "A" mill, opens, heralding the city's supremacy in the flour-milling industry.

1882 The nation's first hydroelectric plant opens at St. Anthony Falls.

1883	Charles Loring establishes the Minneapolis Park Board, and James J. Hill's Northern Pacific Railroad connects the Twin Cities with the West Coast.
1890	The two cities' already heated rivalry goes into overdrive as Minneapolis surpasses St. Paul's census; both are later revealed to have padded their numbers heavily.
1903	The Minneapolis Symphony (later the Minnesota Orchestra) plays its first concert.
1905	Cass Gilbert's imperial State Capitol is dedicated.
1915	The Cathedral of St. Paul is dedicated, and the Minneapolis Institute of Arts opens.
1929	The 32-story Foshay Tower is dedicated in downtown Minneapolis, becoming the tallest building west of Chicago for decades.
1930	St. Paul native Frank B. Kellogg wins the Nobel Peace Prize.
1940	Sister Elizabeth Kenny opens a clinic in Minneapolis specializing in the treatment of the ravages of polio.
1948	Minneapolis Mayor Hubert Humphrey's impassioned speech at the Democratic National Convention sparks the beginning of the Civil Rights movement.
1956	Southdale, the country's first enclosed shopping mall, opens in Edina.
1961	The beloved Metropolitan Building is demolished ("the most inexcusable act of civic vandalism in the city of Minneapolis," according to one critic) in the name of urban renewal, triggering a newfound sense of historic preservation.
1963	The Guthrie Theater opens in Minneapolis to great acclaim, ushering in a new era of the performing arts in the Twin Cities.
1965	The first interstate freeway opens in Minneapolis, clearing the way for large-scale suburban development and simultaneous inner-city decay.
1967	Nicollet Mall is dedicated in downtown Minneapolis, and its design is copied the world over.
1972	Historic preservationists score a huge victory when St. Paul's delightful Old Federal Courts Building (now Landmark Center) is saved from the wrecking ball.
1973	Philip Johnson's 52-story IDS Center opens in downtown Minneapolis, surpassing the Foshay Tower's 44-year dominance on the city's skyline.
1987	The Minnesota Twins win the World Series, a feat they repeat in 1991.
1991	The Twin Cities host the first winter-city Super Bowl game.
1992	Mall of America, the nation's largest shopping and entertainment complex, opens in Bloomington.

Billion-Dollar Twin Citians

Several Twin Citians made Forbes *magazine's 1996 annual list of billionaires, including the Cargill and MacMillan families, who control Cargill, the Minnetonka-based grain giant that is the world's largest privately held company; the Weyerhaeuser family, who made their fortune in lumber and paper; Radisson Hotel magnate Curt Carlson; Dwight Opperman, former chairman of West Publishing, the legal books and data services firm; and Stanley Hubbard, the man behind U.S. Satellite Broadcasting.*

her election in 1992. Alan Page, the former Vikings football legend, has sat on the Minnesota Supreme Court since 1994.

The Twin Cities is home to a large and visible gay and lesbian population, too. Unlike many other urban areas, there isn't a gay neighborhood per se in either Minneapolis or St. Paul, although the Loring Park area in downtown Minneapolis could be considered so.

In terms of religion, while the Twin Cities are a strong Catholic enclave, the area is heavily Protestant, reflecting its German and Scandinavian roots. The American Lutheran Church, now part of the Evangelical Lutheran Church of America, was headquartered in Minneapolis for years, and two of the nation's three largest Lutheran congregations still call the Twin Cities home.

Calendar of Events

JANUARY
New Year's Eve, Historic Main Street, Minneapolis
St. Paul Winter Carnival

MARCH
Hollywood Oscar Party, State Theatre, Minneapolis
Minnesota State High School hockey and basketball tournaments,
     St. Paul Civic Center
St. Patrick's Day Parade, downtown St. Paul

APRIL
Festival of Nations, St. Paul Civic Center

MAY
Cinco de Mayo, St. Paul
Syttende Mai, Minneapolis

JUNE
Gay, Lesbian, Bisexual, Transgender Pride Festival, Loring Park, Minneapolis
Grand Old Day, Grand Avenue, St. Paul
Juneteenth Celebration, Theodore Wirth Park, Minneapolis
Minnesota Fringe Festival, Seven Corners, Minneapolis
Stone Arch Festival of the Arts, St. Anthony Falls, Minneapolis
Svenskarnes Dag, Minneapolis
Symphony Ball, Minneapolis

JULY
Basilica Block Party, Basilica of St. Mary, Minneapolis
Le Grand Aioli Bastille Day Celebration, Minneapolis
Minneapolis Aquatennial
Rondo Days, St. Paul
Taste of Minnesota, State Capitol Mall, St. Paul
Viennese Sommerfest, Orchestra Hall, Minneapolis

AUGUST
Cedarfest, Cedar-Riverside, Minneapolis
Minnesota Renaissance Festival, Shakopee
Minnesota State Fair, St. Paul
Powderhorn Festival of the Arts, Minneapolis
Uptown Art Fair, Minneapolis

SEPTEMBER
American Indian Movement Pow Wow, Minneapolis

OCTOBER
Twin Cities Marathon
University of Minnesota Homecoming, Minneapolis

NOVEMBER
Holidazzle, Nicollet Mall, Minneapolis

DECEMBER
Bright Lights, City Nights, downtown St. Paul
Holidazzle, Nicollet Mall, Minneapolis

Twin Cities' Weather

One of the lures of the Twin Cities is experiencing Minnesota's dramatic theater of seasons. Of course, winter is what most Americans think of when they consider the Gopher State, and with good reason. Although International Falls (often referred to as "the nation's icebox" and often the most frigid place in the lower 48) is thankfully more than 300 miles to the

St. Paul Winter Carnival ice carving

north, it does get cold in the Twin Cities during the winter.

How cold? Temperatures can plummet—and remain—below zero degrees Fahrenheit for days on end (the local record is a bone-chilling 40 degrees below, set in January 1996), although the average January temperature is a comparatively balmy 10 degrees Fahrenheit. On the flip side, Twin Cities summers can be hot and humid; temperatures can easily climb into the nineties, accompanied by stifling humidity. But that's an extreme, too. Most August days hit an average high of 80 degrees Fahrenheit, and most Minnesota summers tend to be dry, much to the angst of area farmers.

Generally missing in the Twin Cities are extended spring and fall seasons, which are lovely but painfully brief. Winter can drag—literally—well into April. Suddenly spring will arrive (much to the relief of residents) and almost without warning, segue directly into summer in a matter of weeks. Ditto the autumn months. Summer often lingers well into late September, and the snow can fly as early as November 1, leaving but a few weeks for the autumn colors to work their magic. How much does it

Celebs in Residence

Judith Guest, *the author of* Ordinary People, *lives in Edina.*

Garrison Keillor, *the man behind the national Saturday-afternoon radio institution known as "A Prairie Home Companion," lives in St. Paul.*

Oscar-winning actress **Jessica Lange** *(and playwright and actor Sam Shepherd) live in Stillwater.*

Singer and composer **Bobby McFerrin** *lives on Lake of the Isles in south Minneapolis.*

Greg LeMond, *the two-time Tour de France-winning bicyclist, lives in Medina.*

The Artist Formerly Known as Prince *lives in Chanhassen.*

snow in the Twin Cities? An infamous blizzard dropped more than 30 inches of snow on Halloween in 1991, and a more deadly (and entirely unexpected) storm on Armistice Day in 1940 left nearly 50 inches of snow and killed scores of Minnesotans. But most winters average 50 inches of the white stuff scattered across the entire season.

Truth to tell, Minnesota winters really don't deserve the bad rap that they have around the rest of the country or even in their own backyard. While it's true that the city made famous by Mary Tyler Moore is at its most hospitable in the summer and autumn months, the Twin Cities can be a great destination during the dead of winter, as well.

Minnesota winters can be very beautiful, too, with gleaming snows, soaring pine trees, and clean, crisp air. Local and regional parks offer all kinds of wintertime activities, including skating, sledding, and Alpine and Nordic skiing. Kids (and adults) temporarily enlarge families with front-yard snow siblings.

Business and Economy

Because of its diversified economy, large number of major hometown corporations, and well-educated work force, business and government leaders often consider the Twin Cities area to be recession-proof.

A number of major American corporations call the Twin Cities home, including Cargill, the commodities concern that is widely considered to be the world's largest privately held company (its annual revenues exceed $50 billion). West Publishing, the legal publishing and information systems behemoth, is headquartered in suburban Eagan, as is Northwest Airlines, the nation's fourth-largest airline. In the manufacturing sector, the list includes 3M (Minnesota Mining and Manufacturing), Honeywell, and

Mother of Invention

Minneapolis and St. Paul are fountains of invention, churning out products that are sold the world over, including Post-It Notes and cellophane tape, both from 3M; heart pacemakers by Medtronic; the entire Big G family of cereals from General Mills; GM's Betty Crocker line of packaged foods; Cream of Wheat hot cereal; Poppin' Freshrolls and every other Pillsbury product, including Totino's frozen pizzas and Green Giant vegetables; Tonka toys; thermostats (invented by Honeywell); supercomputers (perfected by Cray Research); Rollerblades; the Tilt-A-Whirl carnival ride; pacemakers; Salted Nut Rolls and Nut Goodies candy bars; and Mini-Donuts.

Famous Twin Citians

*Eddie Albert, actor (*Roman Holiday, Green Acres*)*
*Loni Anderson, actor (*WKRP in Cincinnati*) and the former
    Mrs. Burt Reynolds*
*Richard Dean Anderson, actor (*General Hospital*; title character,*
    MacGyver*)*
Siah Armajani, sculptor
*James Arness, actor (*Gunsmoke*)*
Merrill Ashley, principal dancer, New York City Ballet
*Joel and Ethan Coen, film directors and producers (*Raising Arizona,
    Blood Simple, Fargo, *and* Barton Fink*)*
*Julia Duffy, actor (*Newhart, Designing Women*)*
*Mike Farrell, actor (*M*A*S*H*)*
*F. Scott Fitzergald, author (*The Great Gatsby, Tender Is the Night*)*
*Al Franken, actor (*Saturday Night Live*) and author (*Rush Limbaugh
    Is a Big Fat Idiot*)*
*Mark Frost, television producer (*Twin Peaks*)*
John Paul Getty, billionaire industrialist
Peter Graves, actor (Mission: Impossible*)*
*Tippi Hedren, actor (*The Birds)*
*George Roy Hill, Oscar-winning film director (*The Sting*)*
*Hubert H. Humphrey, Minneapolis mayor, U.S. senator, U.S.
    vice president, 1968 U.S. presidential candidate*
*Linda Kelsey, actor (*Lou Grant*)*
*Charlie Korsmo, actor (*Hook, Dick Tracy*)*
Meridel Le Sueur, author (Harvest Song, Little Brother of
    the Wilderness, North Star Country, Song for My Time, Winter
    Prairie Women*)*
*Dorothy Lyman, actor (*All My Children, Mama's Family*)*
*Kelly Lynch, actor (*Drugstore Cowboy*)*
*Harvey Mackay, author (*Sharkproof, Swim with the Sharks Without
    Being Eaten Alive, Beware the Naked Man Who Offers You
    His Shirt*)*

Walter Mondale, U.S. senator, U.S. vice president, 1984 U.S. presidential candidate, U.S. ambassador to Japan
Bob Mould, lead singer, Sugar
*Mike Nelson, actor (*Mystery Science Theater 3000*)*
*Prince Rogers Nelson, musician and actor (*Purple Rain*)*
*Gordon Parks, author (*The Learning Tree*) and film director (*Shaft*)*
Dave Pirner, lead singer, Soul Asylum
*Harry Reasoner, journalist (*60 Minutes*)*
Charles Schulz, creator of Peanuts
Eric Severeid, journalist
Kevin Sorbo, actor (title character, Hercules*)*
*Lea Thompson, actor (*Back to the Futures I, II, III; Howard the Duck; *title character,* Caroline in the City*)*
Cheryl Tiegs, model
*Robert Vaughn, actor (*The Man from U.N.C.L.E.*)*
Paul Westerberg, former lead singer, The Replacements

Weyerhauser. Medical products are a key segment of the local economy, led by Medtronic, makers of the first heart pacemaker.

Service giants include American Express Financial Advisors, which operates one of its most successful divisions in Minneapolis, the former Investors Diversified Services; Carlson Companies, the privately held, $2-billion travel and accommodations company whose holdings include the Radisson Hotel chain, Carlson Wagonlit Travel, and TGIFriday's restaurants; First Bank Systems and Norwest Corporation, the region's two largest banks; the St. Paul Companies, one of the nation's largest underwriters of professional and property insurance; and the University of Minnesota, the state's fourth-largest employer and the nation's largest land-grant university.

Retail is big business in the Twin Cities, too. Dayton Hudson Corporation, the nation's fourth-largest retailer, was born—and is still headquartered—on Nicollet Mall in downtown Minneapolis. The $21-billion company owns three of the nation's largest department store chains (Marshall Field's, Hudson's, and Dayton's), the mid-priced Mervyn's chain, and Target, the upscale discounter. SUPERVALU, the nation's largest food wholesaler (annual sales top $16 billion), is in suburban Eden Prairie, as is Best Buy, one of the country's largest electronics chains. Fingerhut, the $2-billion discount catalogue business, is headquartered in suburban Minnetonka.

And the Musicland Group, the brash music retailer (Sam Goody, Musicland, and Media Play) is located in St. Louis Park.

Food processing put Minneapolis on the map, and more than a century after the city's rise to preeminence in the flour-milling industry, the area remains a giant food-processing town, with a roster of name-brand companies including General Mills, Pillsbury (now a division of Grand Metropolitan PLC), Land O' Lakes, Cream of Wheat, and International Multifoods.

Cost of Living

The Twin Cities are a relatively inexpensive place to live compared with other major U.S. cities. Housing is particularly affordable, and while Minnesota's personal income tax is the second-highest in the nation (how else to pay for the state's highly touted quality of life?), the 6.5 percent sales tax is waived for food or clothing, which tends to even things out.

5-mile taxi ride:		$7
Hotel double room:		$75
Average dinner:		$15
Movie admission:		$6.50
Daily newspaper:	(Minneapolis)	$.50
	(St. Paul)	$.25
8 oz. tube of brand-name toothpaste:		$2.50
Hot dog from a downtown vendor:		$1

Dressing in the Twin Cities

The first rule is to dress for the weather, and in winter, that means layers. A heavy, well-insulated coat is a wardrobe staple, and a hat, gloves, a scarf, and sturdy waterproof boots are a must when the temperatures fall. In the spring and autumn months, a lightweight waterproof jacket is advised, as well as a light sweater or two. Most locals break out the shorts as soon as the temps top 60 degrees, sometime in early May, and they remain out until the autumn leaves start to fall.

Both Minneapolis and St. Paul are informal cities, and few upscale restaurants require coats and ties for men. Black tie is reserved for very special—and increasingly rare—occasions. Business dress is also becoming increasingly more relaxed. On Fridays, legions of downtown and suburban office workers are reverting to casual dress, and many companies are spreading these more relaxed apparel rules to other days of the week, too. An evening at Orchestra Hall, the Guthrie Theater, or the Ordway Music Theatre will run the gamut from dark suits and conservative ties to blue jeans and T-shirts for men and sophisticated suits to casual separates for women.

Marc Caryl

2

GETTING AROUND THE TWIN CITIES

City Layout

Orienting yourself in Minneapolis and St. Paul is easy. Both cities are essentially large rectangles laid out along the Mississippi River. Minneapolis hugs the river on a basically north-south axis, and St. Paul lies east-west on both sides of the river.

Minneapolis' primary streets run north-south. Hiawatha Avenue is the principal thoroughfare between Minneapolis/St. Paul International Airport and downtown Minneapolis, and major north-south streets in south Minneapolis include Cedar, Portland, Park, First, Blaisdell, Nicollet, Lyndale, and Hennepin Avenues. On the city's north side, the principal north-south streets are Lyndale and Penn Avenues and Victory Memorial Drive. The city's busiest east-west streets include Broadway on the north side, Washington and University Avenues on the northern end of downtown through the University of Minnesota campus, and Franklin, Lake, and 50th Streets in south Minneapolis.

In St. Paul, the primary east-west routes include 7th Street, Shepard and Warner Roads, and Summit, Marshall, University, Minnehaha, Arlington, and Como Avenues. Primary north-south routes include Cleveland, Snelling, and Hamline Avenues, Lexington Parkway, Dale and Rice Streets, and McKnight Road.

Freeways crisscross the Twin Cities metropolitan area. The major north-south artery is Interstate 35. Coming north into the Twin Cities, I-35 splits into two separate freeways in suburban Burnsville, with I-35W heading north into Minneapolis and I-35E turning north and east into St. Paul;

the two are reconnected about 20 miles north of the Twin Cities in Forest Lake; from there, I-35 continues on to Duluth.

The major east-west freeway is Interstate 94, which splits St. Paul in half, crosses the Mississippi River just south of the University of Minnesota campus, and hooks around the southern and western edges of downtown Minneapolis before heading north and west out of the city on its way to western Minnesota, North Dakota, and points beyond.

The western suburbs are connected to downtown Minneapolis via Interstate 394, a recently completed, $400-million state-of-the-art expressway, complete with separate lanes for car pools and buses. The entire Twin Cities is ringed by Interstate 494 (on the south and west) and Interstate 694 (on the area's north and east sides). The western edges of the metropolitan area are served by two north-south freeways: Highway 100 is just west of the Minneapolis city limits, and Highway 169 is about 5 miles further west. Crosstown 62 hugs the southern edges of Minneapolis, connects Minneapolis/St. Paul International Airport with I-35W, and then heads west, past the Southdale area and on to I-494.

Streets in Minneapolis fall into a fairly predictable and easy-to-follow pattern. East-west streets are numbered, starting at Washington Avenue. In south Minneapolis, Franklin Avenue is also 20th Street, and Lake Street is also 30th Street. Avenues running north-south are numbered east of Nicollet Avenue; west of Lyndale Avenue they take on names in alphabetical order for 52 blocks. The first sequence begins with Aldrich, Bryant, Colfax, and Dupont Avenues, and the second begins with Abbott, Beard, Chowen, and Drew Avenues. Building numbers generally begin at Washington and Nicollet Avenues.

Finding an address in St. Paul can be more confusing. Downtown streets are numbered sequentially, but the order stops there. Throughout most of the city, street names follow no apparent logic. Have a good street map on hand, particularly when navigating through St. Paul.

Public Transportation

Metropolitan Council Transit Operations
612/373-3333 live operator
612/341-0140 TDD/TTY
612/341-4587 automated route information

T i P

The most accurate street maps are made at the Hudson Map Co. (2510 Nicollet Ave. S., Minneapolis, 612/872-8818); a copy of their *Twin Cities Street Atlas* goes for $16.95.

DOWNTOWN MINNEAPOLIS-MCTO

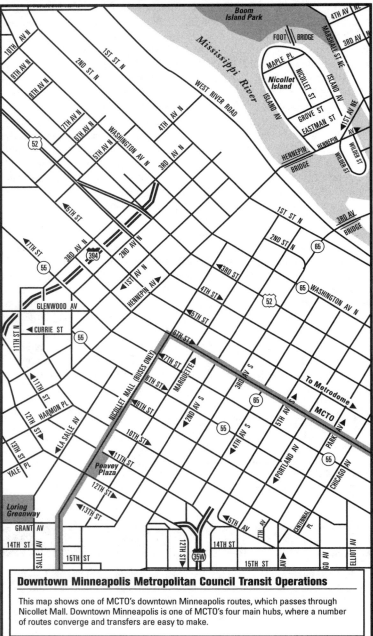

Downtown Minneapolis Metropolitan Council Transit Operations

This map shows one of MCTO's downtown Minneapolis routes, which passes through Nicollet Mall. Downtown Minneapolis is one of MCTO's four main hubs, where a number of routes converge and transfers are easy to make.

Hennepin Avenue streetcar in the 1920s

Not so very long ago the Twin Cities area was crisscrossed by one of the world's largest streetcar systems. Electric streetcars made their debut in downtown Minneapolis in 1889, and by the 1920s, the Twin City Rapid Transit Co. had more than 1,000 cars on 500 miles of track on both city streets and dedicated rights-of-way. The system was so extensive that it was possible to travel via streetcar to nearly every corner of what is now the Twin Cities metropolitan area—from Stillwater on the St. Croix River all the way west to Excelsior on the shores of Lake Minnetonka, and from Anoka 40 miles south to Hastings—although most of the area back then was rural.

The streetcars disappeared in 1954, replaced by the buses that still constitute mass transit in the Twin Cities. Today, the Metropolitan Council Transit Operations (MCTO) transports more than 65 million passengers a year on its fleet of more than 1,000 vehicles over 115 routes, many of which follow the same paths the streetcars did.

Inner-city service is the most frequent and dependable, and it is possible—but not always easy—to live in Minneapolis or St. Paul and not own a car. The same cannot be said for the vast majority of the sprawling suburban communities that surround the two cities. Downtown Minneapolis, downtown St. Paul, Uptown Minneapolis, and the Mall of America are the MCTO's four main hubs, where a number of routes converge and transfers are easy to make.

Much of the MCTO service is designed to serve commuters traveling into both downtowns, and service to most suburban areas is spotty at best outside the morning and evening rush hours. Commuting by bus is often preferable to battling the ever-increasing traffic, particularly since the recent proliferation of dedicated bus lanes on area freeways, which allow buses to bypass the bumper-to-bumper traffic. The MCTO also operates

DOWNTOWN ST. PAUL-MCTO

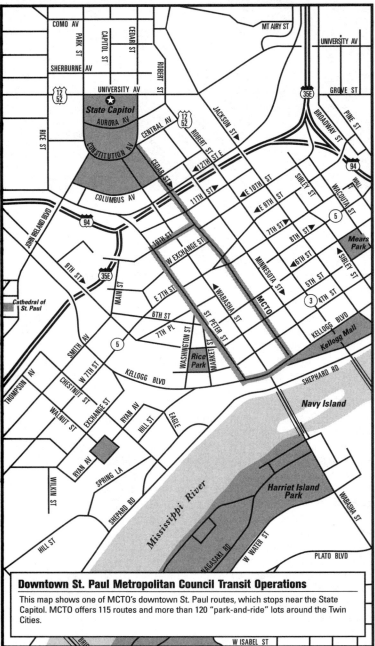

Downtown St. Paul Metropolitan Council Transit Operations

This map shows one of MCTO's downtown St. Paul routes, which stops near the State Capitol. MCTO offers 115 routes and more than 120 "park-and-ride" lots around the Twin Cities.

T i P

For an update on highway conditions, call 612/297-4103 (612/296-9930 TDD/TTY).

more than 120 "park-and-ride" lots all across the Twin Cities, allowing commuters to park free and hop the bus to their destination.

Intra-city bus service between the two downtowns is via route 16, which stops and goes along city streets for what can feel like the longest 45 minutes of your life; or via routes 94B and 94D, which glide along I-94 and make the express trip in around 15 minutes. The MCTO also offers express service between Nicollet Mall in downtown Minneapolis and Mall of America via route 80; the 15-minute trip runs every 20 minutes. Buses are generally safe, and are patrolled by a 150-member police force. During inclement winter weather, the safest and least nerve-racking way to get around is via the MCTO, which manages to run during even the most brutal of blizzards. Most routes end at midnight year-round, a few run until 1 a.m., and all stop by 1:15 a.m.; the earliest resume at 5 a.m.

Off-peak fares are $1 for local trips and $1.50 for freeway service; during rush hours (6:30 to 9 a.m. and 3:30 to 6:30 p.m.) add 50 cents. Children under age 5 ride free at all times; and seniors, persons with disabilities, and children ages 6 to 12 ride for 50 cents during off-peak hours and pay the full fare during peak hours. Ride anywhere within downtown Minneapolis for 25 cents during nonpeak hours and 50 cents during peak hours.

Fare boxes accept exact change only (including dollar bills), and money-saving magnetic cards can be purchased. A stored-value card allows unlimited rides for 31 consecutive days at all fare levels, priced from $38 to $76. Discounted stored-value cards are also sold at three price levels: the $10 card has an $11 value, the $15 card has a $16.50 value, and the $20 card has a $22 value.

Bus drivers run the gamut, from shining examples of "Minnesota nice" to obnoxious and surly. Should you need a transfer, you must ask for it when you pay your fare. Transfers have a two-hour expiration and are not good for the return trip.

The MCTO operates three Transit Stores, which sell transit passes and are staffed by friendly, helpful experts in routes, fares, and other information. In downtown Minneapolis, the store is located across the street from the IDS Center at 719 Marquette Avenue (look for the front of a bus coming out of the building) and is open weekdays from 7:30 a.m. to 5:30 p.m. In downtown St. Paul, it's located on the skyway level of the American Bank Building at 101 East 5th Street and is open weekdays from 7:30 a.m. to 5 p.m. The Mall of America store is located in the Transit Hub just outside the Mall's East Broadway entrance (between Bloomingdale's and Sears) and is open 11:30 a.m. Tuesday through Saturday.

Metro Mobility
612/221-1932

Door-to-door transportation for people with disabilities, with fares similar to the MCTO's. Metro Mobility provides more than 1.2 million rides per year in its fleet of 150 specially equipped vans. Rides can be scheduled up to two weeks in advance.

Minnesota RideShare
612/349-RIDE
612/349-SIGN TDD/TTY

A free car-pool and van-pool matching service operated by the MCTO to encourage fewer cars on the road. RideShare drivers can use the same high-occupancy freeway lanes that buses use to bypass bumper-to-bumper traffic and are eligible for inexpensive or sometimes free parking in a number of parking facilities in downtown Minneapolis and St. Paul.

Taxis

Unless you're in a few rare stretches of downtown Minneapolis or at the airport, don't expect to hail a cab from the curb in the Twin Cities. Call instead and have a dispatcher send one to your door.

Fares vary among companies but average about $1.50 per mile, and there's often a surcharge for extra passengers and trips to the airport. Expect to pay $25 for a taxi from the airport to downtown Minneapolis, $20 for an airport–downtown St. Paul run, and $10 from the airport to Mall of America. Most cabs accept major credit cards.

T I P

TAXI COMPANIES
Airport Taxi, 612/721-0000
Blue & White Taxi, 612/333-3333
Suburban Taxi, 612/884-8888
Yellow Cab Minneapolis, 612/824-4444
Yellow Cab St. Paul, 612/222-4433
Yellow Cab Suburban, 612/824-4000

Airport Express
612/726-6400

If you're staying at a hotel and don't need to rent a car, consider this quick and affordable one-way and round-trip van service, which runs from the airport to a number of hotels and condominiums in downtown Minneapolis, downtown St. Paul, and Minneapolis suburbs. The fare is about a third of what it would cost to take a taxi.

Downtown Minneapolis–airport service is $10 one-way, $15.50 round-trip, and runs every half-hour daily from 5 a.m. to 7 p.m.; downtown St.

Paul–airport service is $8 one-way, $11.50 round-trip, and runs every half-hour daily from 5 a.m. to 7 p.m.; and suburban-airport service ranges from $8 to $22.50, depending on the final destination, and runs every hour from 5 a.m. to 7 p.m.

Driving in the Twin Cities

If you plan to venture outside of the two downtowns, chances are you will need to rent a car. The Twin Cities have never been particularly compact urban areas, and the suburban sprawl of the last 25 years has pushed the metropolitan area's borders far out into the countryside. Outside of the two downtowns and a few adjoining neighborhoods, little of the area is easily walkable, and the MCTO's routes and schedules can be tough to decipher.

However, for all of its endless sprawl, the metropolitan area is surprisingly easy to navigate by car. Drivers are generally courteous but not particularly charitable. Unlike the citizens of freewheeling automobile cities like Los Angeles or Houston, Twin Citians are not known for their generosity on the open road, so don't expect a lot of kindness when merging or changing lanes.

Almost all freeway on-ramps are metered during peak hours, which means that access is limited by a complicated computerized system of stop lights designed to manage traffic flows. Driving the area's overtaxed freeways can be a trying experience during the morning and evening rush hours; the stretch of I-35W between downtown Minneapolis and its southern suburbs can be particularly maddening during these times.

Making matters worse is the old joke that there are two seasons in Minnesota: winter and highway construction. Two of the area's main interstate freeways are undergoing reconstruction projects that will take several years to complete, so expect delays on both I-35W from downtown Minneapolis to the Minnesota River, and I-94 from Cretin Avenue in St. Paul to the Lowry Hill Tunnel in Minneapolis.

Driving Tips

Wintertime driving can be a real test of will. Maintenance crews are surprisingly skilled at clearing roads and keeping them passable with copious amounts of sand and salt. If you've never been in a cold-weather city before, it may alarm you to happen upon a street sign declaring a certain road a "Snow Emergency Route."

If your car is towed in Minneapolis, call 612/673-5777 (the impound lot is located just west of downtown adjacent to I-394 at 51 Colfax Ave. N.). In St. Paul, call 612/292-3642 (the lot is behind Holman Field, near the intersection of Hwy. 52 and Concord St. at 830 Bard's Channel Rd.).

Fear not. This means that after a particularly heavy snowfall, the city will declare a "snow emergency," and that thoroughfare will get the immediate attention of the plowing crews; less-traveled residential streets are cleared within 24 to 48 hours. During a snow emergency, parking is banned on streets according to their priority, and both cities (in what some residents joke is the primary means of filling city coffers) vigorously tag and tow vehicles in violation of plowing regulations. Call 612/348-SNOW in Minneapolis and 612/266-7569 in St. Paul for information about snow emergency schedules and procedures.

Winter conditions also affect parking. If snowfalls are heavy enough, the city of Minneapolis allows parking only on the even-numbered side of most residential streets. Mounds of snow also eliminate metered and unmetered spots all across the Twin Cities.

Driving on icy roads isn't anyone's idea of fun, and the heinous phenomenon known as "black ice" (when the air is so cold that car exhaust freezes upon contact with the pavement) has caused many a fender-bender. Just be sure to drive slowly, give the vehicle in front of you plenty of room, use the brake gingerly, and steer in the direction of a spin should one occur. The Minnesota Highway Patrol also suggests keeping an emergency winter survival kit in your car; it should include a flashlight, a candle, matches, and chocolates or hard candy. A bag of salt, a blanket or two, and a window scraper and brush are also wise supplies to keep in the trunk.

Winter is not easy on automobiles, which is one reason why classic vehicles and the latest expensive new models are a rarity on Minnesota roads during the winter months. The extreme weather can and will freeze just about anything inside a car engine, including the fuel, and the sand and salt that is liberally spread across the roads play havoc on a car's exterior. The rough weather isn't easy on roads, either. Half of the fabled 10,000 Minnesota lakes are really waterlogged potholes, or so you will begin to believe when taking a drive after a long, harsh winter.

Meters within Minneapolis city limits accept only quarters. Be sure to study the meter's hours of operation, because Minneapolis meter-readers watch their beats like prison guards; if you let your time expire, you'll be hit with a $10 ticket. Most meters are enforced Monday through Friday 8 a.m. to 6 p.m., although those closer to the Metrodome and the Minneapolis Convention Center are enforced daily 8 a.m. to 10 p.m.

Parking Tips

Twin Citians love to complain about parking, and a constant criticism about both downtowns is the perceived lack of parking. Actually, both cities have enormous parking capacities. In Minneapolis, three gargantuan city-owned ramps straddle a blocks-long span of I-394, collectively containing space

T
I
P

Commuter Connection (235 Pillsbury Center, Minneapolis, 612/348-2062) sells maps for bike trails in the seven-county metro area as well out-of-state trails maintained by the Department of Natural Resources.
Calhoun Cycle (1622 W. Lake St., Minneapolis, 612/827-8231) has a large selection of single and tandem bicycles for rent by the hour, half-day, day, and weekend at reasonable rates.

for several thousand cars. By day, commuters from the western suburbs fill them (accessed directly from I-394), and by night they are often busy with patrons from Target Center (connected by skyway) or people coming into the city for dinner, a show, or to catch a little nightlife.

Most downtown parking ramps and lots participate in the "Do the Town" program, a joint effort between the city and the Downtown Council that validates parking in a participating facility with a $20 purchase in a long (more than 200) list of stores, restaurants, clubs, and theaters. Just enter any ramp or lot (be sure to look for the "Do the Town" sign) after 4 p.m. on weekdays, or all day on weekends, and don't forget to get the certificate from the participating merchant or restaurateur.

Downtown St. Paul has a similarly huge stockpile of parking, as well as its own validation program; it's good all day, every day for up to three hours with any $20 purchase at a participating merchant.

Biking in the Twin Cities

Both Minneapolis and St. Paul are starting to see the wisdom of dedicated commuter bike paths, and each city has begun realigning city streets to accommodate bikers. In Minneapolis, several principal downtown streets (including Hennepin, Portland, and Park Avenues and 2nd, 4th, 5th, 9th, and 10th Streets) have dedicated bike lanes. In 1995, Minneapolis opened a 3.5-mile bike corridor along a little-used railroad right-of-way that connects downtown Minneapolis with Cedar Lake and the rest of the extensive Minneapolis Park Board bike path system. The downtown entrance is at the intersection of Glenwood Avenue and 12th Street. Call 612/673-2411 for details. With its plethora of buses, as well as a strictly enforced no-passing law, biking on Nicollet

Woodside biking

Minnesota Office of Tourism

Mall is not advised. Minneapolis also has an extensive system (nearly 40 miles) of interconnected paved bike paths running through its parks and along its Grand Rounds parkways.

The city of St. Paul recently created a bike path running the full length of Summit Avenue, and that trail connects with the city's bike trails running along Mississippi Boulevard.

The suburbs have a number of bike trails designed for both serious riders and recreational pedalers. Hennepin County maintains a large system of groomed trails, and the most popular include a 16.5-mile trail that follows an old streetcar route, connecting Hopkins with Victoria. Along the way, the trail skirts Lake Minnetonka, comes within a mile of the lush University of Minnesota Landscape Arboretum, and goes through the lovely Carver Park Reserve. And another former streetcar trail, this one 10.5 miles long, runs through rolling countryside from Hopkins to Chaska, ending at the Minnesota Valley Wildlife Refuge. Picnicking and parking are available on both trails. For more information, call 612/559-9000.

The state of Minnesota also maintains a number of trails, the vast majority outside the seven-county metropolitan area. For more information, call 612/296-6157 or 800/766-6000.

Airports

The Twin Cities area is served by a number of airports, all managed by the Metropolitan Airports Commission, a division of the Metropolitan Council.

Minneapolis/St. Paul International Airport (MSP)
Recently ranked among the world's five safest airports, this busy facility, located at Wold Chamberlain Field, was named after Ernest Wold and Cyrus Chamberlain, two Minnesota aviators killed in action during World War I. There has been an airport on this site since 1923, when an old auto

---

T
i
P

MAJOR AIRLINES
Air Canada, 800/776-3000
American Airlines, 800/433-7300
America West Airlines, 800/235-9292
Continental Airlines, 800/231-0856
Delta Air Lines, 800/241-4141
Frontier Airlines, 800/432-1359
Northwest Airlines, 800/225-2525
Sun Country Airlines, 612/726-5252
Trans World Airlines, 800/221-2000
United Airlines, 800/241-6522
US Air, 800/428-4322
Vanguard Airlines, 800/826-4827

MSP International Airport

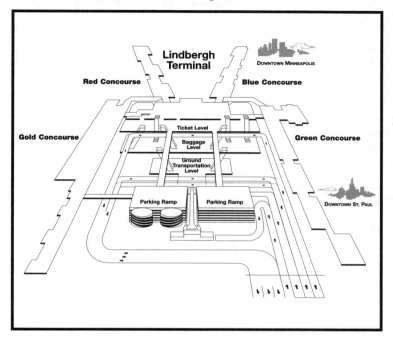

race track was retrofitted as an airfield. Northwest Airlines was born at this field in 1926 as Northwest Airways, starting with a mail route; three years later, the company began regular passenger service.

Northwest is still the big name here, and 80 percent of the airport's gates are controlled by the Eagan-based airline, the nation's fourth largest. More than 22 million people pass through this facility every year, arriving or departing on more than 1,100 daily flights by 18 national and regional carriers. MSP has flights to 160 direct destinations, including 20 international cities.

The airport's urban location, just 8 miles south of downtown Minneapolis and 9 miles east of downtown St. Paul, causes consternation among nearby residents, who have to live with the constant roar of aircraft, but the accessible location is a boon to visitors and residents alike.

There are two terminals at MSP. The main terminal, named for Minnesota native Charles Lindbergh, is located off I-494 just west of Highway 55 and Fort Snelling. Aside from its constant state of expansion or renovation, the terminal is somewhat dowdy but very easy to manage. Parking is available in a series of large ramps just opposite the passenger drop-off and pickup points, and is accessible via skyway from the ticketing floor. Valet parking is also available at the airport, and the entire facility is handicapped-accessible. Car rental and additional parking ramp access is available through a recently completed tunnel; enter at the baggage pickup area.

The second terminal, named for the late Hubert H. Humphrey, the former Minneapolis mayor, U.S. vice president, and Minnesota senator, is located just north of I-494 on 34th Avenue South in Bloomington. This cheerless facility is reserved for charter flights and a number of international arrivals and departures. Its best feature is its manageability; unlike its neighbor to the east, the crowds here are thin, traffic is almost nonexistent, and it's very easy to park. Unfortunately, beyond a small snack bar and gift shop, there is little to do to pass the time if you have a wait ahead of you. The airport's main long-term lot is located just north of the terminal; enter on 34th Avenue.

The two terminals are connected by a frequently running shuttle bus, and the MCTO offers service—but, alas, no express routes—to Lindbergh and Humphrey from both downtowns.

Other Airports
The Twin Cities area is also served by several smaller airports.

AirLake Airport
8140 220th St. W., Lakeville
612/469-4040   MP

Anoka County Airport
2289 85th Ave. N., Blaine
612/784-6614   SP

Crystal Airport
Bass Lake Road and Highway 52, Crystal
612/537-2058   MP

Flying Cloud Airport
10110 Flying Cloud Dr., Eden Prairie
612/941-3545   MP

Lake Elmo Airport
12402 N. 30th St., Bayport Township
612/777-6300   SP

St. Paul Downtown Airport
644 Bayfield St., St. Paul
612/224-4306   SP
Business travelers and private aviators prefer this smaller facility (which is also called Holman Field) to MSP for its inexpensive services and convenient location, right across the Mississippi River from downtown St. Paul.

Train Service

Twin Cities Passenger Station
730 Transfer Rd., St. Paul
612/644-1127   SP

The Empire Builder, Amtrak's major east-west train line between Chicago and Seattle, stops in the Twin Cities at the Amtrak passenger station in St. Paul's Midway area.

MSP International Airport

Currently, Amtrak's daily service (800/872-7245) to Chicago departs from St. Paul at 8:20 a.m. and arrives in Chicago's Union Station at 4:20 p.m.; one-way tickets average $75. Daily service to Seattle departs St. Paul at 11:55 p.m. and arrives in Seattle's King Street Station two calendar days later at 10:30 a.m.; one-way tickets average $219. Because of the long distances between destinations, train travel in the Midwest comes nowhere close to matching the convenience and popularity that it enjoys in other parts of the country, and traffic in this drab, utilitarian station is fairly light.

The station is open daily from 6:30 a.m. to midnight (box office hours are 7:15 a.m. to midnight) and is located two blocks north of the intersection of University and Cleveland Avenues, about ten minutes from both downtowns. MCTO service is via route 16. Expect a $10 taxi fare from downtown St. Paul and a $15 fare from downtown Minneapolis. Free parking.

Bus Service

Greyhound (800/231-2222), a company founded in Minneapolis, has two bus stations in the Twin Cities. The Minneapolis station (29 N. 9th St., 612/371-3323) is located across the street from the Orpheum Theatre and two blocks from the major MCTO routes along Hennepin Avenue and 7th and 8th Streets. The St. Paul station (25 W. 7th St., 612/222-0509) is located at the intersection of 7th and St. Peter Streets, across the street from Mickey's Diner, a greasy spoon housed in an honest-to-God railroad car and a St. Paul institution.

Both terminals are also served by Jefferson Bus Lines (612/332-3224), which also operates a passenger pickup station at Minneapolis/St. Paul International Airport's Lindbergh Terminal.

The Saint Paul Hotel

3

WHERE TO STAY

Thanks to the building boom of the 1980s, there is a hotel or motel room available for just about any price and at any location in the Twin Cities. Most national chains are represented as well as a number of one-of-a-kind hotels and bed and breakfasts. Disabled access is indicated by &.

Price rating symbols:
$	**Under $50**
$$	**$50 to $75**
$$$	**$75 to $125**
$$$$	**$125 and up**

Rates include lodging taxes; in Bloomington and Minneapolis, the rate is 12 percent; in St. Paul, it's 13 percent.

DOWNTOWN MINNEAPOLIS

Most of the 5,000 hotel rooms in downtown Minneapolis are connected to the skyway system.

Hotels and Motels

CROWN PLAZA NORTHSTAR
618 2nd Ave. S.
Minneapolis 55402
612/338-2288
$$ DMP

A sensible, comfortable hotel from the 1960s that just underwent a multi-million-dollar renovation. Located in the heart of downtown, across the street from the Minneapolis Athletic Club. Several nonsmoking floors available. Skyway connected. &

EMBASSY SUITES MINNEAPOLIS
425 S. 7th St.
Minneapolis 55415
612/333-3111
$$$ DMP

DOWNTOWN MINNEAPOLIS

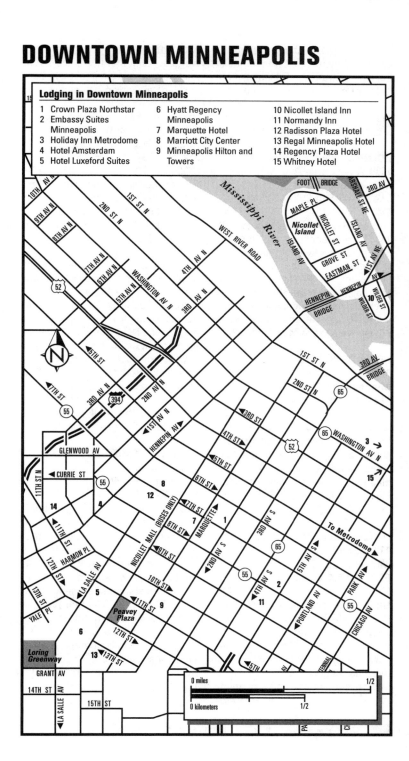

Lodging in Downtown Minneapolis

1 Crown Plaza Northstar
2 Embassy Suites Minneapolis
3 Holiday Inn Metrodome
4 Hotel Amsterdam
5 Hotel Luxeford Suites
6 Hyatt Regency Minneapolis
7 Marquette Hotel
8 Marriott City Center
9 Minneapolis Hilton and Towers
10 Nicollet Island Inn
11 Normandy Inn
12 Radisson Plaza Hotel
13 Regal Minneapolis Hotel
14 Regency Plaza Hotel
15 Whitney Hotel

An all-suites hotel in a large mixed-use development just a few blocks from the Metrodome. The hotel offers 218 two-room suites, modest on-site workout facilities, a so-so in-house restaurant (Cornell's), and a free breakfast. Skyway connected. &

HOLIDAY INN METRODOME
1500 Washington Ave. S.
Minneapolis 55415
612/333-4646 or 800/448-3663
$$$ **DMP**
This quasi–art deco 1980s hotel with 265 rooms anchors the bustling Seven Corners neighborhood, which is home to a number of theaters, nightclubs, and restaurants. The Metrodome is six blocks to the west. There's a small indoor pool and workout area, and free shuttle service to downtown and the Metrodome. &

HOTEL AMSTERDAM
828 Hennepin Ave.
Minneapolis 55402
612/288-0459
$ **DMP**
A small (24 rooms) bare-bones hostelry. Many of the rooms have shared baths, but this new gay- and lesbian-oriented establishment is clean and relatively quiet, considering its location above one of the city's most popular gay bars.

HOTEL LUXEFORD SUITES
1101 LaSalle Ave.
Minneapolis 55402
612/332-6800 or 800/662-3232
$$ **DMP**
One of the best accommodations deals in the city, the Luxeford is a hospitable alternative to the large chains. The hotel's 230 suites aren't particularly large but they are attractive and include a bedroom, kitchenette, and sitting room (complete with sleeper sofa). There's a small workout room located in the hotel. Just beyond the snug lobby is Café Luxeford, a hopping jazz joint. &

HYATT REGENCY MINNEAPOLIS
1300 Nicollet Mall
Minneapolis 55403
612/370-1234
$$$$ **DMP**
One of the city's major convention hotels, the Hyatt's location is choice, but this large hotel is just as impersonal as its big-name rivals. The Hyatt has 532 comfortable rooms and 20 suites, plus four restaurants (including the excellent Manny's for steak and Pronto for Italian). Another attraction is the Regency Athletic Club and Spa (612/343-3131), a well-appointed facility available to hotel guests for a $9 fee, as well as a number of large ballrooms and the city's largest exhibition hall outside of the Minneapolis Convention Center. The Hyatt is two blocks from the convention center and a two-block stroll from Orchestra Hall, shops, and restaurants. Skyway connected. &

MARQUETTE HOTEL
710 Marquette Ave.
Minneapolis 55402
612/332-2351 or 800/445-8667
$$$$ **DMP**
Probably the top spot in town, the Marquette is a luxury hotel that attracts nearly all out-of-town celebrities, who enjoy its big, well-appointed rooms, discreet and thoughtful staff, and prime location in the IDS Center. The Marquette is managed by Hilton International and has 277 rooms. Shopping, business, and entertainment are all within a short walk. There's a small fitness facility on the hotel's fifth floor and a banquet and meeting

room on the 50th floor of the IDS Tower. Basil's, the hotel's restaurant, serves breakfast, lunch, and dinner daily, and the Marq VII bar in the hotel's first-floor lobby is a quiet place to conclude a long day of work or play. Skyway connected. &

MARRIOTT CITY CENTER
30 S. 7th St.
Minneapolis 55402
612/349-4000
$$$$ **DMP**
The big, 31-story, triangular glass monolith in the City Center shopping and office complex offers nearly 600 modern rooms and suites. The hotel has an enormous ballroom and a well-equipped conference center, as well as Gustino's restaurant (entertaining singing waiters but predictable, overpriced food) and the more informal Papaya's. Downtown shopping, entertainment, and business addresses all within walking distance. Skyway connected. &

MINNEAPOLIS HILTON AND TOWERS

1001 Marquette Ave.
Minneapolis 55402
612/376-1000 or 800/445-8667
$$$$ **DMP**
The city's primary convention hotel, built specifically to complement the Minneapolis Convention Center, a block and a half to the south and adjacent to Orchestra Hall. The mammoth Hilton has 814 rooms (including 52 suites), and while its pompous public spaces are grand in a schlocky kind of way, the rooms are comfortable and well-appointed. The hotel has two restaurants (including Carver's, an excellent four-diamond restaurant), an on-site health club and pool, and an enormous ballroom. Skyway connected. &

NICOLLET ISLAND INN
95 Merriam St.
Minneapolis 55401
612-331-1800
$$$ **DMP**
Built within the limestone walls of a nineteenth-century door factory, this antique-filled romantic getaway is smack-dab in the middle of the

Nicollet Island Inn

Nicollet Island Inn

largest island in the Mississippi River and a ten-minute walk to the heart of downtown. The inn has 24 distinctive guest rooms, as well as a fine restaurant and picture-perfect views of the river and downtown Minneapolis. The restaurants and movie theaters of Southeast Main Street are just a two-minute stroll across a vintage iron bridge. &

NORMANDY INN
405 S. 8th St.
Minneapolis 55415
612/370-1400
$$ **DMP**

Owned by the Noble family for two generations, this clean, quiet, family-oriented hotel (160 rooms) has an indoor pool for the kids and free parking. The restaurant makes a mean popover. Pets allowed. &

RADISSON PLAZA HOTEL
35 S. 7th St.
Minneapolis 55402
612/339-4900 or 800/333-3333
$$$ **DMP**

There has been a Radisson on this site since 1909, and this latest incarnation (the flagship of local zillionaire Curt Carlson's worldwide Radisson chain) is geared toward the business traveler, with big, modern, lavishly appointed rooms and plenty of amenities, including an excellent on-site health club and a service-with-a-smile staff. The city-center 288-room hotel is part of a 1987 office and retail project called Plaza VII. The hotel has two restaurants, The Festival and The Cafe, but skip them both; there are far better establishments just footsteps away, including Goodfellow's, right across the street (see Chapter 4, Where to Eat). Skyway connected. &

REGAL MINNEAPOLIS HOTEL
1313 Nicollet Mall
Minneapolis 55403
612/332-6000 or 800/522-8856
$$$ **DMP**

A smart choice for conventioneers on a budget, the Regal is two short blocks from the Minneapolis Convention Center and close to parks, entertainment, and restaurants. The hotel has 325 rooms, a modest health facility, a large banquet hall, and a so-so restaurant, George's on the Park. The airy lobby and many of the rooms were recently remodeled. Skyway connected. &

REGENCY PLAZA HOTEL
41 N. 10th St.
Minneapolis 55402
612/339-9311 or 800/528-1234
$$ **DMP**

This modest Best Western outlet is nothing fancy, but the 200 rooms are clean, the parking is free, and the price is right. The neighborhood is not picturesque (the Greyhound bus depot is across the street), but the Regency is just a block from the Orpheum Theatre and two blocks from the State Theatre. &

WHITNEY HOTEL
150 Portland Ave.
Minneapolis 55401
612/339-9300 or 800/248-1879
$$$$ **DMP**

Downtown's other celebrity destinaion, the Whitney is an intimate (40 rooms and suites) getaway in a renovated brick factory on the banks of the Mississippi River. This European-style hotel is full of luxurious touches, including two exceptional restaurants (the Whitney Grill and Richard's), individually appointed rooms, and grand public spaces. Be sure to ask for a room facing the

Mississippi, or you'll end up over-looking a vast parking lot. &

DOWNTOWN ST. PAUL

The pickings for accommodations are much slimmer in downtown St. Paul than they are in downtown Minneapolis, but that doesn't mean that there aren't several excellent hotels here, as well as some significant bargains.

Hotels and Motels

DAYS INN CIVIC CENTER
175 W. 7th St.
St. Paul 55102
612/292-8929 or 800/325-2525
$ **DSP**
A clean, no-nonsense alternative for travelers on a budget (or with pets), this recently upgraded 200-room hotel is across the street from the St. Paul Civic Center and a quick stroll to the Ordway Music Theatre. Foster's restaurant is in the hotel lobby, but don't bother. &

EMBASSY SUITES SAINT PAUL
175 E. 10th St.
St. Paul 55101
612/224-5400 or 800/443-4600
$$$ **DSP**
Two hundred and ten big, comfortable suites cluster around a sunny, plant-filled atrium in this sensitively designed hotel, which wouldn't feel out of place on the Cote d'Azur. Complimentary breakfast is served in the atrium, and there's a large indoor pool, too. The Minnesota Capitol is six blocks away, and the hotel has a free airport shuttle. &

KELLY INN STATE CAPITOL
161 St. Anthony

St. Paul 55103
612/227-8711 or 800/528-1234
$$ **DSP**
Lots of politicos stay at the Kelly for the convenient location (the State Capitol and surrounding state buildings are three blocks away), low prices, and clean, newly remodeled rooms. This Best Western outlet has a pool and a restaurant, too. Ask for a room on the quieter north side, and you'll get the added bonus of a thrilling view of the capitol dome. &

RADISSON HOTEL ST. PAUL
11 E. Kellogg Blvd.
St. Paul 55102
612/291-1900 or 800/333-3333
$$$$ **DSP**
This 22-story 1960s-era hotel offers lovely vistas of the Mississippi River Valley from many of its 475 recently renovated rooms, and its gorgeous, newly completed ballroom is the city's largest. There's a large pool, too, overlooked by a number of suites and cabana-style rooms. The hotel's kitschy top-floor restaurant, Le Carousel, rotates and offers striking panoramic views that are much better than the food. Skyway connected. &

RADISSON INN
411 Minnesota St.
St. Paul 55102
612/291-8800
$$$ **DSP**
Radisson rescued this property from oblivion in 1996, reopening it as a more affordable alternative to its glitzier hotel a few blocks south. Located in the dreary Town Square office and retail complex downtown, this sleekly modern hotel got a nominal facelift after being dormant for five years, and its 250 rooms are

DOWNTOWN ST. PAUL

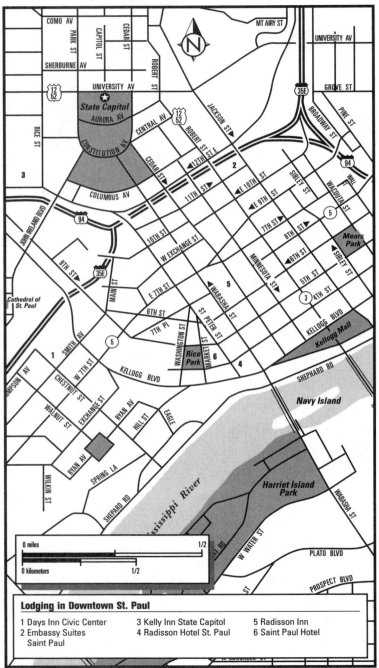

Lodging in Downtown St. Paul

1 Days Inn Civic Center
2 Embassy Suites
  Saint Paul
3 Kelly Inn State Capitol
4 Radisson Hotel St. Paul
5 Radisson Inn
6 Saint Paul Hotel

attractive and quiet. Complimentary breakfast. Skyway connected. &

SAINT PAUL HOTEL
350 Market St.
St. Paul 55102
612/292-9292 or 800/292-9292
$$$$ **DSP**

Minneapolis may have a bevy of gleaming new skyscraper hotels, but those blandly contemporary towers cannot match this grand turn-of-the-century hotel for Old-World sophistication. The 250 deluxe rooms are outfitted for comfort, the two restaurants (the St. Paul Grill and The Cafe) are among the city's finest, and the superb location on Rice Park can't be beat. The ballroom and meeting facilities are excellent, and the concierge service is top-notch. Skyway connected. &

MINNEAPOLIS

BEST WESTERN UNIVERSITY INN
2600 University Ave. SE
Minneapolis 55414
612/379-2313 or 800/528-1234
$$ **MP**

Clean and affordable digs located about six blocks east of the U of M campus, and particularly handy to the U's hockey and basketball arenas. The Best Western offers free shuttle service to the U of M Hospital and Clinic. &

DAYS INN UNIVERSITY
2407 University Ave. SE
Minneapolis 55414
612/623-3999 or 800/325-2525
$ **MP**

No frills, but this 130-room motel does offer free parking, TV, continental breakfast, local phone service, and shuttle service to the U of M's medical complex about six blocks to the east. &

ECONO LODGE
2500 University Ave. SE
Minneapolis 55414
612/331-6000 or 800/553-2000
$ **MP**

Another low-cost, no-nonsense motel (with 80 rooms), in between the Days Inn and the University Inn. The neighborhood has several inexpensive restaurants, including Embers, Arby's, Baker's Square, and the Peking Garden.

FAIR OAKS MOTEL
2335 3rd Ave. S.
Minneapolis 55404
612/871-2000
$ **MP**

Although located across the street from the Minneapolis Institute of Arts, this utilitarian motel isn't in the best of neighborhoods, and the open-air corridors don't do much to ease one's mind. Even so, the rooms are clean, the price is right, and the adjoining Fair Oaks Restaurant is a decent curry house. &

MINNEAPOLIS

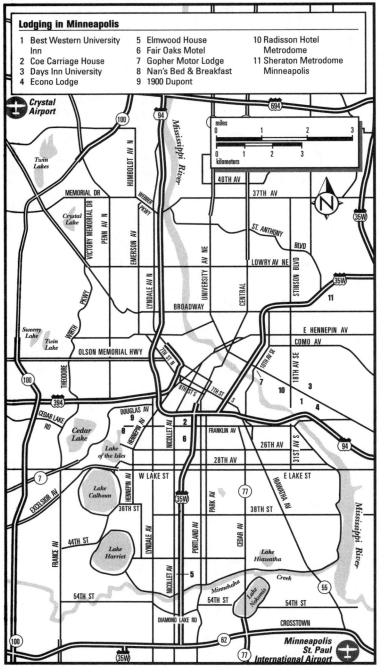

Lodging in Minneapolis

1 Best Western University Inn
2 Coe Carriage House
3 Days Inn University
4 Econo Lodge
5 Elmwood House
6 Fair Oaks Motel
7 Gopher Motor Lodge
8 Nan's Bed & Breakfast
9 1900 Dupont
10 Radisson Hotel Metrodome
11 Sheraton Metrodome Minneapolis

GOPHER MOTOR LODGE
925 4th St. SE
Minneapolis 55414
612/331-3740
$ **MP**

A borderline dump, but it's cheap, the parking is free, and its location (about six blocks west of campus) is convenient to many of the U's sorority and fraternity houses. The plain-Jane rooms are definitely of the "you get what you pay for" variety, but they're clean and quiet, particularly if you request one on the 4th Street side.

RADISSON HOTEL METRODOME
615 Washington Ave. SE
Minneapolis 55414
612/379-8888 or 800/333-3333
$$$ **MP**

A recent name change is somewhat misleading, because this attractive, modern hotel (formerly the Radisson University Hotel) is across the street from the U of M's medical complex and more than 2 miles east of the stadium. Misnomers aside, this 304-room hotel is full of amenities and has two good restaurants: The Meadows, a clubby steak and wild-fowl joint, and McCormick's, a lively deli.

SHERATON METRODOME MINNEAPOLIS
1330 Industrial Blvd.
Minneapolis 55413
612/331-1900
$$ **MP**

Why it's called the Sheraton *Metrodome* is a puzzle, since this former Hilton property is located several miles north of the stadium. This 250-room hotel is convenient to Rosedale, as well as to U of M's St. Paul campus and the state fairgrounds. The Anchorage, the seafood restaurant located in the hotel, isn't what it used to be. &

Elmwood House

Bed and Breakfasts

COE CARRIAGE HOUSE
1700 3rd Ave. S.
Minneapolis 55404
612/871-4249
$$$$ **DMP**

Good and bad location: just two blocks south of the Minneapolis Convention Center but bordering an increasingly marginal neighborhood. The house itself (rented as a single unit) is a stunner, a deluxe three-bedroom unit in a converted 1880s carriage house, with a Jacuzzi, kitchen, fine furnishings, and cable TV. Rates are based on the number of guests.

ELMWOOD HOUSE
1 East Elmwood Pl.
Minneapolis 55419
612/822-4558 or 888/822-4558
$$ **MP**

Three rooms, (one has a private screened porch), shared bath, and a two-bedroom, third-floor suite with bath, in a comfortable 1887 house.

ST. PAUL

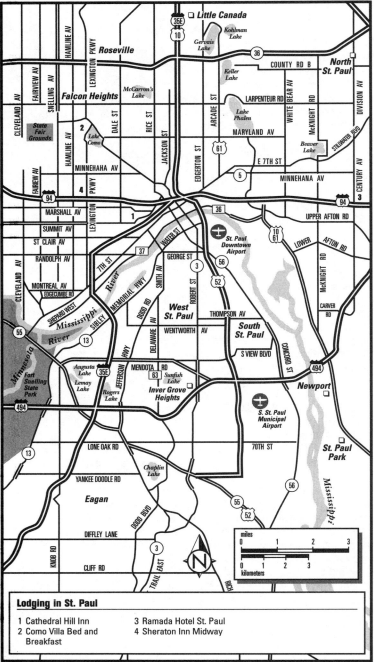

Lodging in St. Paul

1 Cathedral Hill Inn
2 Como Villa Bed and Breakfast
3 Ramada Hotel St. Paul
4 Sheraton Inn Midway

Designed by Henry Wild Jones (architect of Butler Square) for his family, Elmwood House resides in the charming Tangletown neighborhood, ten minutes from both downtown and Mall of America. Minnehaha Creek and its walking and bike paths are one block to the south.

NAN'S BED & BREAKFAST
2304 Fremont Ave. S.
Minneapolis 55405
612/377-5118 or 800/214-5118
$ **MP**
Three rooms with shared bath in a great south Minneapolis location, just six blocks east of picturesque Lake of the Isles and a ten-minute walk to Uptown shops, restaurants, and movie theaters.

1900 DUPONT
1900 Dupont Ave. S.
Minneapolis 55403
612/374-1973
$$ **MP**
Four rooms with private baths in a turn-of-the-century home on Lowry Hill, just a few blocks south of the Guthrie Theater, Walker Art Center, and the Minneapolis Sculpture Garden.

ST. PAUL

RAMADA HOTEL ST. PAUL
1870 Old Hudson Rd.
St. Paul 55119
612/735-2330 or 800/228-2828
$$ **SP**
The best features of this amiable 200-room Ramada Hotel St. Paul are its proximity to the huge corporate campus of 3M (Minnesota Mining and Manufacturing), its comfortable rooms, and its big indoor swimming pool and lounge. &

1900 Dupont

SHERATON INN MIDWAY
400 Hamline Ave. N.
St. Paul 55104
612/642-1234
$$ **SP**
A smart choice for families, this well-maintained 200-room hotel in St. Paul's Midway district is convenient to both downtowns (via I-94), the Minnesota State Fairgrounds, and the adjacent Midway shopping area. &

Bed and Breakfasts

CATHEDRAL HILL INN
341 Dayton Ave.
St. Paul 55102
612/224-7033 or 800/590-6779
$$$ **SP**
This B & B provides a beautiful urban getaway in a beautifully restored Tudor Revival mansion, circa 1908. The Cathedral Hill Inn is open March through December and is located minutes from downtown St. Paul in the historic Cathedral Hill neighborhood.

COMO VILLA BED AND BREAKFAST
1371 W. Nebraska Ave.
St. Paul 55108
612/647-0471
$$ **SP**
An 1870s Victorian home just two blocks off of St. Paul's Como Park and six blocks from the Minnesota State Fairgrounds. Three rooms with private baths.

GREATER TWIN CITIES

The I-494 "strip" is lined with an unusually large number of motels and hotels for three reasons: first, proximity to Minneapolis/St. Paul International Airport; second, proximity to what once was Metropolitan Stadium (now demolished) and the Metropolitan Sports Center (now demolished); third, proximity to the gargantuan Mall of America, built on the site of the Met in 1992.

Quality and prices run the gamut, and the Mall's popularity sometimes can make it difficult to book a room anywhere in the area; many out-of-town Mall shoppers find themselves staying in downtown Minneapolis or downtown St. Paul (both about 15 minutes away) if they haven't planned ahead.

The listings below also include hotels and motels located outside the I-494 strip. These are identified as "suburban."

Hotels and Motels

AFTON HOUSE INN
3291 S. St. Croix Trail
Afton 55001
612/436-8883
$$$ **GTC**
Dating back to 1867, this small,

charming hotel is on the National Register of Historic Places. Most rooms have fireplaces and Jacuzzis. &

BEST WESTERN AMERICAN INN
3924 Excelsior Blvd.
Minneapolis 55416
612/927-7731 or 800/528-1234
$ **GTC**
Just 1 mile west of Lake Calhoun, this unassuming and inexpensive suburban motel is a little-known and conveniently located gem to remember when putting up out-of-town guests on a budget.

BEST WESTERN CANTERBURY INN
1244 Canterbury Rd.
Shakopee 55379
612/445-3644 or 800/528-1234
$ **GTC**
A comfortable, 175-room choice for suburban lodgings, close to the fun of Valleyfair amusement park, the horse races at Canterbury Park, or the gambling at Mystic Lake Casino. &

BEST WESTERN SEVILLE PLAZA HOTEL
8151 Bridge Rd.
Bloomington 55437
612/830-1300 or 800/528-1234
$$ **GTC**
The cheesy mock-Spanish decor can be easily overlooked because the value is pretty good at this 250-room hotel located about five minutes west of the Mall. Free shuttle service to the Mall and the airport. The hotel has an indoor pool, too.

BRADBURY SUITES BEST WESTERN
7770 Johnson Ave.
Bloomington 55435
612/893-9999 or 800/528-1234

$$ **GTC**

Small and affordable, this no-frills hotel has 125 larger-than-usual rooms (all with refrigerators) and is located at the intersection of I-494 and France Avenue, about four minutes west of the Mall and 1 mile south of Southdale.

COUNTRY INN & SUITES BY CARLSON
2221 Killebrew Dr.
Bloomington 55425
612/854-5555 or 800/456-4000
$$ **GTC**

This new hotel features 85 standard rooms and 55 suites, including ten with whirlpools. Carlson Companies (owners of the Radisson chain) put a little extra dough into this high-profile location, so this hotel (across the street from the Mall) is less spartan than its other metro-area compatriots. A TGIFriday's restaurant is located next to the hotel. Additional locations: 2905 Snelling Ave. N., Roseville; 4940 Hwy. 61, White Bear Lake; 6003 Hudson Rd., Woodbury. &

DAYS INN AIRPORT
1901 Killebrew Dr.
Bloomington 55425
612/854-8400
$$ **GTC**

A convenient Mall location (directly across the street from Macy's), attractive rooms, and a big indoor swimming pool make this hotel popular with visiting families. Free shuttle to the Mall and the airport. &

DECATHLON ATHLETIC CLUB
1700 E. 79th St.
Bloomington 55425
612/854-7777
$$ **GTC**

This deluxe health club and spa has extensive sports and fitness facilities

and also operates a well-kept secret: a small hotel of single rooms and suites at remarkably low prices. Attentive service, plus the run of the club, which also includes dining facilities and free shuttle service to the Mall and the airport. Two minutes west of the Mall. &

EMBASSY SUITES HOTEL AIRPORT EAST
7901 34th Ave. S.
Bloomington 55425
612/854-1000 or 800/362-2779
$$$ **GTC**

EMBASSY SUITES HOTEL AIRPORT WEST
2800 W. 80th St.
Bloomington 55431
612/884-4811 or 800/362-2779
$$$ **GTC**

Two branches of the all-suites hotel chain, both organized around lushly landscaped indoor atriums, are located about 4 miles apart. The spacious two-room suites are comfortable and quiet, and both serve complimentary breakfast. The Airport West location is near Southdale (about four minutes west of the Mall), and the Airport East location is about two minutes from the front door of Minneapolis/St. Paul International and a similar distance to the Mall. The eastern location is within a stone's throw of the gorgeous Minnesota Valley National Wildlife Refuge. Both offer free shuttle service to the airport and the Mall. &

EXEL INN
2701 E. 78th St.
Bloomington 55425
612/854-7200 or 800/356-8013
$ **GTC**

This branch of the national no-frills motel chain, located next door to the

GREATER TWIN CITIES

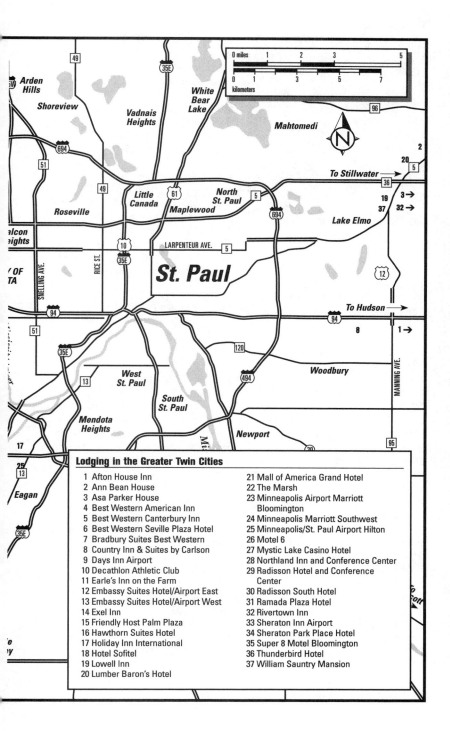

Lodging in the Greater Twin Cities

1 Afton House Inn
2 Ann Bean House
3 Asa Parker House
4 Best Western American Inn
5 Best Western Canterbury Inn
6 Best Western Seville Plaza Hotel
7 Bradbury Suites Best Western
8 Country Inn & Suites by Carlson
9 Days Inn Airport
10 Decathlon Athletic Club
11 Earle's Inn on the Farm
12 Embassy Suites Hotel/Airport East
13 Embassy Suites Hotel/Airport West
14 Exel Inn
15 Friendly Host Palm Plaza
16 Hawthorn Suites Hotel
17 Holiday Inn International
18 Hotel Sofitel
19 Lowell Inn
20 Lumber Baron's Hotel

21 Mall of America Grand Hotel
22 The Marsh
23 Minneapolis Airport Marriott
   Bloomington
24 Minneapolis Marriott Southwest
25 Minneapolis/St. Paul Airport Hilton
26 Motel 6
27 Mystic Lake Casino Hotel
28 Northland Inn and Conference Center
29 Radisson Hotel and Conference
   Center
30 Radisson South Hotel
31 Ramada Plaza Hotel
32 Rivertown Inn
33 Sheraton Inn Airport
34 Sheraton Park Place Hotel
35 Super 8 Motel Bloomington
36 Thunderbird Hotel
37 William Sauntry Mansion

Lowell Inn

Sheraton Inn, isn't anything special, but the prices are affordable, the rooms are clean, and the prime location means easy access to the airport (free shuttle service) and the Mall. &

FRIENDLY HOST PALM PLAZA
1225 E. 78th St.
Bloomington 55425
612/854-3322 or 800/341-8000
$$ **GTC**
A small (47 rooms) and unusually affordable motel, with kitchenettes in every room and an indoor pool. Deluxe it's not, but the proximity to the Mall (two minutes away) and the airport (five minutes away) make this place a great deal if you're on a budget.

HAWTHORN SUITES HOTEL
3400 Edinborough Way
Edina 55435
612/893-9300
$$ **GTC**
This all-suites hotel has 140 two-room suites (with kitchenettes) and offers free breakfast daily and free Happy Hour Monday through Thursday.

Hotel guests have free access to adjacent Edinborough Park, a large indoor park—complete with gardens, a swimming pool, skating rink, and a children's playground—that is especially popular in the winter months. &

HOLIDAY INN INTERNATIONAL
3 Appletree Sq.
Bloomington 55425
612/854-9000 or 800/465-4329
$$ **GTC**
Located two minutes from the airport, this fancy (for a Holiday Inn) 13-story hotel has 430 rooms, an Olympic-size swimming pool, and easy access to the Minnesota Valley National Wildlife Refuge. Free shuttle service to the airport and the Mall, both about two minutes away. &

HOTEL SOFITEL
5601 W. 78th St.
Bloomington 55439
612/835-1900 or 800/763-4835
$$$ **GTC**
It's all très French (or at least a Midwesterner's idea of France) at this congenial and well-appointed getaway, probably the most comfortable hotel in the I-494 area. Nearly 300 rooms (all recently remodeled) are stacked around a lovely interior atrium court, and there's a pool and a fairly plush health spa, too. The Sofitel also has three noteworthy restaurants: Chez Collette does casual bistro fare, La Terrasse is for quick snacks, and Le Cafe Royal is more formal. &

LOWELL INN
102 N. 2nd St.
Stillwater 55082
612/439-1100
$$$$ **GTC**
Expensive and romantic, this 21-room inn (built in 1930) was designed to re-

Camping in the Twin Cities

Campsites are few and far between in the seven-county metropolitan area, but you can still find a quiet place to spend a night in a tent (or under the stars).

*Hennepin County's park system operates a number of camping facilities, including a 210-site location on beautiful Lake Independence in **Baker Park**, about 15 miles west of downtown Minneapolis, and a 54-site location at Lake Auburn in **Carver Park**, about 20 miles southwest of downtown Minneapolis. Baker's rates are $12 per night; Carver's, $9 per night. Call 612/559-6700 for reservations.*

*There are two dozen backpack campsites at **Afton State Park** in Hastings, about 20 minutes southeast of downtown St. Paul. The park has stunning views of the St. Croix River. The year-round campsites cost $8 per night; call 612/922-9000 or 800/246-2267 for reservations. **Bunker Hill Regional Park** in Anoka (30 minutes north of downtown Minneapolis) offers 26 sites (50 cents per night) with a central restroom with running water, but no showers or electricity. Call 612/757-3920 for reservations.*

The Minnesota Alliance of Campground Operators publishes an annually updated roster of private and public campgrounds across the state. For a free copy of Minnesota Campground and RV Parks, call the Minnesota Department of Tourism at 612/296-5029 or 800/657-3700. The department also manages an extensive database of area campgrounds and will help callers find facilities that best serve their needs.

semble Mount Vernon and oozes hospitality. A particular favorite with honeymooners and couples celebrating anniversaries, the inn also has three restaurants and is located in the heart of historic Stillwater.

LUMBER BARON'S HOTEL
127 S. Water St.

Stillwater 55082
612/439-6000
$$$$ GTC
An exquisite 36-room hotel (partially housed in a vintage 1890 commercial building) in the center of Stillwater. The rooms are large and lavishly appointed, and the superior staff aims to please. &

MALL OF AMERICA GRAND HOTEL
7901 24th Ave. S.
Bloomington 55425
612/854-2244 or 800/222-8733
$$$ GTC
Located directly across the street from the Mall, this 320-room quasi-luxury hotel (formerly known as the Registry Hotel and recently renovated) is a great choice for those immersing themselves in the Mall experience. If you feeling like going all-out, consider booking a room on the Concierge Floors, which offer free Happy Hour and breakfast. The hotel's Nine Mile Grill (named for a meandering Bloomington creek) is actually quite good. Free Mall and airport shuttle service. &

MINNEAPOLIS AIRPORT MARRIOTT BLOOMINGTON
2020 E. 79th St.
Bloomington 55425
612/854-7441 or 800/228-9290
$$$ GTC
A standard Marriott with a superb location across the parking lot from the Mall. This sprawling hotel has nearly 500 rooms, a big indoor pool, and shuttle service to the Mall and the airport. &

MINNEAPOLIS MARRIOTT SOUTHWEST
5801 Opus Pkwy.
Minnetonka 55343
612/935-5500
$$$ GTC
A big, 325-room suburban hotel in a campus-like office park about five minutes west of Southdale and just north of the intersection of Highways 62 and 169. There's a large fitness center on the premises, as well as access to a miles-long system of jogging and biking paths. &

MINNEAPOLIS/ST. PAUL AIRPORT HILTON
3800 E. 80th St.
Bloomington 55425
612/854-2100 or 800/673-7453
$$ GTC
Another big, impersonal, but comfortable airport hotel, located about two minutes west of the airport. Big pool and a fancy conference center, too. &

MOTEL 6
7640 Cedar Ave. S.
Richfield 55423
612/861-4491 or 800/466-8356
$ GTC
Clean, cheap (around $40 per night), but exceedingly basic accommodations. The Mall is just across the confusing I-494/Highway 77 interchange.

MYSTIC LAKE CASINO HOTEL
2400 Mystic Lake Blvd.
Prior Lake 55372
612/445-9000 or 800/262-7799
$$ GTC
The only hotel at the state's largest—and most lavish—casino (and the nation's second-largest Native American—owned gaming operation), located 30 minutes southwest of downtown Minneapolis. This comfortable 220-room suburban hotel is constantly booked solid, so call ahead for reservations. &

NORTHLAND INN AND CONFERENCE CENTER
7025 Northland Dr. N.
Brooklyn Park 55428
612/536-8300 or 800/441-4622
$$$ GTC
More than 200 deluxe two- and three-room suites are arranged around a sunny, eight-story atrium at this popular destination for business travelers, located 20 minutes north-

west of downtown Minneapolis. The suburban hotel has extensive conference facilities, two on-site restaurants, and a lavishly appointed exercise facility. &

RADISSON HOTEL AND CONFERENCE CENTER
3131 Campus Dr.
Plymouth 55441
612/559-6600 or 800/333-3333
$$ GTC

The former Scanticon Conference Center is now under Radisson management, which renovated the suburban complex's 240 guest rooms and its spacious conference center. There's a major fitness center, and the surrounding grounds are lovely. &

RADISSON SOUTH HOTEL
7800 Normandale Blvd.
Bloomington 55439
612/835-7800 or 800/333-3333
$$$$ GTC

Bloomington's largest hotel (575 large rooms) is also a popular meeting and convention facility. It's located at the intersection of I-494 and Highway 100, about five minutes west of the Mall. Request a room around the big indoor pool for a private balcony. Shipside, the hotel's seafood restaurant, isn't thrilling, but the more informal Cafe Stuga does a pretty good job with Scandinavian-themed fare. You'll do better if you dine across the street at one of the restaurants in the Hotel Sofitel. &

RAMADA PLAZA HOTEL
12201 Ridgedale Dr.
Minnetonka 55343
612/593-0000 or 800/228-2828
$$$ GTC

A popular stop for business travelers working in the western suburbs (General Mills' headquarters is 2 miles east on I-394). For a suburban chain hotel, this one's unusually attractive and has the added bonus of being on the edge of a wetlands preserve; ask for a room overlooking the park so you can avoid a view of the parking lot at Ridgedale shopping center. &

SHERATON INN AIRPORT
2500 E. 79th St.
Bloomington 55425
612/854-1771
$$ GTC

A low-lying, 230-room hotel that's a favorite with flight crews, who praise its big indoor pool, large exercise area, ruggedly handsome lobby, and close proximity to Mall of America, which is just up the street. Airport and Mall shuttle service, of course. &

SHERATON PARK PLACE HOTEL
5555 Wayzata Blvd.
St. Louis Park 55416
612/542-8600 or 800/542-5566
$$ GTC

Just five minutes west of downtown Minneapolis, this attractive 300-room suburban hotel has a huge indoor swimming pool and extensive meeting and banquet facilities. Dover's, the hotel's casual restaurant, doesn't thrill, but there are a number of interesting places to eat within walking distance of the hotel. &

SUPER 8 MOTEL BLOOMINGTON
7800 2nd Ave. S.
Bloomington 55420
612/888-8800 or 800/800-8000
$$ GTC

This Super 8 Motel offers reliable, no-frills accommodations, located about 2 miles west of the Mall at I-494 and Nicollet Avenue. Complimentary shuttle service to the Mall and the airport. &

THE THUNDERBIRD HOTEL
2201 E. 78th St.
Bloomington 55425
612/854-3411 or 800/528-1234
$$ GTC

This Best Western property is in a class all its own and worth checking out even if you don't intend to book a room. Every square inch of *chez* Thunderbird seems to be covered in Native American art and artifacts (some of it of dubious origin), and what isn't extraordinarily beautiful is supremely tacky. The faux Native American motif continues in the guest rooms. The Totem Pole Dining Room has forgettable food but equally unforgettable atmosphere. The hotel boasts three swimming pools (indoor, outdoor, and kiddie) and a small workout area. The Mall is just across the street, and shuttle service to both the Mall and the airport is available.

Bed and Breakfasts

ANN BEAN HOUSE
319 W. Pine St.
Stillwater 55082
612/430-0355
$$$ GTC

Five rooms (all with private baths) in an 1870s mansion, adorned with oak woodwork and elaborate fireplaces.

ASA PARKER HOUSE
17500 N. St. Croix Trail
Marine on St. Croix 55047
612/433-5248
$$$$ GTC

Five guest rooms (all with private baths) in a picture-perfect house from the 1850s.

EARLE'S INN ON THE FARM
6150 Summit Dr. N.
Brooklyn Center 55430
612/569-6330 or 800/428-8382
$$$ GTC

Eleven wonderfully decorated rooms (all with private baths) housed in restored, turn-of-the-century farm buildings on the old Earle Brown Farm, the estate of the founder of the Minnesota Highway Patrol. Dinner at Earle's restaurant (Friday and Saturday only) is a special treat. The gardens are lovely, too. Ten minutes north of downtown Minneapolis. ♿

THE MARSH
15000 Minnetonka Blvd.
Minnetonka 55435
612/935-2202
$$$ GTC

A half-dozen comfortable rooms located in a soothing and luxurious health and wellness facility. ♿

RIVERTOWN INN
306 W. Olive St.
Stillwater 55082
612/430-2955
$$$ GTC

A lumber fortune was behind this 1882 Victorian mansion, and many of its eight rooms have dazzling views of the St. Croix River valley.

WILLIAM SAUNTRY MANSION
626 N. 4th St.
Stillwater 55082
612/430-2653
$$$ GTC

This glorious 1890 Queen Anne house has five antique-filled rooms with private baths and fireplaces and is located in the heart of historic Stillwater. Smoke-free.

SPCVB/Thomas K. Perry

4

As little as a decade ago, the Twin Cities were strictly meat-and-potatoes towns. Eating ethnic meant grabbing egg rolls at the local chow mein house, and French toast was about as nouvelle as it got.

The Twin Cities' restaurant renaissance has been remarkable, not only for its range—nearly every kind of cuisine is now represented here— but also for the sheer number of new and interesting food-and-drink establishments to savor. Today there is a restaurant for every taste and pocketbook, and taking in the gastronomical side of Minneapolis and St. Paul is as fun as exploring the area's parks, cultural institutions, and sights.

This chapter begins with a list of restaurants organized by type of food each offers. For details about each restaurant, consult the pages that follow—dining spots are listed alphabetically within each geographic zone. Dollar-sign symbols indicate how much you can expect to spend per person for a meal (one appetizer, one entrée, and dessert). Disabled access is indicated by the wheelchair symbol.

Price rating symbols:
$ **Under $10/person**
$$ **$11 to $20**
$$$ **$21 and up**

All restaurants listed accept credit cards unless otherwise noted.

Bakeries

Blackie's Bakery (MP)
French Meadow Bakery
    and Cafe (MP)
Isles Bun & Coffee Co. (MP)
Sindbad International Foods and
    Imports (MP)
Turtle Bread Company (MP)

Breakfasts

Al's Breakfast (MP)
Isles Bun & Coffee Co. (MP)
No Wake Cafe (DSP)
Ruby's Cafe (MP)

Cafeterias

Cafe Latte (SP)
New French Kitchen (MP)

Casual

Harvest Restaurant (GTC)
Linguini & Bob (DMP)
Lucia's Restaurant (MP)
Monte Carlo Bar & Cafe (DMP)
Muffuletta in the Park (SP)

Nicollet Island Inn (DMP)
Oak Grill (DMP)
128 Cafe (SP)
Palomino (DMP)
River Room (DSP)
Sidney's Pizza Cafe (GTC)
Tavern on Grand (SP)
W.A. Frost & Co. (SP)

Ethnic

Asia Grille (GTC)
August Moon (GTC)
The Barbary Fig (SP)
Black Forest Inn (MP)
Brit's Eating and Drinking
    Establishment (DMP)
Cafe Havana (DMP)
Chez Bananas (DMP)
Curry Leaf Deli (SP)
Gardens of Salonica (MP)
Juanita's Restaurante
    Mexicano (SP)
Nankin Cafe (DMP)
Origami (DMP)
Rainbow Chinese Restaurant (MP)
Sawatdee (DMP, DSP)
Shilla (SP)
Singapore Chinese Cuisine (GTC)

Dining at the Mall of America

Java Jive

The Twin Cities' caffeine landscape is dominated by seemingly countless outlets of **Starbucks** and **Caribou Coffee** (with 12 and 19 locations, respectively, and counting), the two dominant chain competitors. But if cookie-cutter surroundings aren't your cup of coffee, there are a number of one-of-a-kind joints in which to sip and scope the crowd. In **south Minneapolis**, the coffee habit can be satisfied at the eclectic **Coffee Gallery** (715 Franklin Ave. W., 612/870-9508) or the dark and quiet **Caffetto** (708 W. 22 St., 612/872-0911). Grungers hang at **Muddy Waters** (2401 Lyndale Ave. S., 612/872-2232), which is famous for its quirky menu of Rice Krispie bars, Spaghettios, and other quasi-suburban treats; while bikers and Harley wannabes congregate down the street at **Bob's Java Hut** (2649 Lyndale Ave. S., 612/871-4485). **Cyber X** (3001 Lyndale Ave. S., 612/824-3558) melds two hot trends—caffeine and cyberspace—and **Crema Cafe** (3403 Lyndale Ave. S., 612/824-3868) is probably the prettiest place in the Twin Cities to enjoy a cup of coffee—or a scoop of Sonny's Ice Cream. Friendly **Ole & Lena's** (3255 Bryant Ave. S., 612/824-6611) sells sandwiches and salads as well as a decent cup of joe.

The **Uptown** neighborhood's most popular java joints include **Cafe Wyrd** (1600 W. Lake St., 612/827-5710), which attracts a young gay and lesbian crowd; **Uncommon Grounds** (2809 Hennepin Ave. S., 612/872-4811), which is romance personified; and the intimate **Cafe Tazza** in Calhoun Square (3001 Hennepin Ave. S., 612/825-9707).

Best bets in **downtown Minneapolis** include sunny **Coffee News** (910 Nicollet Mall, 612/359-0889), laid-back **Prairie Star** (119 N. 1st St., 612/341-3526), and mellow **Moose & Sadie's** (212 3rd Ave. N., 612/371-0464). In the **Dinkytown** neighborhood near U of M, young scholars debate the vagaries of Proust over cappuccino at the **Purple Onion** (326 14th Ave. SE, 612/378-7763) and **Espresso Royale** (411 14th Ave. SE, 612/623-8127).

Late-Night Dining

The Twin Cities aren't exactly night-owl towns, but there are a few places that stay open past the 10:00 news.

*Cheap, delicious eats, a great beer and wine selection, bowling on six lanes, and a busy cabaret scene make the **Bryant-Lake Bowl** (180 W. Lake St., Minneapolis, 612/825-3737; $) a south Minneapolis hot spot. No reservations; open until 1 a.m. daily.*

***Caffe Solo** (123 N. 3rd St., Minneapolis, 612/332-7108; $$) serves tasty pastas and pizzas in an open, animated warehouse space. Good wine list and fab breakfasts. No reservations; open Sunday through Thursday until 11 p.m., Friday and Saturday until 3 a.m.*

*The open kitchen at **Figlio** (3001 Hennepin Ave. S., Minneapolis, 612/822-1688; $$) prepares vaguely Italian fare, including terrific wood-fired pizzas, plus pastas, salads, and sandwiches. The crowd is young and fashionable. No reservations; open Sunday through Thursday until 1 a.m., Friday and Saturday until 2 a.m.*

*You'll find the best pizza in the Twin Cities at **Pizza Luce** (119 N. 4th St., Minneapolis, 612/333-7359; $). Chewy, hearty, herby crusts are topped with fresh, homemade ingredients (and plenty of garlic) but not a lot of cheese (luce is Italian for "light"). Luce delivers to a limited area. No reservations; open Thursday until 2 a.m., Friday and Saturday until 3 a.m.*

Taco Morales (MP)
Tejas (GTC)

Fine Dining

Bayport American Cookery (GTC)
cafe un deux trois (DMP)
California Cafe (GTC)
Campiello (MP)
Chez Foley (GTC)
D'Amico Cucina (DMP)
510 Restaurant (DMP)
Forepaugh's (SP)
Goodfellow's (DMP)
Gustino's (DMP)
Lord Fletcher's on Lake
  Minnetonka (GTC)
Loring Cafe and Bar (MP)
Lowell Inn (GTC)
Napa Valley Grill (GTC)
The New French Cafe and
  Bar (DMP)
Pronto Ristorante and Caffe (DMP)
St. Paul Grill (DSP)
Sophia (DMP)
Table of Contents (SP)

Inexpensive

Best of Phillie Deli (DMP)
Birchwood Cafe (MP)
Byerly's Restaurants (GTC)
Convention Grill (GTC)
Highland Grill (SP)
Loretta's Restaurant (MP)
Mayslack's Polka Lounge (MP)
Modern Cafe (MP)
Peter's Grill (DMP)
Punch Woodfire Pizza (SP)

Italian

Broder's Cucina Italiana (MP)
Buca Little Italy (DMP, SP, GTC)
D'Amico & Sons (MP, GTC)
Giorgio (MP)
Giorgio on Lake (MP)
Ristorante Luci (SP)

Novelty

Minnesota Zephyr (GTC)
Planet Hollywood (GTC)
Rainforest Cafe (GTC)
Twin City Grill (GTC)

Ribs

Famous Dave's BBQ
   Shack (MP, GTC)
Market Bar-B-Que (MP)

Seafood

Anthony's Wharf (DMP)
Blue Point Restaurant & Oyster
   Bar (GTC)

Steak

Kincaid's (GTC)
Manny's Steakhouse (DMP)

Morton's of Chicago (DMP)
Murray's (DMP)

Vegetarian

Cafe Brenda (DMP)

DOWNTOWN MINNEAPOLIS

BEST OF PHILLIE DELI
112 N. 3rd St., Minneapolis
612/673-9595
$ **DMP**
Awesome Philadelphia steak sandwiches, plus the tastiest sub
sandwiches in town. The walls of this
small Warehouse District hangout
are covered with mementos from the
City of Brotherly Love. No reservations; no credit cards; lunch and dinner daily; closed Sunday. ♿

BRIT'S PUB AND EATING
ESTABLISHMENT
1110 Nicollet Mall, Minneapolis
612/332-3908
$$ **DMP**
Minneapolis' most popular sidewalk
cafe, this quaint, pub-like place
serves traditional English food as
well as a long list of Brit teas, beers,
and ales. Lots of British pastimes,
too, including darts, cribbage, and
backgammon. High tea every after-
noon, and one of the few places in
town that stays open late (until
1 a.m.). No reservations; lunch and
dinner daily. ♿

BUCA LITTLE ITALY
11 S. 12th St., Minneapolis
612/638-2225
$$ **DMP**
One of "the ten best new restaurants
in America," according to *Bon Ap-
petit* magazine. A series of amusingly
overdecorated rooms house this

DOWNTOWN MINNEAPOLIS

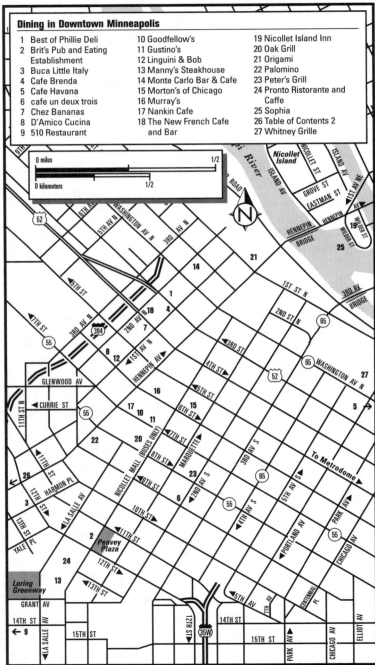

Dining in Downtown Minneapolis

1 Best of Phillie Deli
2 Brit's Pub and Eating Establishment
3 Buca Little Italy
4 Cafe Brenda
5 Cafe Havana
6 cafe un deux trois
7 Chez Bananas
8 D'Amico Cucina
9 510 Restaurant
10 Goodfellow's
11 Gustino's
12 Linguini & Bob
13 Manny's Steakhouse
14 Monte Carlo Bar & Cafe
15 Morton's of Chicago
16 Murray's
17 Nankin Cafe
18 The New French Cafe and Bar
19 Nicollet Island Inn
20 Oak Grill
21 Origami
22 Palomino
23 Peter's Grill
24 Pronto Ristorante and Caffe
25 Sophia
26 Table of Contents 2
27 Whitney Grille

over-the-top, popular Italian red-sauce house. The portions have *abbondanza* written all over them (to encourage sharing), and the garlicky food, while it doesn't stray too far from what most Americans consider to be Italian, is pretty darned good. Kill time in the tiny bar, or hang on the sidewalk during warm weather. Two other locations: 2728 Gannon Ave., St. Paul, 612/772-4388; and 7711 Mitchell Rd., Eden Prairie, 612/724-7266. The downtown Minneapolis spot has the most interesting ambience. Reservations for the first hour only; dinner only. ♿

CAFE BRENDA
300 1st Ave. N., Minneapolis
612/342-9230
$$$ **DMP**

A serene, contemporary palace for vegetarians and seafood lovers. Brenda's spectacular nouvelle cuisine uses organic ingredients and eschews red meat in favor of freshwater fish, chicken, and an occasional seafood selection. The quiet and attractive dining room is decidedly urban, with its high ceilings, enormous arching plate-glass windows, and minimalist decor. There's a small bar. The kitchen closes at 9 p.m. on weekdays and 10 p.m. on weekends. Reservations recommended; lunch Monday through Friday, dinner Monday through Saturday; closed Sunday; smoke-free. ♿

CAFE HAVANA
231 Cedar Ave. S., Minneapolis
612/338-8484
$$ **DMP**

Home-cooking, Cuban style, in a small storefront operation in the Seven Corners neighborhood. Cafe Havana does not accept reservations; lunch and dinner are served

Monday through Saturday; closed Sunday. ♿

CAFE UN DEUX TROIS
114 S. 9th St., Minneapolis
612/673-0686
$$$ **DMP**

More business is probably transacted over lunch at un deux trois than at any other downtown address, and dinner draws a heady crowd, too. Power brokers return to this stylish restaurant with the e.e. cummings complex for its luxurious French bistro fare, attentive service, and chic (acres of *trompe l'oeil*) atmosphere. On Wednesday night, the kitchen rolls out recipes from Asia, and on Sunday evening, the emphasis is on delectable *cassoullet* (and other simple French country favorites), accompanied by the song stylings of chanteuse Francine Roche. Reservations recommended; lunch Monday through Friday; dinner daily; Sunday brunch September through May. ♿

Brit's Pub and Eating Establishment, p. 55

GMCVA

CHEZ BANANAS
119 N. 4th St., Minneapolis
612/340-0032
$$ **DMP**
Hot-hot Caribbean food in amusing, quirky surroundings. Longstanding hits include the jerk chicken and jerk pork. The adventurous daily specials almost always offer something intriguing (and spicy). No reservations; lunch Monday through Friday, dinner Monday through Saturday; closed Sunday. ⅋

D'AMICO CUCINA
100 N. 6th St., Minneapolis
612/338-2401
$$$ **DMP**
The top of the Twin Cities' food chain. Elegant, understated, and very expensive, this crown jewel of the D'Amico brothers' food empire serves sublime contemporary northern Italian cuisine in serene surroundings. Fabulous wines and impeccable service. Reservations recommended. Dinner only, daily. ⅋

510 RESTAURANT
510 Groveland Ave., Minneapolis
612/874-6440
$$$ **DMP**
Housed in an imposing dining room of a still-regal 1920s luxury apartment hotel, the 510 serves sophisticated American cuisine. Two prix-fixe dinner packages (three courses for $29, or a pre-theater limited-choice menu for $19) are some of the best dining bargains in the Twin Cities. The appealing wine list is reasonably priced. Valet parking. Reservations are recommended; dinner only, Monday through Saturday. ⅋

GOODFELLOW'S
40 S. 7th St., Minneapolis
612/332-4800

$$$ **DMP**
A food-lover's paradise. Exquisite but approachable American regional cuisine, in drop-dead-gorgeous surroundings. Foodies argue over Goodfellow's supreme eminence on the Twin Cities dining scene, but one thing is certain: Goodfellow's new digs, the art deco showplace that was once the Forum Cafeteria, are splendiferous. Polished service and an enviable wine list, too. If you don't want to drop a wad at dinner, do the lunch thing; the surprisingly affordable noon menu is one of the best bargains in the Twin Cities. Reservations recommended; lunch Monday through Friday; dinner Monday through Saturday; closed Sunday. ⅋

GUSTINO'S
30 S. 7th St., Minneapolis
612/349-4075
$$$ **DMP**
The talented singing waiters and waitresses are the main draw to this Marriott City Center Hotel restaurant. Gustino's attracts large birthday/anniversary crowds, and people tend to dress up for a big night out. Unfortunately, the food is the low note here; with luck, you will be so enchanted by the well-sung light opera and Broadway musical selections that you won't notice how mediocre—and expensive—your dinner is. Great service and a decent wine list. Reservations recommended; dinner only, Monday through Saturday; closed Sunday. ⅋

LINGUINI & BOB
100 N. 6th St., Minneapolis
612/332-1600
$$$ **DMP**
Casual, contemporary food and decor (it's all very Pottery Barn) by the D'Amico brothers, and a lower-

Top Ten Outdoor Dining Spots

Twin Citians take any chance they can get to break bread under the open sky. Here are ten particularly wonderful places to enjoy a summer's day.

1. Black Forest Inn, 1 E. 26th St., Minneapolis, 612/872-0812.
2. Brit's Pub and Eating Establishment, 1110 Nicollet Mall, Minneapolis, 612/332-3908.
3. Campiello, 1320 W. Lake St., Minneapolis, 612/825-2222.
4. The Loring Cafe, 1624 Harmon Place, Minneapolis, 612/332-1617.
5. Lord Fletcher's on Lake Minnetonka, 3746 Sunset Dr., Spring Park, 612/471-8513.
6. Sidney's Pizza Cafe, France Avenue at 69th Street, Edina, 612/925-2002.
7. Sophia, 65 SE Main St., Minneapolis, 612/379-1111.
8. Tejas, 3910 W. 50th St., Edina, 612/926-0800.
9. W.A. Frost & Co., 374 Selby Ave., St. Paul, 612/224-5715.
10. Whitney Grille, 150 Portland Ave., Minneapolis, 612/372-6405.

priced (but not much) alternative to their D'Amico Cucina, also located in Butler Square. The food is simpler than the fare at the Cucina, but you can't go wrong with the pastas or the refreshing apricot chicken salad. Fashionable crowd, too: the bar is something of a see-and-be-seen place. No reservations; lunch and dinner Monday through Saturday, dinner only Sunday. &

MANNY'S STEAKHOUSE
1300 Nicollet Mall, Minneapolis
612/339-9000
$$$ **MP**
The restaurant to head for when someone else is picking up the check. Magnificently prepared steaks, lamb, pork chops, and lobster

are the draw here, along with sublimely crisp hash browns, delectable French-fried onions, and beautiful vegetables, all served à la carte. Portions are Fred Flintstone–sized, and that includes the cocktails and the desserts. The surroundings are disarmingly low-key, and the congenial service is nothing short of perfect. Reservations recommended; dinner only, daily. &

MONTE CARLO BAR & CAFE
219 3rd Ave. N., Minneapolis
612/333-5900
$$ **DMP**
Loud, busy, and dark, this Warehouse District magnet features a reliable menu of well-prepared American standards. The meat-loaf sandwich is

outstanding, as is Charlie's Steak Sandwich. Don't let the host steer you into the Monte's two Siberias: the small and secluded front or back dining rooms. The beautiful bar is worth a visit all on its own. Reservations recommended; lunch Monday through Saturday; dinner daily; brunch Sunday. &

MORTON'S OF CHICAGO
555 Nicollet Mall, Minneapolis
612/673-9700
$$$ **DMP**
The epitome of expense-account dining. Serious steaks, lobsters, swordfish, and prime rib in a wood-paneled but not overly staid dining room. The service is genteel, and the desserts are as straightforward and gigantic as the rest of the food. Reservations recommended; lunch Monday through Friday; dinner daily. &

MURRAY'S
26 S. 6th St., Minneapolis
612/339-0909
$$$ **DMP**
Soaked in glamorous 1940s atmosphere, Murray's has been a downtown Minneapolis draw for more than 50 years. The steaks are sublime (try the famous Silver Butter Knife steak for two; the name says it all), and the garlic toast is a City of Lakes tradition. Those under 40 may find it a little pokey, but anyone with a sense of nostalgia will eat Murray's up with a spoon. Reservations recommended; lunch and afternoon tea Monday through Friday; dinner daily. &

NANKIN CAFE
2 S. 7th St., Minneapolis
612/333-3303
$$ **DMP**
One of the city's largest restaurants,

Monte Carlo Bar & Cafe, p. 59

devoted to Cantonese specialties. The food is ordinary (the menu is huge) and seldom veers from the bland, Americanized idea of Chinese food, but the decor is a panic, and the dim sum on Sunday is remarkable. Reservations recommended; lunch Monday through Friday; dinner daily; dim sum Saturday and Sunday. &

THE NEW FRENCH CAFE AND BAR
128 N. 4th St., Minneapolis
612/338-3790
$$$ **DMP**
Few Twin Cities restaurants have enjoyed the influence of the New French. This café sparked the revitalization of the long-neglected Warehouse District in the 1970s, and its sense of adventure and obvious love of good food spawned a whole new generation of foodies in the Twin Cities area. Now under new management, the spare dining room received a much-needed remodeling and the kitchen has been revitalized. This is also the place for power breakfasting in the Twin Cities. Service can be

spotty. Reservations recommended; breakfast and lunch Monday through Friday; dinner daily; brunch Saturday and Sunday. &

NICOLLET ISLAND INN
95 Merriam St., Minneapolis
612/331-3035
$$$ **DMP**

Regional specialties (including walleye and Minnesota-raised poultry and beef) are the focus in this irresistible old-fashioned dining room, with lovely views of the Mississippi River. Reservations are recommended; breakfast and lunch Monday through Saturday; dinner daily; brunch Sunday. &

OAK GRILL
700 on the Mall, Minneapolis
612/375-2938
$$ **DMP**

The dark oak paneling, red leather chairs, 300-year-old carved Tudor fireplace, and snug, blood-red bar (which, unfortunately, is the smoking section) haven't changed one iota since the Oak Grill on the twelfth floor of Dayton's opened in 1947, and the food (and the value) remains equally fine. Try the Mandarin chicken salad or the meat loaf with Yukon gold potatoes. The hot popovers are addicting, and the apple praline pie has stretched more than a few waistlines. The Oak Grill does not accept reservations; lunch Monday through Saturday; dinner Monday through Friday (closes at 7 p.m.); closed Sunday. &

ORIGAMI
30 N. 1st St., Minneapolis
612/333-8430
$$ **DMP**

French-Japanese fusion food, with often brilliant results. The sushi has no equal in the Twin Cities, and the dining room, which is carved out of a renovated, late-nineteenth-century storefront a stone's throw from the Mississippi River, is comfortable and unassuming. Origami does not accept reservations; lunch Monday through Friday; dinner daily. &

PALOMINO
825 Hennepin Ave.,
Minneapolis
612/339-3800
$$$ **DMP**

Wildly overdecorated and always crowded, this restaurant pulses with energy and is the top pre-theater destination in downtown Minneapolis. The spit-roasted garlic chicken is always a good bet, as are the thin-crust pizzas and generously large pastas. The adjacent bar is the city's most sophisticated (but hardly understated) pickup joint. Reservations are recommended; lunch Monday through Saturday; dinner daily; smoke-free. &

PETER'S GRILL
114 S. 8th St., Minneapolis
612/333-1981
$ **DMP**

Peter's Grill has been a downtown home-cooking destination since 1919. Roast turkey with mashed potatoes and gravy, club sandwiches, chef's salad, and pot roast are just some of the standards you'll find. Lunch is big business, and it's tough to leave without a slice of one of the legendary pies. (President Clinton didn't.) The big wooden booths date from the original (and long-gone) Peter's on 9th Street, as do many of the no-nonsense waitresses. Peter's does not accept reservations; breakfast and lunch Monday through Saturday; dinner Monday through

TIP

Too tired to cook or go out? For a $7 fee (tip not included) Gourmet Express (612/922-3463) will deliver just about anything from several dozen restaurants in Minneapolis and its southern and western suburbs directly to your door, Monday through Friday 9 a.m. to 9 p.m., Saturday and Sunday 3 p.m. to 9 p.m.

Friday; closed Sunday; no credit cards; no liquor. &

PRONTO RISTORANTE AND CAFFE
1300 Nicollet Mall, Minneapolis
612/333-4414
$$$ DMP
The ristorante is a serious and rather luxurious Northern Italian house, offering creative and adventurous food; the more laid-back (and significantly cheaper) caffe does tasty pastas, pizzas, and salads. Reservations recommended in the ristorante, no reservations in the caffe. Lunch daily and dinner daily in the caffe, dinner-only in the ristorante. &

SOPHIA
65 SE Main St., Minneapolis
612/379-1111
$$$ DMP
Dimly lit and bewitchingly romantic in a swanky, 1930s-nightclub kind of way, Sophia serves continental American food to an older, well-heeled crowd. Live music and a small dance floor add to the allure, as do the vistas of the downtown Minneapolis skyline. Polished service adds to the experience. Reservations are recommended; lunch Monday through Saturday; dinner daily. &

TABLE OF CONTENTS 2
1310 Hennepin Ave., Minneapolis
612/339-1133
$$$ DMP
This offspring of a popular St. Paul

restaurant has style to burn and has been luring well-dressed crowds since its debut in June 1995. The food is as chic and sophisticated as the surroundings; don't leave without nibbling one of the fabulous cracker-crust pizzas, the stunning tuna tartare, or the peppery lamb shank. Lunch is a great value, and the *soigné* bar features a naughty martini menu. Reservations recommended; lunch Monday through Friday; dinner daily; brunch Sunday. &

WHITNEY GRILLE
150 Portland Ave. S., Minneapolis
612/372-6405
$$$ DMP
Quiet, elegant, and expensive, this is a hotel dining room that's quite a cut above its competition. The menu changes seasonally, but it's always contemporary American in tone. The wood-paneled dining room is designed for privacy. Reservations recommended; breakfast and lunch Monday through Saturday; dinner daily; brunch Sunday. &

DOWNTOWN ST. PAUL

NO WAKE CAFE
100 Yacht Club Rd., St. Paul
612/292-1411
$ DSP
If you like your breakfast on a boat on the Mississippi, then head over to Harriet Island (opposite downtown St. Paul) and greet the day on this

DOWNTOWN ST. PAUL

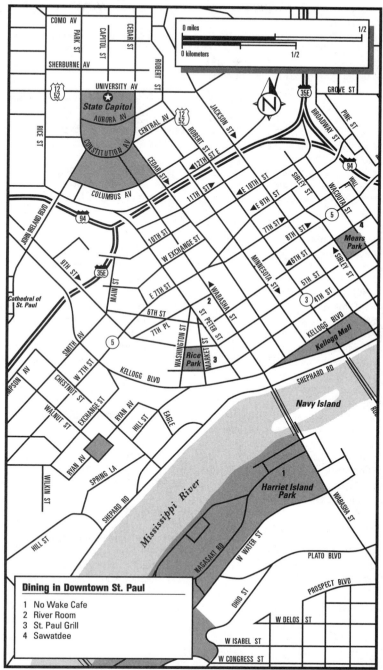

Dining in Downtown St. Paul

1 No Wake Cafe
2 River Room
3 St. Paul Grill
4 Sawatdee

tiny and thoroughly delightful floating restaurant. &

RIVER ROOM
411 Cedar St., St. Paul
612/292-5174
$$ **DSP**

This debonair restaurant (black lacquered walls, mirrors, pink tablecloths, and crystal chandeliers), on the second floor of Dayton's downtown St. Paul store, is a smart choice for a quiet, secluded meal. The menu features a tempting selection of salads, sandwiches, and entrées, plus an excellent wild-rice soup and Dayton's signature popovers. Don't skip the Frango mint cheesecake. Reservations recommended; lunch daily; dinner Monday through Friday (closes at 7 p.m.). &

ST. PAUL GRILL
350 Market St., St. Paul
612/224-7455
$$$ **DSP**

The first place that pops into people's heads when they want to eat in downtown St. Paul. The classic grill fare (steaks, chops, salads) is also a draw, and the handsome-as-all-getout bar lures a heady mix of state politico types and business leaders. The Grill is also the number-one pre-Ordway Music Theatre destination, and offers stunning views of the Rice Park area. Reservations recommended; lunch Monday through Saturday; dinner daily; brunch Sunday; late-night bar menu (until midnight) daily. &

SAWATDEE
289 E. 5th St., St. Paul
612/222-5859
$$ **DSP**

Thai food, from merely hot to scorching, in often-creative combinations.

Also at 607 Washington Ave., Minneapolis, 612/338-6451; and 8501 Lyndale Ave., S., Bloomington, 612/888-7177. Reservations recommended (parties of six or more only); lunch and dinner daily. &

MINNEAPOLIS

AL'S BREAKFAST
413 14th Ave. SE, Minneapolis
612/331-9991
$ **MP**

A U of M legend, this claustrophobic (14 stools) but charming joint has been feeding hungry students for almost a half-century. Get the blueberry pancakes. &

BIRCHWOOD CAFE
3311 E. 25th St., Minneapolis
612/722-4474
$ **MP**

Tasty, inexpensive, and full of surprises, this cheerful café is run by several talented expatriates from Lucia's Restaurant. A constantly rotating menu of sandwiches, soups, a hot entrée or two, and three or four pasta salads. The desserts are noteworthy, and the house-baked bread is equally fine. A great spot for a weekend breakfast, too. No reservations; no credit cards; lunch and dinner daily; closed Monday; no liquor. &

BLACK FOREST INN
1 E. 26th St., Minneapolis
612/872-0812
$$ **MP**

German food in comfortably Teutonic surroundings equals lots of fun. Try the *spaetzel*, the sauerkraut, and the Wiener schnitzel. Vegetarians will have to content themselves with the dessert tray, but the wide range of imported beers is impressive. The

MINNEAPOLIS

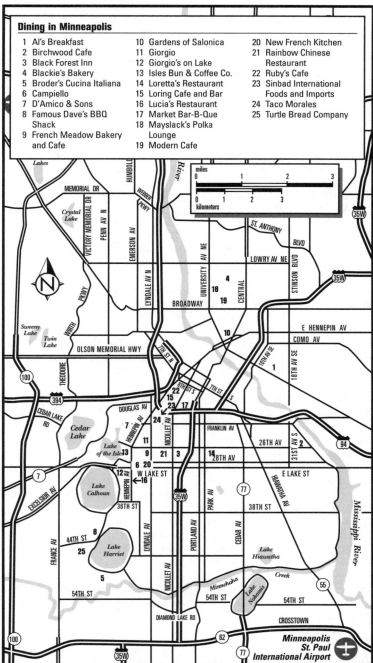

Dining in Minneapolis

1 Al's Breakfast
2 Birchwood Cafe
3 Black Forest Inn
4 Blackie's Bakery
5 Broder's Cucina Italiana
6 Campiello
7 D'Amico & Sons
8 Famous Dave's BBQ Shack
9 French Meadow Bakery and Cafe
10 Gardens of Salonica
11 Giorgio
12 Giorgio's on Lake
13 Isles Bun & Coffee Co.
14 Loretta's Restaurant
15 Loring Cafe and Bar
16 Lucia's Restaurant
17 Market Bar-B-Que
18 Mayslack's Polka Lounge
19 Modern Cafe
20 New French Kitchen
21 Rainbow Chinese Restaurant
22 Ruby's Cafe
23 Sinbad International Foods and Imports
24 Taco Morales
25 Turtle Bread Company

walled urban garden, complete with splashing fountains, statues, a pergola, and tons of blooming plants, is lovely. No reservations; lunch and dinner daily. &

BLACKIE'S BAKERY
639 22nd Ave. NE, Minneapolis
612/789-5326
$ MP
Seventeen varieties of hearty Danish bread are baked daily. There's a wide variety of sweets, too, including Mahjoner, a tasty Danish Christmas cookie (sold year-round). &

BRODER'S CUCINA ITALIANA
2308 W. 50th St., Minneapolis
612/925-3113
$ MP
The lines are always long at this tiny Italian deli, as shoppers queue up for its array of imported Italian treats and salads, pastas, sandwiches, and calzones. The house-baked bread and desserts (particularly the chocolate-dipped biscotti) are also quite good. No reservations; breakfast, lunch and dinner daily; no credit cards. &

CAMPIELLO
1320 W. Lake St., Minneapolis
612/825-2222
$$$ MP
Uptown's smoothest restaurant serves standard Italian pastas, pizzas, poultry, and salads—but it's all eye-catching and a treat to eat. Don't let the host seat you in the back room, which has all the appeal of a conference room in a second-rate law firm. The no-reservation policy is a drag, especially since the place is perpetually packed, but you can call up to an hour ahead and put your name on the waiting list. Reservations recommended at lunch, no reservations at dinner; lunch Monday

through Saturday; dinner daily; Sunday brunch. &

D'AMICO & SONS
2210 Hennepin Ave. S.,
Minneapolis
612/374-1858
$$ MP
Fast food the way it should be. D'Amico & Sons specializes in quick salads, sandwiches, pizzas, pastas, and desserts with an Italian twist. The service (a counter and table service hybrid) isn't all it could be, but the creative preparations, fresh ingredients, affordable prices, and attractive surroundings more than make up for it. Take-out, too. Other locations at 2724 W. 43rd St., Minneapolis, 612/920-2646; 555 Nicollet Mall, Minneapolis, 612/342-2700; and 810 E. Lake St., Wayzata, 612/476-8866. Wine and beer at the Hennepin Avenue and Lake Street locations. No reservations; lunch and dinner daily; brunch Saturday and Sunday. &

FAMOUS DAVE'S BBQ SHACK
4264 Upton Ave. S., Minneapolis
612/929-1200
$ MP
Dave slathers his secret sauce on absurdly large portions of tender pork and beef ribs, as well as chicken, burgers, beef sandwiches, and a pretty mean brisket. If you've got a party of four or more (or just a few folks with major appetites), then consider the "All-American BBQ Feast," amusingly served on a garbage can lid. Fun, friendly atmosphere, low prices, and a hot-hot blues band at the Calhoun Square location (3001 Hennepin Ave. S., Minneapolis, 612/822-9900). Also at Greater St. Paul location, in Roseville (2131 Snelling Ave. N., 612/633-4800). No reservations; lunch and dinner daily; smoke-free. &

While most of the coffeehouses in the Twin Cities are in Minneapolis, you can find a good cup o' joe in St. Paul, too. Artists kill time in Lowertown's sprawling Kuppernicus (308 Prince St., 612/290-2718), while Cahoots Coffee Bar (1562 Selby Ave., 612/644-6778) draws a younger crowd.

FRENCH MEADOW BAKERY AND CAFE
2610 Lyndale Ave. S., Minneapolis
612/870-7855
$ **MP**

Organic breads (including a wicked sourdough) and sweets (killer muffins), plus a perpetually packed cafeteria-style restaurant. &

GARDENS OF SALONICA
19 5th St. NE, Minneapolis
612/378-0611
$ **MP**

A small and appealing Greek café, specializing in *boughatsas*, delicious little triangles of flaky phyllo dough stuffed with savory ingredients. Other specialties include pita-crust pizzas and tantalizing Greek spreads served with pita bread. Lots for vegetarians, and a small to-go deli counter. Reservations are not accepted; lunch and dinner Monday through Saturday; closed Sunday; no credit cards; no liquor. &

GIORGIO
2451 Hennepin Ave., Minneapolis
612/374-5131
$$ **MP**

Small and cluttered—but in a good way—this tiny storefront operation specializes in rustic Tuscan food with a kick. The Caesar has more garlic than any other in town, the pasta is homemade, and the tiny bar next door is an engaging place to linger over a glass of wine or a luscious dessert. No reservations; lunch Tuesday through Friday; dinner daily; no credit cards. &

GIORGIO'S ON LAKE
1601 W. Lake St., Minneapolis
612/822-7071
$$ **MP**

Rustic Italian food in urbane surroundings. This crowded corner storefront buzzes with pleasant activity every night of the week. Salads are special, the focaccias are divine, and the mouth-watering roasted meats are worth the wait. Yummy roasted vegetables, too. The handsome wine bar next door is a smart choice for a quiet night out. No reservations; lunch Tuesday through Friday; dinner daily; no credit cards. &

ISLES BUN & COFFEE CO.
1422 W. 28th St., Minneapolis
612/870-4466
$ **MP**

Out-of-this-world sweet rolls. Slather on the frosting from the big bowl on the counter, and grab a cup of their excellent coffee on your way out. Open daily 6:30 a.m. to 5:00 p.m.; no credit cards. &

LORETTA'S RESTAURANT
2615 Park Ave. S., Minneapolis
612/871-1660
$ **MP**

The restaurant your grandmother

would run if she were so inclined. Loretta's has been serving simple comfort food in its cozy dowager surroundings since 1929. It's the kind of place where the daily special might be chicken à la king over baking-powder biscuits, where the meat loaf is heaven-sent, and the mashed potatoes and gravy are made from scratch. This being Minnesota, there's also a Jell-O salad du jour, and a turkey dinner with all the trimmings is served the first Wednesday of every month. No reservations; lunch only, Sunday through Friday; no credit cards; no liquor. &

LORING CAFE AND BAR
1624 Harmon Pl., Minneapolis
612/332-1617
$$$ **MP**
The epitome of romance, this beguiling getaway is a slice of Montemartre right in the heart of Minneapolis. The inspired regional food is as ambitious as the surroundings are bohemian, and the kitchen often lives up to its formidable reputation. The exotic desserts are spectacular. If you can

handle the wait staff's you-should-be-thrilled-to-be-here attitude, then you'll start a love affair with the Loring. The sprawling, atmospheric bar next door features live music and hordes of yuppie grungers. Reservations recomended; lunch Monday through Friday, dinner daily. &

LUCIA'S RESTAURANT
1432 W. 31st St., Minneapolis
612/825-1572
$ **MP**
One of the Twin Cities' most consistently appealing restaurants. Owner Lucia Watson has been making the most of Midwestern farms' abundance for years in her unpretentious storefront restaurant. The small and surprisingly affordable menu changes weekly, but there's always something for chicken and fish lovers—as well as for vegetarians. Weekend brunches are a distinct pleasure, desserts are dreamy, and the wine bar next door features tasty, inexpensive fare. Reservations are recommended; lunch Tuesday through Friday, dinner

Loretta's Restaurant

Tuesday through Sunday, brunch Saturday and Sunday; closed Monday; restaurant is smoke-free. ᕇ

MARKET BAR-B-QUE
1414 Nicollet Ave., Minneapolis
612/872-1111
$$ **MP**

A 50-year Minneapolis institution specializing in smoky, St. Louis–style spare ribs; you add the sauce. The side dishes can be uneven (except for the baked beans, which are flat-out fabulous), but nobody notices because not only are the ribs that good, but the fun, 1940s atmosphere is eye-catching, too. Also at 1532 Wayzata Blvd., Minnetonka, 612/475-1770. Reservations recommended; lunch and dinner daily. ᕇ

MAYSLACK'S POLKA LOUNGE
1428 NE 4th St., Minneapolis
612/789-9862
$ **MP**

The essence of old "Nordeast" Minneapolis. The massive and wonderfully garlicky roast-beef sandwiches draw folks from all over the city, from factory workers, to pin-striped lawyers, to Minneapolis City Council member Walt Dziedzic. No reservations; lunch and dinner daily. ᕇ

MODERN CAFE
337 13th Ave. NE, Minneapolis
612/378-9882
$ **MP**

A neighborhood joint with a city-wide draw. You might find New England–style pot roast and a winter squash puree for six bucks, a pair of pan-roasted chicken breasts with skin-on mashed potatoes for $6.50, or a BLT with skin-on fries for $4.50. Mondo breakfasts on the weekends, too, including fluffy buttermilk pancakes and a heaping platter of *huevos*

rancheros. No reservations; lunch Tuesday through Friday; dinner Tuesday through Saturday; breakfast Saturday and Sunday; closed Monday.ᕇ

NEW FRENCH KITCHEN
1300 Lagoon Ave., Minneapolis
612/825-2525
$ **MP**

Easygoing, cafeteria-style dining from the folks at the New French Café. Conveniently located next to the Lagoon Cinema, the Kitchen is the obvious place to go for a quick bite before or after the movie. The food can be uneven and a little bland, but if you steer toward the excellent desserts (from the New French Bakery), the rotisserie meats, the imaginative soups, and the composed-while-you-wait salads, you'll have a perfectly fine meal. No reservations; continental breakfast Monday through Friday; lunch and dinner daily; brunch Saturday and Sunday. ᕇ

RAINBOW CHINESE RESTAURANT
2750 Nicollet Ave. S., Minneapolis
612/870-7084
$$ **MP**

There are Chinese restaurants and then there is Rainbow. Seafood is one of owner Tammy Wong's specialties, but she does wonders with pork and beef, too, and there's lots for vegetarians. Fans sing the praises of the sesame noodles, and the roast beef with mustard greens and the tempura-style prawns with broccoli and red curry sauce are to-die-for. Reservations recommended (no same-day reservations, however); lunch and dinner daily. ᕇ

RUBY'S CAFE
1614 Harmon Pl., Minneapolis
612/338-2089

$ **MP**

Great views of Loring Park and huge helpings of biscuits and gravy, scrambled eggs, and awesome pancakes keep the crowds (gays and lesbians in particular) coming back morning after morning. &

SINDBAD INTERNATIONAL FOODS AND IMPORTS
2528 Nicollet Ave. S., Minneapolis
612/871-6505

$ **MP**

The local source for flatbreads, pitas, and a Persian version of focaccia, plus an encyclopedic Middle Eastern deli and gourmet shop. &

TACO MORALES
14 W. 26th St., Minneapolis
612/870-0053

$ **MP**

You know it's authentic Mexican when everyone behind the counter—and most of the customers—are speaking Spanish. Try the tamales, the *sopas*, and the *gorditas*, or the wonderful corn-tortilla tacos. Blistering salsa and tons of fresh cilantro, along with a fun selection of south-of-the-border soft drinks. No reservations; lunch and dinner daily; no credit cards; no liquor. &

TURTLE BREAD COMPANY
3415 W. 44th St., Minneapolis
612/924-6013

$ **MP**

Beautiful and unusual breads, sold in one of the city's most appealing cafés. The chocolate bread stops traffic. &

ST. PAUL

THE BARBARY FIG
720 Grand Ave., St. Paul

612/290-2085

$$ **SP**

The tastes of northern Africa are the focus of this couscous restaurant. The menu offers lots for vegetarians (the kitchen has quite a way with eggplant), and the surroundings are modest but attractive. No reservations; lunch Monday and Wednesday through Saturday; dinner Monday and Wednesday through Sunday; closed Tuesday. &

CAFE LATTE
850 Grand Ave., St. Paul
612/224-5687

$ **SP**

A dream cafeteria. Fresh soups, sandwiches, salads, and hot entrées compete with awesome desserts (the Turtle Cake is legendary) for the attention of a steady horde of admirers. The dining room is a little on the mid-1980s side, but it's sunny and genial and the food is so good you'll end up loving it anyway. No reservations; breakfast Monday through Friday; lunch and dinner daily; brunch Saturday and Sunday; smoke-free. &

CURRY LEAF DELI
1278 Grand Ave., St. Paul
612/699-9330

$ **SP**

A hole-in-the-wall specializing in tantalizing Sri Lankan fare, served deli-style. Beautiful salads and snacks, perfect for take-out or an impromptu picnic. Huge portions. No reservations; lunch and dinner daily; no credit cards; no liquor. &

DAY BY DAY CAFE
477 W. 7th St., St. Paul
612/227-0654

$ **SP**

Funky, affordable, and delicious breakfasts. &

ST. PAUL

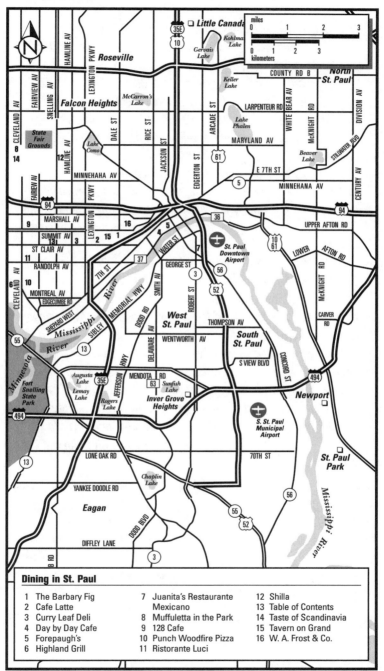

Drive-Ins

The proliferation of fast-food drive-up windows has put a serious dent in their business, but a few authentic drive-ins from the 1950s and 1960s remain in the Twin Cities.

For nearly 40 years, **Wagner's** (3712 Quebec Ave. S., St. Louis Park, 612/933-1857) has drawn a devoted clientele under its modest carports, serving tasty burgers, crisp fried chicken, and eight flavors of rich, creamy malts. Friendly service, too. Also at 7000 W. Broadway, Brooklyn Park, 612/533-8262.

Not only does the **Dari-Ette** (1440 Minnehaha Ave., St. Paul, 612/776-3470) fry up a mean hamburger, this family-owned operation also prepares fairly tasty Italian fare. The big sundaes and malt selections include fun flavors like black raspberry and crème de menthe.

The **Minnetonka Drive-In** (4658 Shoreline Dr., Spring Park, 612/471-9383) features a big menu that has all the burger and hot-dog standards, plus barbecued ribs, fried chicken, and fish and chips; plus a large kids' menu. The "Minnetonka Twin" burger is a special treat.

Porky's (1890 University Ave., St. Paul, 612/644-1790) is not a drive-in per se, but it still rates as a must-visit if you're into car culture. The fried chicken; rich, thick malts; and battered catfish are pretty darned good. Porky's biggest draw: the impromptu classic car show that swarms the parking lot (and spills over to University Avenue) every Friday and Saturday night during the warm-weather months.

FOREPAUGH'S
276 S. Exchange St., St. Paul
612/224-5606
$$$ SP

A gorgeous special-event kind of place, housed in a beautifully restored Victorian mansion on the edge of historic Irvine Park. The house is the lure here, but the quasi-French food is OK, and the pastry cart is heavenly. Reservations recommended; lunch Monday through Friday; dinner daily; brunch Sunday. &

HIGHLAND GRILL
771 Cleveland Ave., St. Paul
612/690-1173
$ SP

A friendly neighborhood joint with flair. You won't notice the modest decor once you've dug into the huge servings of simple, imaginative fare, the kind you'd imagine Martha Stewart would serve were she on a limited budget. Mondo breakfasts, friendly service, and low, low prices. No reservations; breakfast, lunch, and dinner daily. &

JUANITA'S RESTAURANTE MEXICANO
201 Concord St., St. Paul
612/290-2511
$ SP

The real thing. A center of St. Paul's thriving Hispanic neighborhood, Juanita's serves cheap, hearty, and spicy Mexican food in the tiniest of spaces. No reservations; lunch and dinner daily; breakfast Saturday and Sunday; no credit cards; no liquor. &

MUFFULETTA IN THE PARK
2260 Como Ave., St. Paul
612/644-9116
$$ SP

Comfort food with flair, including thick grilled burgers served on focaccia buns with homemade catsup, beef tips in mushroom gravy over garlic mashed potatoes, salad Nicoise with grilled salmon, and big desserts. Large, comfy booths and a pleasant outdoor deck. Reservations are recommended; lunch Monday through Saturday; dinner daily; brunch Sunday; smoke-free. &

128 CAFE
128 Cleveland Ave. N., St. Paul
612/645-4128
$$ SP

Fine seasonal fare, from the hands of a youthful and talented kitchen staff, served in a cozy little dining room near the College of St. Thomas. No

reservations; dinner only, Monday through Saturday; closed Sunday.

PUNCH WOODFIRE PIZZA
704 Cleveland Ave., St. Paul
612/696-1066
$ SP

This smart and stylish little open-kitchen café offers a lengthy roster of single-serving pizzas, and everything from thin, herb-filled crusts, to imported Italian tomatoes, to picholine olives conspire to make this some of the tastiest pizza in the Twin Cities. Fab salads, too. No reservations; lunch and dinner Monday through Saturday; closed Sunday. &

RISTORANTE LUCI
470 Cleveland Ave. S., St. Paul
612/699-8258
$$$ SP

This intimate, family-owned delight serves deliriously tasty Italian food, including homemade pasta. The four-course prix-fixe option is a steal, but the no-reservations policy only exacerbates the problems of the cramped, no-nonsense dining room. No reservations; dinner only, daily; smoke-free. &

SHILLA
694 Snelling Ave. N., St. Paul
612/645-0006
$$ SP

Korean food at its best. You'll get the most out of Shilla if you order lots of different dishes and share them with your dining buddies. Shilla winners include the *bi bim bop* (vegetable salad with a snappy sauce and a boiled egg), *man do* (pork and vegetable dumplings), *bul go gi* (tender sliced beef), *jungal* (seafood gumbo), and *chop chae* (cold vermicelli noodles in a red-pepper sesame sauce). The decor suggests a gussied-up

Outdoor dining at W.A. Frost & Co.

VFW hall, and the best day to visit is Sunday afternoon, when the place is packed with post-church Koreans. No reservations; lunch and dinner daily; no credit cards. &

TABLE OF CONTENTS
1648 Grand Ave., St. Paul
699-6595
$$$ **SP**
Sly, adventurous food served in chummy surroundings. Named for its close proximity to the Hungry Mind Bookstore next door, the Table is known for its creative hybrid of American cuisine with Asian and European accents. The cracker-crust pizzas are perfection, as are the grilled duck, pork tenderloin, and heavenly grilled pound cake, the kitchen's signature dessert. Reservations recommended; lunch Monday through Friday; dinner daily; brunch Sunday; smoke-free. &

TASTE OF SCANDINAVIA
2232 Carter Ave., St. Paul
612/645-9181
$ **SP**

Finnish, Swedish, and Norwegian baked goods, open-faced sandwiches, salads, and drinks in an enchanting, self-serve setting. &

TAVERN ON GRAND
656 Grand Ave., St. Paul
612/228-9030
$$ **SP**
Walleye-lovers central. The atmosphere has "lake cabin" written all over it, and the kitchen serves more walleye (in ceaselessly creative ways) than any other restaurant in the state, if not the world. Heaps of fun, and the food ain't bad, either. No reservations; lunch and dinner daily. &

W.A. FROST & CO.
374 Selby Ave., St. Paul
612/224-5715
$$ **SP**
Elegant dining rooms graced with French doors, high ceilings, and ornate woodwork in a historic and carefully restored commercial building create a romantic setting for fine food, wine, and service. There's no better place in St. Paul to while away a quiet

evening or a rainy afternoon than in Frost's clubby bar overlooking Western Avenue. The shady, well-tended garden is the most romantic outdoor spot in the city. Reservations recommended; lunch Monday through Saturday; dinner daily; brunch Sunday. &

GREATER TWIN CITIES

AUGUST MOON
5340 Wayzata Blvd., Golden Valley
612/544-7017
$$ **GTC**
Top-notch Asian fusion food. Even though it offers little in the decor department, the clever, fresh, and often intensely spicy food has created quite a loyal following over the years. Reservations for parties of five or more only; lunch Monday through Friday; dinner daily. &

ASIA GRILLE
549 Eden Prairie Center Dr.,
Eden Prairie
612/944-4095
$$ **GTC**
A culinary journey across Asia from Leeann Chin, the queen of Twin Cities Chinese cooking. The sleek surroundings—straight out of the pages of *Elle Decor*, a surprise for the strip-mall location—are the chief lure here, although the food can be OK, particularly if you stick with the appetizers (the Asian tacos, Eurasian spring rolls, and Thai chicken satay are all sure-fire choices) or the tea-smoked rotisserie chicken. No reservations; lunch and dinner daily. &

BAYPORT AMERICAN COOKERY
328 5th Ave. N., Bayport
612/430-1066
$$$ **GTC**
Don't let the modest surroundings fool you: this unassuming storefront café is one of the most agreeable dining experiences in the Twin Cities. Nightly five-course prix-fixe dinners at a single seating are the Cookery's standard operating procedure. The innovative recipes, highest quality ingredients, and meticulous attention to detail will help you overlook the sometimes makeshift quality of the place. Definitely worth the drive (about 25 minutes east of downtown St. Paul). Reservations recommended; single nightly seating at 6:30 p.m. on Wednesday, Thursday, and Sunday, and at 7:30 p.m. Friday and Saturday; closed Monday and Tuesday. &

BLUE POINT RESTAURANT & OYSTER BAR
739 E. Lake St., Wayzata
612/475-3636
$$$ **GTC**
Superbly grilled, broiled, sauteed, and poached ocean-fresh seafood, a rarity in Minnesota. The catch-of-the-day list usually features eight or more selections, and the side dishes are often pretty special, as well. Other hallmarks include excellent house-baked breads, an engaging wine list, and killer Key lime pie. The dining room recalls an upscale 1940s roadhouse. The bar up front is snug and inviting. Reservations recommended; dinner only, daily. &

CALIFORNIA CAFE
Third floor, South Avenue, Mall of America, Bloomington
612/854-2233
$$ **GTC**
Bathed in contemporary chic, the Mall of America outlet of this West Coast chain does such wonderful things with pastas, pizzas, and appetizers, you'll forget you're sitting inside a suburban shopping mall.

GREATER TWIN CITIES

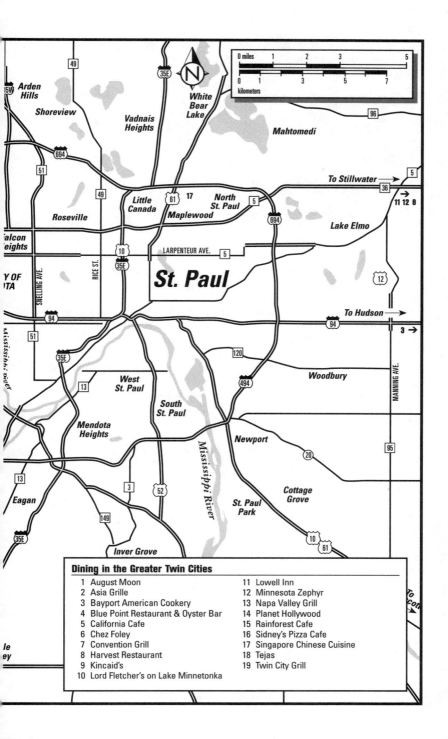

Dining in the Greater Twin Cities

1 August Moon
2 Asia Grille
3 Bayport American Cookery
4 Blue Point Restaurant & Oyster Bar
5 California Cafe
6 Chez Foley
7 Convention Grill
8 Harvest Restaurant
9 Kincaid's
10 Lord Fletcher's on Lake Minnetonka
11 Lowell Inn
12 Minnesota Zephyr
13 Napa Valley Grill
14 Planet Hollywood
15 Rainforest Cafe
16 Sidney's Pizza Cafe
17 Singapore Chinese Cuisine
18 Tejas
19 Twin City Grill

Lord Fletcher's on Lake Minnetonka

Great wine list, featuring a heady roster of Napa Valley labels. A well-trained staff of servers. Steer clear of the deafening "outdoor" seating area, which overlooks the pandemonium of Knott's Camp Snoopy. Reservations recommended; lunch and dinner daily. ♿

CHEZ FOLEY
331 Broadway Ave. S., Wayzata
612/476-8120
$$$ GTC
Chic and sophisticated—if not downright *soigné*—this bistro has a modest and constantly changing menu of delights, and the room and the crowd both exude a patina of quiet wealth. Reservations recommended; lunch and dinner daily. ♿

CONVENTION GRILL
3912 Sunnyside Rd., Edina
612/920-6881
$ GTC
Unparalleled hamburgers and obscenely rich malts, served in an authentic neighborhood grill atmosphere. A half-order of fries could

serve an army, the big burgers are thick, hand-formed affairs, and each malt comes with the can. Decent chicken soup, a mean grilled-cheese sandwich, and a heavenly hot fudge-banana sundae, too. You can get the same menu at several Annie's Parlour restaurants around town, but none of them match the Grill's no-nonsense surroundings—or great jukebox. No reservations; lunch and dinner daily; no liquor. ♿

HARVEST RESTAURANT
114 E. Chestnut St.,
Stillwater
612/430-8111
$$ GTC
A tiny (35-seat) treat, housed inside the oldest frame building (an 1848 Greek Revival treasure) in the historic town of Stillwater. The menu changes seasonally, but there are always a few salads, soups, appetizers, poultry dishes, and seafood items, all prepared with exquisite care. Reservations recommended; lunch Monday through Friday; dinner daily. ♿

KINCAID'S
8400 Normandale Blvd., Bloomington
612/921-2255
$$$ **GTC**

Sublime steaks and seafood, in elegant but informal surroundings in the atrium of an office complex. Preparations are simple and straightforward, so the high-quality beef, poultry, and seafood can shine on its own merits. A big suburban business-lunch destination, and rather clubby at dinner time. The large bar is also a draw, and the well-rehearsed service is a distinct pleasure. Reservations recommended; lunch Monday through Friday; dinner daily; brunch Sunday; smoke-free. &

LORD FLETCHER'S ON LAKE MINNETONKA
3746 Sunset Dr., Spring Park
612/471-8513
$$$ **GTC**

A superb Lake Minnetonka view is the draw here, along with tremendous people-watching possibilities and a dining room fashioned out of a grandly timbered English country manor. Fletcher's is at its best during the summer, when its perpetually mobbed deck becomes ground zero for the lake's boating crowd (Fletcher's has its own 70-slip marina). As for the food, it's strictly supper-club genre (steaks, chops, walleye), but it works. Reservations recommended; lunch Monday through Saturday; dinner daily; brunch Sunday. &

LOWELL INN
102 N. 2nd St., Stillwater
612/439-1100
$$$ **GTC**

A time warp. The exterior of this Stillwater landmark recalls Mount Vernon, and the main dining room is named for George Washington. The Matterhorn Room is designed strictly for fondue, and it can be a lot of fun; the Garden Room is just plain tacky. The food is American country-club fare: expensive and dull but well-prepared. Nothing has changed at this country inn in at least 50 years, and its dowdiness will either charm the socks off you or drive you nuts. Reservations recommended; breakfast, lunch, and dinner daily. &

MINNESOTA ZEPHYR
601 N. Main St., Stillwater
612/430-3000 or 800/992-6100
$$$ **GTC**

All aboard! Enjoy dinner in a restored 1940s-era railroad dining car as you journey for three hours and 15 miles through the picturesque countryside of the St. Croix River valley. The experience is rife with nostalgia and romance, but the humdrum five-course dinner ($56 per person) isn't anything you can't have at any nearby hotel dining room. Reservations recommended; dinner departs Wednesday through Saturday at 6:30 p.m.; brunch Sunday at 11:30 a.m. &

NAPA VALLEY GRILL
Third floor, West Market, Mall of America, Bloomington
612/858-9934
$$$ **GTC**

Along with its sibling, the California Café, this sophisticated spot is one of the Mall of America's genuine destination restaurants. The food, decor, and service are so understated, it's easy to forget that the Mall's roaring consumerism is right outside the door. The discriminating wine list features a bevy of (surprise) labels from California's wine country.

Popular menu items at the Rainforest Cafe

Rainforest Cafe

Reservations recommended; lunch Monday through Saturday; dinner served daily; brunch Sunday; smoke-free. &

PLANET HOLLYWOOD
Fourth floor, South Avenue, Mall of America, Bloomington
612/854-7829
$$ **GTC**

If *tourista* is what you seek, look no further. Planet Hollywood is loud, vulgar, and silly, and somehow only seems to get better with age. The Minnesota version of movieland excess can be a hoot for pop-culture buffs (the clay pots thrown by co-owner Demi Moore in *Ghost*—enshrined in Lucite cases as if they were priceless Etruscan artifacts—bring the kitsch level all the way up to stratospheric), and kids love it. The bar is decked out like a swimming pool, à la *Sunset Boulevard*, Dick Van Dyke's carousel horse from *Mary Poppins* hangs from the ceiling, and a Judy Garland dress from *Easter Parade* is at the front

door. The food offers no surprises, but it ain't bad. There's a huge gift shop, of course. No reservations; lunch and dinner daily; open daily until 1 a.m. &

RAINFOREST CAFE
First floor, South Avenue, Mall of America, Bloomington
612/854-7500   **GTC**

If waiting two hours for a $10 bacon cheeseburger is your idea of a good time, then look no further. This hugely popular jungle-themed restaurant is all about phony ambience: a downpour is simulated every 20 minutes (lightning, thunder, water, the works), and there is a menagerie of live and fake animals, live and fake plants, and live and fake food. The most genuine element at work here is the rampant commercialism and cheesy "family" entertainment. If you must go, the late-afternoon waits (especially mid-week) are the shortest. No reservations; lunch and dinner daily; smoke-free. &

SIDNEY'S PIZZA CAFE
France Ave. at 69th St., Edina
612/925-2002
$ **GTC**
Outdoor dining, suburban shopping-mall style (in the Galleria), with a well-tended garden and lots of shade.

SINGAPORE CHINESE CUISINE
1715 Beam Ave., Maplewood
612/777-7999
$$ **GTC**
Where insiders go for Malaysian food. The decor (of the humble strip-mall variety) gives no clue to the astonishing culinary treats that await. Call ahead and order the sea bass wrapped in banana leaves. Lunch and dinner Tuesday through Sunday; closed Monday. &

TEJAS
3910 W. 50th St., Edina
612/926-0800
$$$ **GTC**
Suburban Tex-Mex. Before this popular café moved here from downtown Minneapolis in 1994, it was one of the city's most glamorous restaurants. Unfortunately, its sense of adventure was tamed considerably when it moved to the 'burbs, but the food is still quite good and pleasantly presented. The desserts are worth a visit, too, and the low-key, vaguely Santa Fe–ish decor is comfortable and attractive. Reservations are not accepted; lunch Monday through Saturday; dinner daily; brunch Sunday; smoke-free. &

TWIN CITY GRILL
Mall of America, Bloomington
612/854-0200
$$ **GTC**
American standards are given a fresh twist here. Start your meal with one of the awesome grilled flatbreads. While the huge Chinese chicken salad is delicious, the menu also features hearty "diner plates" (meat loaf, pork chops, baked chicken, and the like), served with outstanding mashed potatoes and gravy. Desserts are monumentally large. The ambience is sturdy 1930s-style diner. Reservations recommended; lunch and dinner daily. &

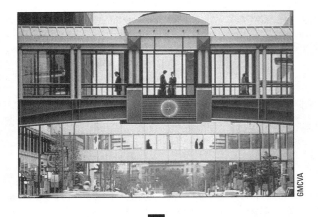

GMCVA

5

SIGHTS AND ATTRACTIONS

Unlike its twin across the Mississippi, Minneapolis is decidedly modern, almost willfully progressive. Downtown Minneapolis showcases a contemporary collection of structures and, while the past several decades of construction have yielded a dynamic city center, the architectural links to the past are not nearly so evident here as they are in St. Paul. Even so, some of the best examples of the historic preservation movement can be found in downtown Minneapolis.

St. Paul has a greater appreciation for history than does its flashy neighbor to the west, and much of its late-nineteenth- and early-twentieth-century architecture remains intact. Rich in urban treasures, the downtown area's relatively compact size makes it easy to navigate on foot.

DOWNTOWN MINNEAPOLIS

BUTLER SQUARE
100 N. 6th St., Minneapolis
612/339-4343   DMP
Butler Square is one of the finest examples of adaptive-reuse restoration in the country, and the anchor of the Warehouse District. Designed by Harry Jones and built in 1907, this rugged, Italianate palazzo building was originally designed as a warehouse for the Butler Bros. Its brilliant renovation (done in two stages, 1974 and 1981) converted an underused

and endangered building into a popular office and retail complex without compromising its historic value. Architects Miller, Hanson and Westerbeck and Arvid Elness Architects turned the massive structure inside out by carving two soaring atriums out of its interior.

FARMERS AND MECHANICS SAVING BANK
88 S. 6th St., Minneapolis
612/973-1111   DMP
The last remaining grand banking hall in the city. The two-story lobby

DOWNTOWN MINNEAPOLIS

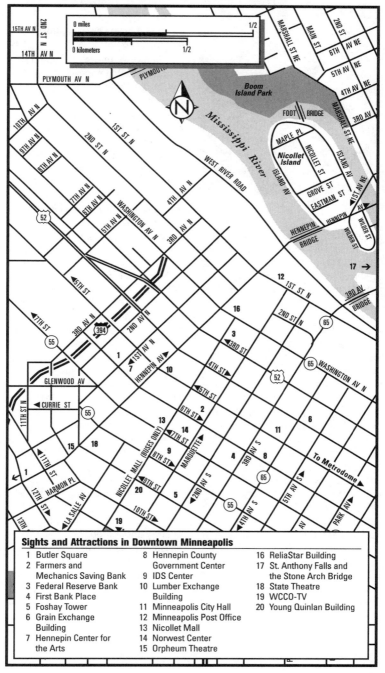

Sights and Attractions in Downtown Minneapolis

1 Butler Square
2 Farmers and Mechanics Saving Bank
3 Federal Reserve Bank
4 First Bank Place
5 Foshay Tower
6 Grain Exchange Building
7 Hennepin Center for the Arts
8 Hennepin County Government Center
9 IDS Center
10 Lumber Exchange Building
11 Minneapolis City Hall
12 Minneapolis Post Office
13 Nicollet Mall
14 Norwest Center
15 Orpheum Theatre
16 ReliaStar Building
17 St. Anthony Falls and the Stone Arch Bridge
18 State Theatre
19 WCCO-TV
20 Young Quinlan Building

Foshay Tower

(from 1942, by McEnary and Kraft) sports fine art deco lines, a gorgeous circular staircase, and sculpted lights, making it the city's most enchanting place to open a checking account.

FEDERAL RESERVE BANK
250 Marquette Ave., Minneapolis
612/340-2345 **DMP**
Downtown's most unusual structure, the Fed is actually two buildings: The first is a multifloor secured area buried beneath the sloping, windswept, and rather forbidding granite plaza that gets little if any use; the second is literally hung above it, à la suspension-bridge construction. Architect Gunnar Birkerts argued that the Fed's need for unobstructed office space was the reason behind the suspension-bridge technology. Such justification seems beside the point because the building is a stunner, more sculptural than architectural. And possibly endangered. In 1997, the Fed is abandoning this 1971 landmark for sumptuous new digs a few blocks north on a site overlooking the Mississippi River.

FIRST BANK PLACE
601 2nd Ave. S., Minneapolis
612/672-0036 **DMP**
The last of a series of major 1980s skyscrapers that aggressively altered the Minneapolis skyline. The semicircular 775-foot office tower of rosy granite and glass (designed by James Ingo Freed of Pei Cobb Freed & Partners) is crowned with the skyline's most unique feature: a delicate tiara of translucent glass, which is dramatically lit at night. As for the rest of the complex, it is skillfully rendered but surprisingly cold, and its Winter Garden, poised at the corner of 6th Street and 3rd Avenue, is mundane and uninviting.

FOSHAY TOWER
821 Marquette Ave., Minneapolis
612/341-2522 **DMP**
Plumbing magnate Wilbur Foshay built this endearing homage to the Washington Monument in 1929. Shortly after its completion, he was sent to prison for financial irregularities. At the tower's pompous three-day opening, he commissioned oom-pa-pa king John Philip Sousa to write a rousing march—and his check to Sousa bounced.

The 32-story tower (by Magney and Tusler) featured such a unique design that its architects had it patented, and Foshay's limitless ego led him to carve his name in 10-foot letters at the top of the tower. The Foshay dominated the Minneapolis skyline for more than 40 years, until it was dwarfed by the IDS Tower in 1973. The public outdoor observation deck on the 31st floor (open April to September) is the only one in town indoors or out; on a clear day, you can see for 30 miles. The art deco lobby is magical.

GRAIN EXCHANGE BUILDING
400 S. 4th St., Minneapolis
612/321-7101   DMP

Kees and Colburn designed this lyrical gem in 1902 for the Minneapolis Chamber of Commerce, borrowing liberally from Louis Sullivan's Wainwright Building in St. Louis. Note the ears of corn and stalks of grain in terra cotta on the building's facade. For tours, call the above number.

HENNEPIN CENTER FOR THE ARTS
528 Hennepin Ave., Minneapolis
612/332-4478   DMP

In a Richardsonian Romanesque frame of mind, architects Long and Kees piled rock-faced masonry up eight floors but still managed to give this graceful beauty a number of endearing quirks. The 1889 building was saved from the wrecking ball in the mid-1970s and reopened in 1979 as a center for the arts. Today this former Masonic Temple teems with dancers, actors, singers, writers, and audiences.

HENNEPIN COUNTY GOVERNMENT CENTER
300 S. 6th St., Minneapolis
612/348-3000   DMP

Architect John Warnecke designed this twin-tower complex; the east tower houses the county courts; the west tower, the county administrative offices. The two are connected by a soaring 24-story atrium that is aligned to frame the City Hall clock tower.

When the building opened in 1973, it was widely considered to be too lavish for a Minnesota government building—the onyx panels in the county boardroom and the not-so-durable imported Swiss tiles on the north plaza were both cited. But today the building endures because of its fine materials, particularly the extensive use of purple-grey granite, carved from the same quarry as the stone for City Hall. The Government Center's two plazas—one cold and formal, with a dramatic waterfall; the other grassy and inviting—are both

The Guthrie Theater, p. 99

Michal Daniel

Finding Frank Lloyd Wright

The master architect designed several homes in the Twin Cities area. Two homes worth driving by (unfortunately, they're not open to the public) are at 225 Bedford St. SE in Minneapolis' Prospect Park neighborhood (built for University of Minnesota president Malcolm Willey in 1934), and at 2815 Burnham Boulevard, between Cedar Lake and Lake of the Isles in south Minneapolis. Wright's best local work—the Little House—was built on the shores of Lake Minnetonka in 1914 and was razed in 1972. Its living room was saved and now resides in New York City's Metropolitan Museum of Art; the Minneapolis Institute of Arts owns the house's hallway.

popular destinations that serve as the town square that downtown Minneapolis lacks.

IDS CENTER
80 S. 8th St., Minneapolis
612/376-8000   **DMP**
The construction of this peerless urban complex ushered Minneapolis into a new era. Unfortunately, the soaring, light-filled IDS Crystal Court, the centerpiece of the complex, is a shadow of its former self, thanks to several insensitive remodelings by a parade of owners, including Heitman Properties, its current landlord. When the IDS Center opened in 1973, the Crystal Court instantly became the vibrant indoor town square that its architect, Philip Johnson envisioned it to be, something along the lines of the Galleria in Milan, Italy. Now devoid of the trees, flowers, benches, and shops—and people—that gave it its *joie de vivre*, the court is nothing more than a vast and rather chilly extended lobby for the IDS Tower.

But what a lobby. Johnson carved out the center of a city block, ringing the perimeter with four blue glass–sheathed buildings and creating an enormous public space inside. From the granite floor he installed a white metal canopy eight stories high and covered it in hundreds of clear Plexiglas pyramids. The city's skyway system converges on the Crystal Court, poured through every day by thousands of pedestrians, many of whom cast a crooked glance at sculptor Jonathan Borofsky's ironic *Hammering Man*.

As for the IDS Tower, it's the city's tallest building (777 feet) and one of the best skyscrapers in America. Johnson ingeniously cut back the tower's four corners, giving the landlord an added bonus of 32 corner offices per floor. The tower's highly reflective blue glass often throws the building into a *pas de deux* with the sky. The imperious lobby was subjected to a ghastly and unnecessary renovation in 1994, hopefully not a sign of things to come for the rest of this unparalleled mid-century masterpiece.

LUMBER EXCHANGE BUILDING
10 S. 5th St., Minneapolis
612/334-3011   DMP
A Long and Kees exercise in Richardsonian Romanesque, the Lumber Exchange Building is the grand dame of Hennepin Avenue. Built of rustic Lake Superior brownstone, it has been lovingly restored to its original 1885 condition, and the lavish marble lobby is worth a peek. Minneapolis was the world's largest lumber milling center from the 1880s until World War I, and this building (the city's first skyscraper and its first fireproof structure) served as the center of that vital trade.

MINNEAPOLIS CITY HALL
350 S. 5th St., Minneapolis
612/673-3000   DMP
This beloved heap of Ortonville granite is the creation of architects Long and Kees. Encompassing an entire city block, the project took 16 years (1889–1905), and its construction nearly bankrupted the city coffers. But when it was completed, the new municipal building was an immediate stamp of legitimacy for a city emerging from infancy into adulthood.

The 345-foot clock tower (its faces are larger than Big Ben's) no longer dominates the city's skyline as it once did, but City Hall still exudes solid, implacable grandeur. A series of renovations have returned parts of the building to their original splendor, including the grand 4th Street entrance. Just inside, in a lavishly appointed interior court, sits the massive *Father of Waters* statue by sculptor Larkin Goldsmith Mead.

Across 4th Street is the new Federal Courts Building, a $103-million monstrosity designed by Kohn Ped-
ersen Fox Associates. The best feature about this 1996 building is its plaza, which fronts City Hall and finally allows passers-by to take in its muscular facade in one appreciative glance.

MINNEAPOLIS POST OFFICE
100 S. 1st St., Minneapolis
612/321-5957   DMP
The Minneapolis Post Office, a broad-shouldered 1933 Moderne jewel, spans two city blocks. Inside, the main concourse is a restrained example of art deco at its finest. The mighty Mississippi River—and St. Anthony Falls—are just beyond these monumental buildings, but you'd never know it; Minneapolis has turned its back on the river almost from its very beginnings, a mistake that only recently has begun to be rectified.

NICOLLET MALL
Between Washington Ave. and
Grant Street, Minneapolis   DMP
In 1967, San Francisco landscape architect Lawrence Halprin (along with Barton Aschman Associates) converted fading Nicollet Avenue into one of the country's first automobile-free pedestrian thoroughfares. Halprin replaced the traffic-clogged street with an undulating 30-foot roadway for buses and taxis, then turned the rest over to shady, flower-filled promenades. The result was an urban revolution that was fomented in dozens of cities around the world.

Halprin's classic design ensured that Nicollet Mall would remain healthy and vibrant for years. In 1981, the Mall was such a success that it was extended, using Halprin's design elements, several blocks from its original terminus at 10th Street all the

Nicollet Mall

never to be seen again. The list goes on and on.

Happily, there are some things worth seeing on the new Nicollet Mall, still the city's main shopping artery. The rich granite paving is a vast improvement over Halprin's original terrazzo. The new Mall is also liberally sprinkled with art, including George Morrison's intriguing pavement mosaic in front of the IDS Center, between 7th and 8th Streets. Stanton Sears' curved, anthropomorphic *Stone Boats* of solid granite are a sculptural treat; one is located in front of City Center at 7th Street, the other is opposite Barnes & Noble at 8th Street. A lovely clock, a holdover from the Halprin Mall, perches on Peavey Plaza at 11th Street. But the slow exodus of retail stores from downtown Minneapolis cannot be pinned solely on competition from the runaway success of the Mall of America; another culprit is this design disaster. (Also see Chapter 9, Shopping.)

way south to Grant Street. Unfortunately, the choice of pavement proved ill-suited for the harsh climate, and after 20 years of hard use, the Mall was looking its age. Rather than simply repave the street, a number of ambitious business and civic leaders decided to rethink the Mall; the results have been mediocre at best, disastrous at worst.

The new Nicollet Mall, designed by Minneapolis-based BRW and completed in 1992, is a depressing and strikingly unoriginal reworking of Halprin's ingenious scheme. BRW flattened Halprin's sinuous roadway, changing the s-curve he imprinted on every block (his "urban dance," as he described it) with a flatter c-curve. The leafy honey locusts that once lined the Mall were chopped down (on Earth Day!) and replaced with Austrian pines, most of which quickly died. Halprin's quirky and elegant lights were replaced with quasi-Victorian horrors. The simple and sturdy bus shelters were torn down, and ghastly fake gazebos erected. Fountains and art were removed,

NORWEST CENTER
90 S. 7th St., Minneapolis
612/344-1200   DMP

The RCA Building at New York City's Rockefeller Center was architect Cesar Pelli's inspiration for this 775-foot, 52-story tower, which became an instant landmark upon its completion in 1988. Pelli's tower is a gracious neighbor to Philip Johnson's coolly modern IDS Tower. Gracious Pelli even permitted the IDS to retain its claim as the city's tallest tower, designing his tower to be several feet shorter.

Pelli sheathed his masterpiece in warm Kasota sandstone, and accented it with white marble and gleaming bronze, and the results almost, but not quite, usurp the spotlight from the IDS. By night, when floodlights bathe it in a warm glow, Norwest becomes almost absurdly romantic. Pelli skillfully incorporated elements from the site's previous building, the stodgy Northwestern National Bank, which burned in a spectacular fire on Thanksgiving Day in 1982. From its ruins he pulled ornate chandeliers, railings, and other decorative elements, and reinstalled them in his understated but luxurious full-block lobby and banking hall—and they look as if they have always been part of the place. The lobby is particularly noteworthy for its ongoing display of Norwest Bank's astounding collection of twentieth-century decorative arts.

ORPHEUM THEATRE
910 Hennepin Ave., Minneapolis
612/339-0075 DMP

When it opened in 1921, the Orpheum was the second-largest vaudeville house in the nation, with a seating capacity of 2,900; for a time in the mid-1980s, it was owned by singer Bob Dylan and had seen better days. After the roaring success of the State Theatre renovation, the city stepped up to the plate in 1988, bought the Orpheum, and pumped nearly $9 million into its restoration, which was completed in 1994. The results are more subdued—but no less triumphant—than its delightfully overdressed neighbor across the street. The Orpheum's most stunning element is the auditorium's glittering dome, lined with 30,000 silvery 4-inch aluminum squares and lit by a 2,000-pound brass chandelier.

RELIASTAR BUILDING
20 Washington Ave., Minneapolis
612/372-5432 DMP

The work of Minoru Yamasaki (who later went on to design the World Trade Center in New York City), this 1963 Greek-temple-as-office-building was intended to be the crown jewel of the Gateway Center, an ambitious slum-clearance program in the late 1950s and early 1960s. Unfortunately, the bulldozers also took some amazing bits of history with them, including the universally beloved Metropolitan Building. As for the ReliaStar (formerly the Northwestern National Life Insurance Building), its striking open-air portico is a clever terminus for Nicollet Mall, and the well-tended grounds and reflecting pool are thoughtful touches. The lobby's centerpiece is a lively Henry Bertoia sculpture of spiky golden rods.

SKYWAY SYSTEM
Various downtown sites DMP

On 7th Street between 2nd and Marquette Avenues is the oldest skyway bridge in Minneapolis. Now ubiquitous, this second-story span was revolutionary when it debuted in 1962, heralding a whole new era for downtown Minneapolis. Now the skyway system (which is predominantly privately owned) connects more than 54 downtown blocks, and it is possible to walk 16-block stretches without ever dealing with the often-harsh weather. The public's love of skyways has clearly played a part in downtown Minneapolis' continued commercial vitality, but the system's influence hasn't been completely rosy. For example, first-floor street life has been in a serious decline ever since the system took off, and the bridges themselves can be hideous to look at, as well as devastating to the buildings they pierce and the vistas they block. One exception is the inviting terra-cotta bridge spanning

Marquette Avenue between the Norwest Center and the Firstar Bank Building, designed by Minneapolis sculptor Siah Armajani.

ST. ANTHONY FALLS AND THE STONE ARCH BRIDGE
125 Main St. SE, Minneapolis
612/627-5433   DMP
The only falls on the Mississippi River are also the *raison d'etre* of the city of Minneapolis. The roaring cataract that Father Louis Hennepin christened St. Anthony Falls was a sacred spot for the area's native Sioux and Chippewa residents. White settlers harnessed the falls' power starting in the 1820s. By the 1880s, the area was clogged with ugly mills and became the hub of the nation's flour—and lumber—milling industries. The falls' natural beauty was destroyed when an ill-advised tunnel project collapsed in a disastrous accident in 1869. The falls were saved an unremarkable future as mere rapids by the construction of a concrete apron. Today St. Anthony Falls retains its might, particularly during the spring and early summer, when water levels are high.

Railroad czar James J. Hill built the Stone Arch Bridge just below the falls in 1883 to replicate a Roman viaduct. He sought to offer his railroad passengers sweeping views of the powerful waterworks as well as create a majestic entry into the city. Built entirely of massive limestone blocks (although it leapfrogs across the river as if it were light as feather), "Jim Hill's folly" is the second-oldest bridge still spanning the Father of Waters, and its gently curving simplicity and strength make it one of the most beautiful. The bridge was extensively renovated in 1994 and is now open to bike and pedestrian traffic only. Guided hour-long tours of the St. Anthony Falls area, sponsored by the Minnesota Historical Society, are available from May through October. Admission: $4 adults, $3 seniors, $2 children. Hours: Wed–Sun 12–4.

STATE THEATRE
805 Hennepin Ave., Minneapolis
612/339-0075   DMP
Painstakingly restored in 1991 to its giddy, joyously overdecorated glory, the State's 2,200 seats now showcase a steady diet of touring plays and musicals, concerts, and lectures. This 1920 wonder—which was remarkably well-preserved, given its checkered history as a vaudeville house, movie theater, and church—was the center of a protracted battle among city officials, preservationists, and the developers of the LaSalle Plaza project, which eventually was built around the theater's outer shell. That the theater was almost razed now seems unimaginable: every element of the place—from the golden proscenium arch, to the glittering chandeliers, to the intricate murals—conspires to put a smile on the face of every patron.

WCCO-TV
Nicollet Mall at 11th Street, Minneapolis
612/339-4444   DMP
The WCCO Television Communications Center, designed by Hardy, Holzman & Pfeiffer Associates and opened in 1981, is probably the most sensitively rendered building in downtown Minneapolis. Built of beige Kasota stone, the building exudes warmth, and the TV elements (the news studio in the big front window and the television monitors on the sidewalk) are fun touches.

YOUNG QUINLAN BUILDING
81 S. 9th St., Minneapolis
612/333-6128 **DMP**

At 9th Street and Nicollet Mall stands one of the country's prettiest retail buildings. The Young Quinlan Company was the brainchild of Elizabeth Quinlan, a brilliant retailer who brought ready-to-wear to Minneapolis at the turn of the century and built this gem of a store in 1926. Until she sold her business in 1945—and for some time after—Y-Q was the Midwest's most elegant store (Neiman-Marcus modeled its Dallas store after Miss Quinlan's French-inspired emporium), and, in its current incarnation as an office and retail complex, her palace remains a soothing and urbane presence on the Minneapolis streetscape. Don't miss the big Y-Q clock just inside the Nicollet Mall entrance, the lanterns and iron railings on the mezzanine, or the strikingly handsome "Paris–New York–Minneapolis" bronze placard on the building's facadeat the corner of 9th Street and Nicollet Mall. Miss Quinlan's elegant Lowry Hill home, designed in the same style as her downtown emporium, still stands at 1711 Emerson Avenue South.

DOWNTOWN ST. PAUL

CAPITOL MALL
St. Paul **DSP**

The park-like Capitol Mall is a product of post–World War II urban planning, when a massive slum clearance rid the area of dilapidated structures—as well as a few historically and architecturally significant ones. In their places, the state government erected several bland office buildings ringing a wide greensward approach to architect Cass Gilbert's exquisite white marble Capitol building.

Today, the Capitol Mall is a pleasant respite, dotted with statues and memorials (including a moving new Minnesota Vietnam Veterans' Memorial). It is also the site for annual festivals including Taste of Minnesota (Fourth of July weekend) and the St. Paul Winter Carnival. The green sweep of the Mall terminates at the understated Veterans Service Building, which is highlighted by Alonzo Hauser's graceful fountain, *The Promise of Youth*.

CATHEDRAL OF ST. PAUL
239 Selby Ave., St. Paul
612/228-1767 **DSP**

The magisterial Cathedral of St. Paul holds court at the foot of Summit Avenue. French architect Emmanuel Masqueray, a practitioner of the Beaux Arts style, was lured to Minnesota by Archbishop John Ireland to design a cathedral of grandeur, and his Renaissance-inspired work resulted in one of Minnesota's most magnificent architectural triumphs.

Stone Arch Bridge

GMCVA

The building was completed in 1915. Masqueray's massive copper dome rises 300 feet and rests atop a modified Greek cross of Minnesota granite. The Summit Avenue facade is flanked by a pair of carillon towers. The nave seats 3,000 worshipers. Open daily from 7 a.m. to 6 p.m.

ECOLAB CENTER
320 N. Wabasha, St. Paul
612/293-2233   DSP
Located in the Capital Centre district, the Ecolab Center (formerly the Osborn Building) is a stellar example of mid-century skyscraper design. Designed by Bergstedt, Wahlberg and Wold in 1968, the minimalist, aloof building is set back from the street by a shallow moat, and its restrained facade of black granite, stainless steel, and glass rises a modest 19 stories. The plaza to the rear is pedestrian-scaled and features a fun, bright steel sculpture by Alexander Liberman titled *Above, Above*.

FIRST NATIONAL BANK BUILDING
332 Minnesota St., St. Paul
612/225-3666   DSP
When it was built in 1931, the First National Bank Building instantly became the symbol of the city—rather, the gigantic neon "1st" sign atop the limestone 31-story tower did—and still is. The building's red and beige marble lobby is as rich as ever, but the bank moved its teller lobby to a nondescript skyway location in the mid-1970s.

FIRST TRUST CENTER
176 E. 5th St., St. Paul
612/224-6000   DSP
Designed by Charles S. Frost as the gargantuan nerve center of James J. Hill's railroad and banking empire,

this 1916 structure has 1 million square feet of space and was the state's largest office building until the opening of the IDS Center in 1973. The giant banking hall—once the heart of the First National Bank and the Northwestern Trust Co.—lost much of its dignity in a hideous 1986 renovation that relegated the space to that of a glorified banquet facility. On the skyway level (4th Street side) a treasure trove of photos and architectural drawings chronicles the building's original splendor.

JEMNE BUILDING
305 St. Peter St., St. Paul   DSP
Named for its architect, this refined 1931 art deco beauty, decked out in Kasota stone, was once home to the Women's City Club and later the Minnesota Museum of Art. Plans are afoot to retrofit the building as a museum showcasing the colorful paintings of St. Paul native LeRoy Neiman.

KELLOGG MALL
Kellogg Boulevard between Robert and Wabasha Streets, St. Paul   DSP
This three-block esplanade was originally conceived in the 1930s to provide vistas of the Mississippi River Valley, and it was extensively retooled in 1989. From the top of the river bluffs, it's easy to see the vital role the river played in the city's development. Several memorials dot the Mall, including a spot near the intersection of Kellogg Boulevard and Robert Street that marks the site of Father Galtier's 1841 log-cabin church, which was named for the apostle Paul and was the city's first building. The Mall and the boulevard are both named in honor of Frank B. Kellogg, a St. Paul native and an important American diplomat.

LANDMARK CENTER
75 W. 5th St., St. Paul
612/292-3225 **DSP**

The anchor of Rice Park is the giddy Landmark Center, a beloved 1904 pile of French-accented pink granite, red tile roofs, turrets, clock towers, gables, and other whimsical details. Built in 1906 and designed by Willoughby J. Edbrooke as a federal courts building and post office, this Victorian beauty was almost razed in the late 1960s, until an enterprising group of preservationists fought for its survival. Inside, the opulence continues, with a soaring five-story skylight courtyard, 20-foot ceilings, Vermont marble fireplaces, and exquisite hand-carved mahogany and marble details. The breathtaking cortile and four major courtrooms are now used for public receptions, and the remainder of the building is devoted to office space for arts organizations and exhibition space for the Minnesota Museum of American Art, the Ramsey County Historical Society, and the Schubert Club. Free tours on Thursday at 11 a.m. and Sunday at 1 p.m.

MINNESOTA STATE CAPITOL
Park and Aurora Streets, St. Paul
612/296-2881 **DSP**

The Capitol itself crowns one of the two hills that dominate old St. Paul; the other is topped by the mighty Cathedral of St. Paul, and the two imposing buildings stare each other down from opposite ends of John Ireland Boulevard.

This building—which cost $4 million and took six years to build—is actually the third Minnesota State Capitol; the first burned to the ground, and the second was outdated even before it was completed. St. Paul architect Cass Gilbert beat

Cathedral of St. Paul, p. 91

Marc Caryl

out 40 other competitors to win the commission in 1898, and he modeled the supremely symmetrical building on St. Peter's in Rome. The Capitol is considered by many critics to be the most striking state capitol in the United States, and with good reason: its beautifully proportioned unsupported marble dome is the world's largest of its kind, and the interior is lavishly (some might say grossly) detailed. Climb the front steps for an unparalleled view of downtown St. Paul, the Cathedral of St. Paul, and the Mississippi River valley. Just above the main entrance is *Quadriga*, a gilded (and recently restored) statue by Daniel Chester French and Edward Potter. The legislature convenes for the first three to four months of every year, and when the House and Senate are in session, all galleries and hearings are free and open to the public. The Minnesota Historical Society offers free tours daily every hour from 9 a.m. to 4 p.m. weekdays, 10 a.m. to 3 p.m. Saturday, and 1 p.m. to 3 p.m. Sunday.

MINNESOTA WORLD TRADE CENTER
30 E. 7th St., St. Paul
612/291-8900   **DSP**

The pedestrian 40-story marble and bronze-glass skyscraper (St. Paul's tallest) with the ziggurat top is the Minnesota World Trade Center. Designed by WZMH Group and Winsor-Faricy Architects, the center opened in 1987 to great fanfare about increasing import-export trade in the state. While some overseas economic growth has actually occurred, the building is really just a fancy office tower, and much of its square footage is leased to lawyers, accountants, and the like.

ORDWAY MUSIC THEATRE
345 Washington St., St. Paul
612/282-3000   **DSP**

Designed by St. Paul native Benjamin Thompson and opened to great acclaim in 1984 (*Time* magazine called it "a jewel on the Mississippi"), the Ordway has been a hub of the city ever since, exactly the role that benefactor Sally Irvine had in mind when she donated $10 million in her father's name to create a performing arts center for sleepy downtown St. Paul. Rich in contemporary details, the handsome 1,800-seat theater is laid out in the manner of a European opera house. The spacious lobbies overlook Rice Park (see Chapter 8, Parks and Gardens) from a continuous, three-story bank of windows. This popular building is the principal home of the St. Paul Chamber Orchestra, Minnesota Opera, and Schubert Club, as well as a variety of theatrical and dance performances. The adjacent and brilliantly scaled 300-seat McKnight Theatre is just off the first-floor lobby.

Irvine Park

The focal point of 1880s high society in St. Paul, this green Victorian square was in serious decline by the 1970s. A restoration of the park and its enclave of homes (some of the oldest in the state) reversed that slide, and today the area is one of the most charming districts in the city. The gracious Alexander Ramsey House (265 S. Exchange St.) is the 1872 home of the state's first governor, today managed by the Minnesota Historical Society. The Second Empire house is open for tours May through December; crowds are particularly heavy during December, when the house is festooned with period Christmas decorations. Admission: $4 adults, $3 seniors, $2 children. Hours: Tues–Sat 10–3. Reservations recommended; call 612/296-8760. Irvine Park is located two blocks south of the intersection of West 7th and Walnut Streets.

DOWNTOWN ST. PAUL

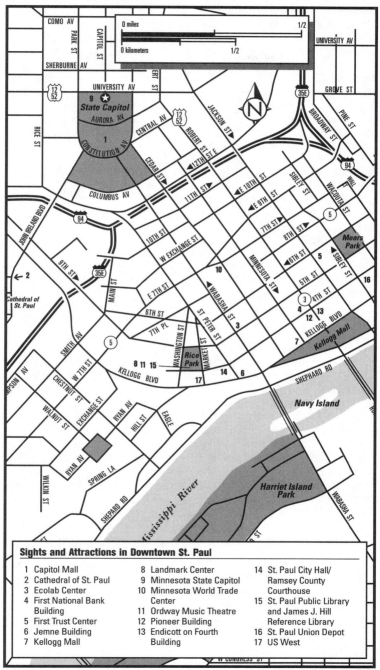

Sights and Attractions in Downtown St. Paul

1 Capitol Mall
2 Cathedral of St. Paul
3 Ecolab Center
4 First National Bank Building
5 First Trust Center
6 Jemne Building
7 Kellogg Mall
8 Landmark Center
9 Minnesota State Capitol
10 Minnesota World Trade Center
11 Ordway Music Theatre
12 Pioneer Building
13 Endicott on Fourth Building
14 St. Paul City Hall/ Ramsey County Courthouse
15 St. Paul Public Library and James J. Hill Reference Library
16 St. Paul Union Depot
17 US West

PIONEER BUILDING
336 Robert St., St. Paul   **DSP**
ENDICOTT ON FOURTH BUILDING
141 4th St. E., St. Paul   **DSP**

The Pioneer (built in 1889 and named for its original tenant, the *St. Paul Pioneer Press*) was St. Paul's first skyscraper. Its red-brick-and-granite exterior by architect Solon Beman remain as handsome as ever; duck inside for a peek at the open elevator shaft and dizzying 15-story iron spiral staircase. The Endicott (which dates from 1890) is the more refined of the two buildings, featuring a subdued Italian palazzo facade of sandstone and red brick by Cass Gilbert and James Knox Taylor. Note the delicate pink marble lobby and carved stone pilasters.

ST. PAUL CITY HALL/RAMSEY COUNTY COURTHOUSE
15 Kellogg Blvd., St. Paul
612/266-8023   **DSP**

Many Minnesota natives consider this 20-story structure to be the finest municipal building in the state. The 1932 masterpiece is a study of contrasts. Its restrained, monochromatic art deco exterior gives no indication of the madcap goings-on inside its jazzy, ornate Zigzag Moderne interior. Designed by Holabird and Root and Ellerbe Architects, this landmark was given a magnificent restoration and seamless addition in 1993 by Wold Architects and Architectural Alliance.

Memorial Hall, the building's 4th Street lobby, has few rivals for sheer drama: a three-story sweep of blue/black Belgian marble excess, worthy of any opera stage, culminating in *Vision of Peace*, Carl Milles' stunning 36-foot, 60-ton statue of an Indian god (carved in Mexican white onyx), which pivots 130 degrees every 2.5 hours. The third-floor city council chambers are dominated by four giant murals by John Norton, a Chicago painter working in the WPA Moderne style. The entire building is a study in exquisite detailing (the Depression-era budget of $4 million went a long, long way) and deserves serious exploration. Free tours are available by appointment only.

ST. PAUL PUBLIC LIBRARY AND JAMES J. HILL REFERENCE LIBRARY
90 W. 4th St., St. Paul
612/292-6311   **DSP**

This subdued Northern Italian Renaissance palace, designed by Electus Litchfield in 1916, was commissioned by railroad baron James J. Hill (1838–1916) to house his extensive private collection as well as the city's central library. The exterior—modeled after the Morgan Library in New York City—is clad in pink Tennessee marble, and the interior is slathered with tons of intricately carved sandstone cut from the Kettle River in northern Minnesota. Portions of the building have been sadly neglected for years.

An exception is the stately reading room of the James J. Hill Reference Library, which occupies the entire east wing. One of the city's most attractive spaces, this beautifully maintained three-story room looks just like a library should: classical, dark, and serious. Besides being the repository of the James J. Hill and Louis B. Hill Papers, the Hill Library and its skilled staff are an excellent resource for free business research, and there's always a pot of coffee (caffeinated, of course) on.

Ten Structures by Cass Gilbert

Although not a Minnesota native, the architect of the neo-Gothic Woolworth Building in New York City and the imposing Supreme Court Building in Washington, D.C., lived in St. Paul for several decades and left quite an imprint on the Twin Cities' urban landscape. Besides the magnificent State Capitol building in St. Paul and the grand Mall at the U of M campus in Minneapolis, Gilbert worked on a number of commercial structures, homes, and churches throughout the Twin Cities, including the ten below:

1. 705 Summit Ave., St. Paul. An 1899 yellow limestone mansion for department-store magnate Jacob Dittenhofer.

2. 322–24 Summit Ave., St. Paul. An 1886 double house for the families of law partners George Young and William Lightner.

3. Endicott on Fourth Building, 141 E. 4th St., St. Paul. Gilbert had his office in this building.

4. Endicott on Robert Building, 350 N. Robert St., St. Paul. The red-brick building is adjacent to the Endicott on Fourth Building.

5. St. Paul Seminary, 2190 Summit Ave., St. Paul. Built from 1892 to 1894 on a striking promontory overlooking the Mississippi River. The land was donated by Archbishop John Ireland, and construction for the entire six-building campus was funded by James J. Hill; only Gilbert's North Residence (now Loras Hall), South Residence (Cretin Hall), and Gymnasium (Heating Plant) remain.

6. St. Clement's Church, 901 Portland Ave., St. Paul. A re-creation of a small English parish church.

7. St. Martin's by the Lake Episcopal Church, 2801 Westwood Rd., Minnetonka Beach. Another small, charming church in the English country-parish tradition.

8. Virginia Street Church, 170 Virginia St., St. Paul. A whimsical confection of wood and stone.

9. American Beauty Macaroni Building, 352 Wacouta St., St. Paul. A five-story brownstone commercial structure from 1895, now converted to loft apartments.

10. Wacouta Street Warehouse, 413 Wacouta St., St. Paul. Designed in 1894 for the T.L. Blood & Company, a paint manufacturer and wholesaler.

Ordway Music Theatre, p. 94

ST. PAUL UNION DEPOT
214 E. 4th St., St. Paul   DSP
This severe limestone structure was one of the busiest passenger terminals in the country during its heyday. Built from 1917 to 1923 by architect Charles Frost, the Union Depot's no-nonsense exterior (highlighted by an imposing row of ten huge Doric columns) belies its vast and lavish interior spaces, which were scrupulously restored in 1983 and realigned for a number of restaurant tenants, including a museum-like LeeAnn Chin Chinese Cuisine restaurant located in what used to be the station's women's waiting room.

US WEST
70 W. 4th St., St. Paul
612/344-5569   DSP
A trio of buildings houses the various functions of telecommunications giant US West. Each structure represents a different generation in twentieth-century commercial architecture. The finest is the earliest: the Tri-State Telephone Building, designed by Clarence Johnston Jr. in

1937. The splendid lobby of this restrained art deco tower (sheathed in warm Kasota stone) was restored in 1986. It is now home to the fascinating Pioneer Telephone Museum, which chronicles the history of the telephone and is managed by the Telephone Pioneers of America; free tours by appointment only.

MINNEAPOLIS

BASILICA OF ST. MARY
88 N. 17th St., Minneapolis
612/333-1381   MP
Emmanuel Masqueray, who was responsible for the Cathedral of St. Paul, also designed this enormous white marble church, completed in 1926. It is now undergoing a multi-year, much-needed restoration that is revealing overlooked marvels on the exterior, but the site has been seriously compromised by a series of ill-placed freeways.

CHRIST LUTHERAN CHURCH
3244 34th Ave. S., Minneapolis

612/721-6611   **MP**

The final work of the Finnish architect Eliel Saarinen truly fashions something out of nothing. In a lesser architect's hands, the modest materials and forgettable site would have been entirely undistinguished, but Saarinen imbues this building with timeless dignity and stature.

THE GUTHRIE THEATER
725 Vineland Pl., Minneapolis
612/347-1100   **MP**

When director Sir Tyrone Guthrie announced his intention to establish a permanent repertory company somewhere outside New York City, Minneapolis business, academic, and social leaders lured him to the city (the promise of a new theater, built to his specifications, didn't hurt). The American regional theater movement was born on May 7, 1963, when the theater opened with a production of *Hamlet*, directed by Guthrie and starring George Grizzard and Jessica Tandy.

The theater itself, designed by Minnesota architect Ralph Rapson, rejected the traditional proscenium for a thrust design, with the audience wrapped around a minimalist stage. Rapson's concept was highly original, but lousy construction led to the facade's demise a decade later, and a 1993 renovation did away with any remaining elements, replacing them with a blandly smooth wall of glass facing the Minneapolis Sculpture Garden. The interior was slightly tweaked, but it remains an exciting and very comfortable place to take in a Guthrie production.

IRENE HIXON WHITNEY BRIDGE
Loring Park, Minneapolis   **MP**

This yellow-and-blue pedestrian bridge is the handiwork of Minneapolis sculptor Siah Armajani. Leaping across 16 terrifying lanes of fast-moving traffic, it acts as a psychological link between what the construction of I-94 plowed asunder: the natural connection between downtown, Loring Park, and Lowry Hill (see Chapter 8, Parks and Gardens). Like most of Armajani's works, this one incorporates the written word, in this case, a poem by John Ashberry.

A Capitol Error

One of the biggest blunders in St. Paul city-planning history was the decision to separate downtown St. Paul from the Capitol area by I-94. Even before it was completed in 1967, the freeway cut deep emotional scars through the city. Since then, a 1-mile stretch (from John Ireland Boulevard to East 7th Street) has been given an imperial makeover, complete with stone walls, iron railings, classical lighting fixtures, and other ornate and vaguely Beaux Arts touches, and the impressive results go a long way toward restoring some of the area's long-wounded civic pride.

Native Son

In 1919, St. Paul native F. Scott Fitzgerald wrote his first published book, This Side of Paradise, *while living in the house at 599 Summit Ave. Fitzgerald's childhood was spent as a second-class citizen, at least in the eyes of Cathedral Hill society. As a result, he didn't exactly have a soft spot in his heart for his hometown.*

LAKEWOOD CEMETERY
3600 Hennepin Ave. S.,
Minneapolis
612/822-2171   MP
The cemetery's Memorial Chapel—designed by Harry Wild Jones, built in 1908, and modeled after the Hagia Sophia in Istanbul—is a Byzantine delight. The chapel's intimate, mosaic-filled space is crowned by a 65-foot-high central dome, and its 24 stained-glass windows are not merely decorative but also ingeniously double as a sundial. As for the cemetery, its rolling, beautifully tended grounds (which overlook Lake Calhoun and were first opened in 1871) are a restorative escape. Hubert H. Humphrey is buried here, as are Horace Cleveland, the man who conceived the Minneapolis park system; Emil Oberhoffer, the first musical director of the Minneapolis Symphony; and many other Twin Cities luminaries, including Walkers, Lorings, Blaisdells, and Elliots. The cemetery is open 8 a.m. to 8 p.m. daily; the chapel is open from 8 a.m. to 4:30 p.m. Monday through Friday.

MILWAUKEE AVENUE
24th Ave. South and
Franklin Ave., Minneapolis   MP
This two-block street of homes built in the 1880s for working-class immi-grants was painstakingly restored during the 1970s. Now on the National Register of Historic Places, this compact neighborhood is a living monument not only to the rich history of the working class that did so much to shape the city, but also to the perseverance of a neighborhood determined to hold on to its history. The avenue is located about a mile west of the Mississippi River.

ORCHESTRA HALL
1111 Nicollet Mall, Minneapolis
612/371-5600   MP
The building with the ocean-liner vents coming out of its roof is Orchestra Hall, designed by Hardy, Holzman & Pfeiffer Associates and Hammel, Green and Abrahamson in 1974. Actually, this home to the Minnesota Orchestra is two buildings: the brown-brick auditorium, and the glass and metal-paneled lobbies, offices, and practice spaces built around it. The hall's near-perfect acoustics are due in large part to its unique design, which utilizes hundreds of cubes, sprayed playfully across the back of the stage and all the way across the ceiling of the 2,500-seat house. Stylistically, the high-tech hall has its enemies, and with good reason; the orchestra threw all of its money into creating an

MINNEAPOLIS

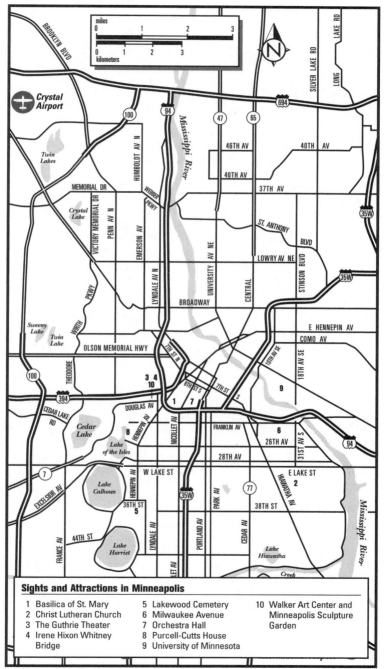

Sights and Attractions in Minneapolis

1 Basilica of St. Mary
2 Christ Lutheran Church
3 The Guthrie Theater
4 Irene Hixon Whitney
  Bridge
5 Lakewood Cemetery
6 Milwaukee Avenue
7 Orchestra Hall
8 Purcell-Cutts House
9 University of Minnesota
10 Walker Art Center and
   Minneapolis Sculpture
   Garden

acoustic marvel, with bare-bones architectural results—some kindly refer to this as good old-fashioned Scandinavian practicality. Lovely Peavey Plaza is just outside (also see Chapter 8, Parks and Gardens).

PURCELL-CUTTS HOUSE
2328 Lake Pl., Minneapolis
612/870-3131 **MP**

A 1913 Prairie School house of great distinction, owned and managed by the Minneapolis Institute of Arts. The house—built by Purcell and Elmslie for Purcell's family and bequeathed to the Institute by Anson Cutts Jr.—was painstakingly restored in 1991. Its intricate and delicate decorative touches, including colorful stencils, 80 art-glass windows, and original furniture, make it a treat to explore. Admission is free. Open the second Saturday of each month from 10 a.m. to 4:30 p.m. Reservations required.

RAND TOWER
527 Marquette Ave., Minneapolis
612/673-0747 **MP**

Step back 70 years to the Rand Tower, a Holabird and Root design that's worlds apart from their sleek First National Bank (now One Financial Plaza). Once a dominant force on the Minneapolis skyline, this 27-story art deco stunner keeps getting better with age. The 1930s lobby is straight out of an RKO/Ginger Rogers–Fred Astaire movie, and a recent renovation is restoring its built-in luster.

UNIVERSITY OF MINNESOTA
612/626-8687 **MP**

The Minneapolis campus of the U of M is one of the largest in the country, and its jumble of architectural styles makes for a varied if somewhat discordant academic landscape. But there are a handful of buildings with genuine merit. Besides the thrilling new Frederick R. Weisman Art Museum (333. E. River Rd.), campus highlights include Cass Gilbert's stately Mall, patterned after Thomas Jefferson's Forum Romanum design at the University of Virginia and presided over by Northrop Auditorium (84 Church St. SE); Pillsbury Hall (310 Pillsbury Dr. SE), a massive 1980 Richardsonian Romanesque fortress designed by L. S. Buffington; Williamson Hall (231 Pillsbury Dr. SE) and Civil/Mineral Engineering Building (500 Pillsbury Dr. SE), both were designed by BRW and are prime examples of the 1970s' trend towards submerged, energy-conscious structures; and the Law School (229 19th Ave. S.), a spacious and gracious design by Leonard Parker. Tours are available; call the number above for information.

WALKER ART CENTER AND MINNEAPOLIS SCULPTURE GARDEN
725 Vineland Pl., Minneapolis
612/375-4444 **MP**

This contemporary art museum and 11-acre garden combine to create one of the country's great urban wonderlands. Perhaps the most superb piece of sculpture in the garden is the Walker itself, a magnificent minimalist object looming above its outdoor galleries.

The building dates from 1972 and is the second gallery to occupy the site. Lumber baron T.B. Walker moved his odd collection of paintings, Japanese porcelain, and ceramics to this site in 1921. The current museum is the work of Edward Larrabee Barnes, and the minute the doors were opened, it became one the city's liveliest places.

ST. PAUL

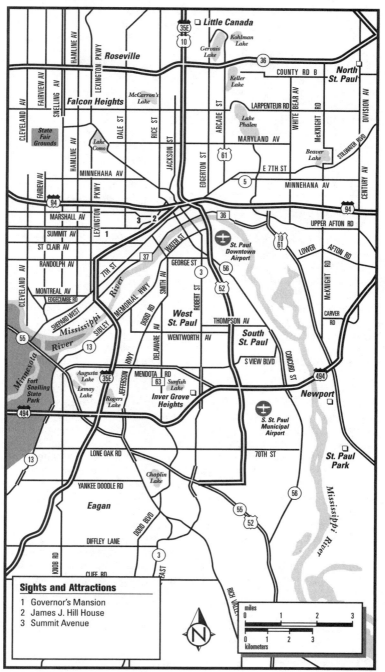

Sights and Attractions

1 Governor's Mansion
2 James J. Hill House
3 Summit Avenue

As for the Minneapolis Sculpture Garden, this joint effort between the Walker Arts Center and the Minneapolis Parks and Recreation Department is the most-visited site in Minneapolis, and with good reason: its works of art, ever-changing landscape, and intriguing design make it a year-round delight. For more information on the Walker Art Center and Minneapolis Sculpture Garden, see Chapter 7, Museums and Art Galleries.

ST. PAUL

GOVERNOR'S MANSION
1006 Summit Ave., St. Paul   SP
The governor's house is a stately Jacobean affair that was built as the home of Horace Irvine and donated to the state in the 1960s. Governor Arne Carlson doesn't live here, however; he isn't a fan of the fishbowl aspect of the place and prefers to reside in suburban St. Paul.

JAMES J. HILL HOUSE
240 Summit Ave., St. Paul
612/297-2555   SP
The base of Summit Avenue is anchored not only by the Cathedral of St. Paul but by the forbidding stone mansion of one of the city's most generous benefactors, James J. Hill. A tour through these palatial digs, now owned by the Minnesota Historical Society, provides a jaw-dropping glimpse into the life of one of the country's great industrialists. Designed by Peabody & Stearns, the richly detailed house took more than three years to complete (at a cost of nearly $1 million, an astronomical

sum for the time) and was ready for occupancy in 1891. The Richardson Romanesque structure stretches for nearly 200 feet along what is—next to the Cathedral and the State Capitol—one of the most commanding locations in the Twin Cities. Inside, it sprawls across nearly 36,000 square feet of space; its 32 rooms (including 13 bathrooms) make it the largest house in the state. Aside from its two-story art gallery, pipe organ, grand staircase, and 100-foot reception room, the house also contains what were the latest inventions in domestic technology, including an ingenious central-heating system and electric lights. The house is open for tours (adults $4) Wednesday through Saturday from 10 a.m. to 3:30 p.m.

SUMMIT AVENUE
St. Paul   SP
From its starting point at the Cathedral, Summit Avenue winds its way through St. Paul for 5 miles and terminates at the Mississippi River and the campus of the St. Paul Seminary. Along the way, this lovely, tree-lined boulevard showcases the longest and best-preserved span of Victorian residential architecture in the United States, punctuated by several beautiful churches and well-tended college campuses. No one style dominates—which is part of the fun of exploring Summit—and you'll see wonderfully overblown examples of Gothic, Italianate, French and Greek Revival, and everything in between. The drive (or bike ride; the entire boulevard is lined with bike paths) is particularly alluring in autumn, when the avenue is ablaze with color.

6

KIDS' STUFF

It's an old adage, but residents have long extolled the virtues of raising a family in the Twin Cities. One reason is that there is so much to offer in terms of family fun, whether it's instructional, recreational, or some combination thereof. For example, the Twin Cities are home to one of the country's most fascinating zoos, a brand-new Children's Museum, and the nation's largest and oldest children's theater company, as well as two large amusement parks (one indoors, the other outdoors), the country's newest aquarium, and a bevy of affordable and interesting historical sites and museums that will fascinate and educate kids of all ages.

ANIMALS AND THE GREAT OUTDOORS

COMO ZOO
Midway Pkwy. and Kaufman Dr.
St. Paul
612/488-5571   **SP**
More than 300 animals are on display at this small zoo, which has been a St. Paul draw for nearly a century. The exhibits are fashioned after natural habitats. Crowd favorites include the primate house and the "Sparky" the Sea Lion's show. Zoodale, the gift shop, has lots of inexpensive trinkets for kids. Admission: Free. Hours: Vary by season.

MINNESOTA ZOO
13000 Zoo Blvd., Apple Valley
612/432-9000 or 800/366-7811
612/297-5353 TTY   **GTC**
This 500-acre zoological garden with five separate habitat trails—Ocean, Tropics, Minnesota, Northern, and Discovery—merits continual exploration. On the Northern Trail, visitors ride on an overhead monorail for treetop views of wolves, moose, musk oxen, caribou, red pandas, Siberian tigers, trumpeter swans, bison, and Asian wild horses. On the Tropics Trail, sights include Komodo dragons, leopards, gibbons, sharks, and exotic tropical fish; and Ocean

Siberian tigers at the Minnesota Zoo

foot acrylic tunnel that simulates a scuba-dive experience in four different habitats: the Gulf of Mexico, a coral reef, the Mississippi River, and a frozen Minnesota lake. A moving walkway (complete with audio tour) takes about 35 minutes, and the average visit runs about 1.5 hours. Admission: $8.95 adults, $6.95 seniors ages 62 and up, $4.95 children ages 3–12, free to children under 2. Hours: Vary by season; tours begin every 15 minutes. Reservations are strongly recommended, and can be made by phone with a Visa or MasterCard ($1.50 surcharge per ticket) or in person.

Trail visitors can see dolphins and a host of other sea creatures.

The zoo has an excellent gift shop, bookstore, concessions, and picnic areas. The Weesner Family Amphitheater hosts family-oriented entertainment. Come winter, the groomed cross-country ski trails are tops. A new $21-million Discovery Bay aquarium is scheduled to open in late spring 1997, along with an $8-million giant-screen, 600-seat 3-D movie theater. The zoo is about 20 minutes south of both downtowns. Admission: $8 adults, $5 seniors, $4 children ages 3–12, free to children under 2. Hours: Daily 9–4.

UNDERWATER WORLD
First floor, East Broadway, Mall of America, Bloomington
888/DIVETIME GTC
The Mall's latest don't-miss attraction is this new $26 million aquarium. More than 15,000 saltwater and freshwater fish in tanks that hold 1.2 million gallons of water call Underwater World home. The ingenious design features a meandering 400-

MUSEUMS

FORT SNELLING
Hwys. 5 and 55, St. Paul
612/726-1711 GTC
Built at the strategic confluence of the Mississippi and Minnesota Rivers—to protect the interests of the U.S. Government—Fort Snelling has been completely restored as a living-history museum that teaches visitors about the harsh realities of frontier life, circa 1827. Sponsored by the Minnesota Historical Society, this 1821 limestone fort comes to life with soldiers, servants, cooks, wives, officers, and laundresses. Admission: $4 adults, $3 seniors, $2 children ages 6–15, free to children under 5. Hours: May–Oct, Mon–Sat 10–5, Sun 12–5.

GIBB'S FARM MUSEUM
2097 W. Larpenteur,
Falcon Heights
612/646-8629 GTC
Get a peek at life on a turn-of-the-century farm at one of the few remaining farmsteads in the Twin Cities area. Owned and operated by

DOWNTOWN MINNEAPOLIS

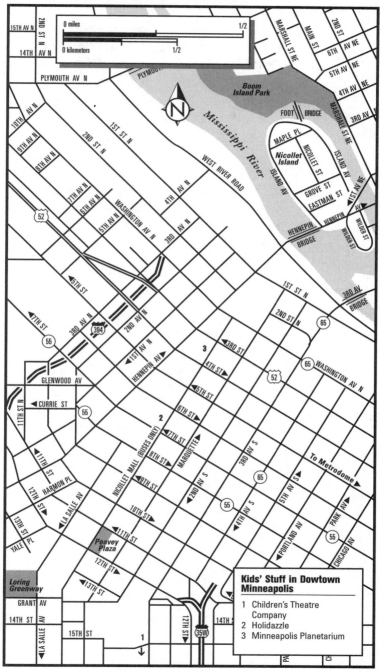

Kids' Stuff in Dowtown Minneapolis

1 Children's Theatre Company
2 Holidazzle
3 Minneapolis Planetarium

A Day at the Farm

Although apple- and berry-picking farms abound around the Twin Cities area, **Rush River Produce** *(W4098 200th Ave., Maiden Rock, Wisconsin, 715/594-3648) is the most friendly and uncommercial. You and the kids can pick blueberries, raspberries, lingonberries, and gooseberries, plus garden produce and red, black, and white currants. The farm has beautiful views of Lake Pepin and lovely flower gardens. There's a picnic ground, too. Prime picking time is July through September. Located an hour southeast of the Twin Cities. Hours: Daily 8–dusk.*

Other popular area orchards include **Aamodt's Apple Farm** *in Stillwater (612/439-3127),* **Afton Apple Orchard** *in Afton (612/436-8385),* **Emma Krumbee's** *in Belle Plaine (612/873-4334),* **Pine Tree Orchards** *in White Bear Lake (612/429-7202), and* **Sponsel's** *in Jordan (612/492-2785).*

the Ramsey County Historical Society, the site includes the Gibbs' fully furnished 1854 farmhouse, two barns, a one-room school, working gardens, and farm animals, all presided over by costumed guides. Admission: $3 adults, $2.50 seniors, $1.50 children. Hours: May–Oct, Tue–Fri 10–4, Sat and Sun 12–4.

MINNEAPOLIS PLANETARIUM
300 Nicollet Mall, Minneapolis
612/372-6644   DMP
Countless Twin Cities schoolchildren are veterans of this popular attraction. The half-hour show changes about every ten weeks, and includes an animated whirl through the current sky, vividly reproduced on a domed ceiling, and a spin through topical astronomical subjects. Laser rock-music shows on Friday and Saturday. Admission: $4

adults, $2.50 children ages 3–12, free to children under 2. Hours: Daily, but showtimes vary.

MINNESOTA CHILDREN'S MUSEUM
10 W. 7th St., St. Paul
612/225-6001
612/225-6057 TDD   DSP
Any kid under age 10 will love this colorful, playful place. Housed in a sleek, cheerful new facility in downtown St. Paul, the museum has five different exhibition areas as well as several touring exhibitions. Habitot is scaled for infants and toddlers, World Works is designed for inventors ages 3 to 7, Earth World opens up four different Minnesota animal habitats for nature-conscious 4- to 8-year-olds, One World takes 6- to 10-year-olds on a journey through several international communities,

DOWNTOWN ST. PAUL

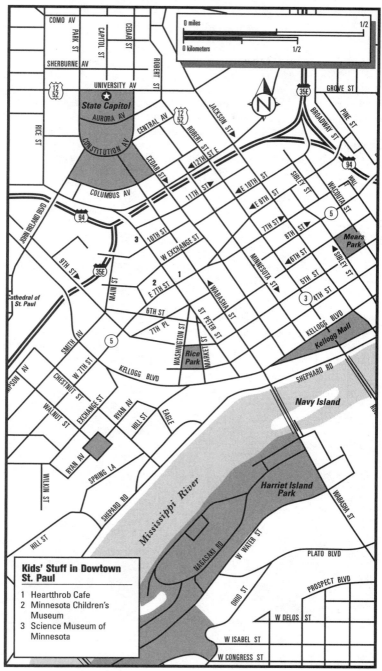

0 miles 1/2

0 kilometers 1/2

COMO AV

PARK ST

CAPITOL ST

CEDAR ST

SHERBURNE AV

ROBERT ST

GROVE ST

UNIVERSITY AV

State Capitol

AURORA AV

JACKSON ST

N

BROADWAY ST

PINE ST

RICE ST

CENTRAL AV

ROBERT ST E

CONSTITUTION AV

12TH ST E

CEDAR ST

SIBLEY ST

WACOUTA ST

COLUMBUS AV

11TH ST

E 10TH ST

E 9TH ST

7TH ST

Mears Park

JOHN IRELAND BLVD

10TH ST

W EXCHANGE ST

8TH ST

6TH ST

SIBLEY ST

9TH ST

MAIN ST

MINNESOTA ST

5TH ST

4TH ST

Cathedral of St. Paul

E 7TH ST

WABASHA ST

6TH ST

ST PETER ST

KELLOGG BLVD

SMITH AV

7TH PL

WASHINGTON ST

MARKET ST

Rice Park

Kellogg Mall

CHESTNUT ST

KELLOGG BLVD

SHEPHARD RD

Navy Island

WALNUT ST

EXCHANGE ST

RYAN AV

HILL ST

EAGLE

WILKIN ST

RYAN AV

SPRING LA

Harriet Island Park

WABASHA ST

SHEPARD RD

Mississippi River

NAGASAKI RD

W WATER ST

PLATO BLVD

HILL ST

OHIO ST

PROSPECT BLVD

W DELOS ST

W ISABEL ST

W CONGRESS ST

Kids' Stuff in Dowtown St. Paul

1 Heartthrob Cafe
2 Minnesota Children's Museum
3 Science Museum of Minnesota

and Changing World and World of Wonder house traveling exhibitions from children's museums around the world.

The best day for families to visit is the first Tuesday of every month, when groups are not allowed. Creative Kidstuff, an innovative toy-and-book store, is in the lobby, and an intimate, 150-seat theater schedules performances and readings for children. The museum is a terrific place to throw a kid's birthday party, too; call 612/225-6036 for b-day bash details. All children must be accompanied by an adult. Admission: $5.95 ages 3 to adult, $3.95 seniors and kids ages 1–2, infants free. Hours: Tue–Sun 9–5; Memorial Day–Labor Day, Mon 9–5.

MURPHY'S LANDING
2187 E. Hwy. 101, Shakopee
612/445-6900   GTC

A unique living-history museum, Murphy's Landing is a collection of 40 different period buildings relocated to an 88-acre wooded site along the Minnesota River. A fur-

trading post, two farmsteads, a country schoolhouse, shops, and homes as well as costumed interpreters and craftspeople provide a fascinating glimpse into nineteenth-century immigrants' lives in rural Minnesota. Located 1 mile west of Valleyfair, about 35 minutes southwest of downtown Minneapolis. Admission: $7 adults, $6 seniors and students, $5 groups, $4 student groups, free to children 5 and under. Hours: Memorial Day–Labor Day, daily 10–5; Sept–Dec, open weekends.

SCIENCE MUSEUM OF MINNESOTA
30 E. 10th St., St. Paul
612/221-9488   DSP

An exploratorium for kids of all ages, geared to stimulate an interest in scientific knowledge. The museum's extensive permanent collections include several dramatic dinosaur fossils. Constantly changing exhibitions, too. The museum's most popular attraction is the William T. McKnight 3M Omnitheater. Admission: $5 adults, $4 seniors and children ages

Science Museum of Minnesota

Science Museum of Minnesota

ST. PAUL

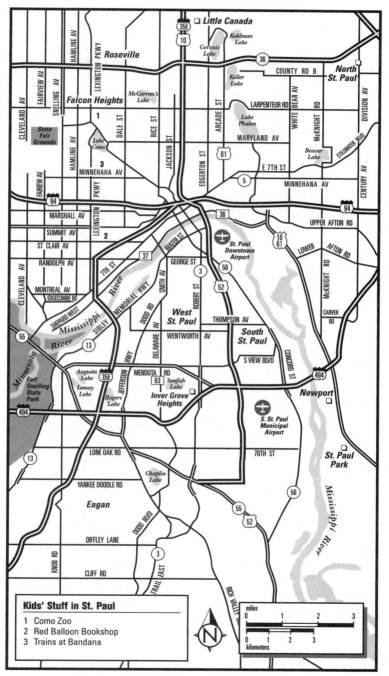

Little Canada

Roseville

Kohlman Lake

Gervais Lake

COUNTY RD B

North St. Paul

Falcon Heights

McCarron's Lake

Keller Lake

LARPENTEUR RD

State Fair Grounds

Lake Como

Lake Phalen

MARYLAND AV

Beaver Lake

MINNEHAHA AV

E 7TH ST

MINNEHANA AV

MARSHALL AV

UPPER AFTON RD

SUMMIT AV

ST CLAIR AV

RANDOLPH AV

St. Paul Downtown Airport

LOWER AFTON RD

GEORGE ST

MONTREAL AV

EDGECUMBE RD

SHEPARD WEST

Mississippi River

West St. Paul

THOMPSON AV

South St. Paul

CARVER RD

WENTWORTH AV

S VIEW BLVD

Minnesota

Augusta Lake

Lemay Lake

MENDOTA RD

Sunfish Lake

Fort Snelling State Park

Rogers Lake

Inver Grove Heights

Newport

S. St. Paul Municipal Airport

LONE OAK RD

70TH ST

St. Paul Park

Chaplin Lake

YANKEE DOODLE RD

Eagan

Mississippi River

DIFFLEY LANE

KNOB RD

CLIFF RD

Kids' Stuff in St. Paul

1 Como Zoo
2 Red Balloon Bookshop
3 Trains at Bandana

miles
0   1   2   3

kilometers
0   1   2   3

N

4–15, free to children under 3. Hours: Mon–Sat 9:30–9, Sun 10–9. For Omnitheater information, including hours and ticket prices, call 612/221-9444.

TRAINS AT BANDANA
1021 Bandana Blvd., St. Paul
612/647-9628 SP
Exact model O-scale replicas of trains from the 1930s, 1940s, and 1950s whir around meticulously landscaped settings in this fun museum, the handiwork of the Twin Cities Model Railroad Club. Admission: Free. Hours: Fri 10–8, Sat 10–6, Sun 12–5.

WALKER ART CENTER
725 Vineland Pl., Minneapolis
612/375-7600
612/375-7685 TDD MP
The contemporary art museum opens its doors to families the first Saturday of every month for Free First Saturday, a day-long series of activities that introduce children and their parents to the worlds of art, music, theater, and performance. Kids also love the 11-acre Minneapolis Sculpture Garden just outside the museum. Admission: $4 adults, $3 seniors and students, and free every Thursday and the first Saturday of each month. Hours: Tue, Wed, Fri and Sat 10–5, Thur 10–8, and Sun 11–5. Closed Monday. Minneapolis Sculpture Garden admission: Free. Hours: Daily 6 a.m. to midnight. *(Note: This sight appears on the Greater Twin Cities map, page 114.)*

ENTERTAINMENT

THE AMAZING SPACE
Second floor, West Market, Mall of America, Bloomington
612/851-0000 GTC

You'll feel good about dropping the kids (while you shop) at this exploratory, instructive play space for kids and adults. Admission: $5.50 adults and children over age 3, $3 for children ages 2–3, free to children under 2. Hours: Mon–Sat 10–9:30, Sun 11–7.

CHILDREN'S THEATRE COMPANY
2400 3rd Ave. S., Minneapolis
612/874-0400 DMP
The nation's largest professional children's theater, CTC's talented company of children and young-at-heart adults produces imaginative adaptations of classic children's works (including *The Story of Babar, The Reluctant Dragon, The Hobbit, Cinderella, Little Women, Not Without Laughter, A Wrinkle in Time, The 500 Hats of Bartholomew Cubbins, How the Grinch Stole Christmas*, and dozens more), as well as new plays commissioned for the company. Adults will appreciate the superb production values, and kids will be entranced by the storytelling. Season runs September through June and usually features seven to nine productions. Admission: Ticket prices vary, but usually run $8 to $25; deeply discounted rush tickets are available 15 minutes before curtain.

CHILD'S PLAY THEATRE COMPANY
1001 Hwy. 7, Hopkins
612/931-2290 GTC
A more modest alternative to the CTC, performed at the Eisenhower Community Center just outside downtown Hopkins. Ticket prices are affordable, and the casts of nearly every play—which includes reworked fairy tales and other children's stories—consist almost entirely of kids. Season runs October

Nuts for *The Nutcracker*

For reasons unknown, it is possible in some seasons to see more than 12 different productions of The Nutcracker *in the Twin Cities. Some are quite good, including:*

- *City Children's* **Nutcracker**, *a rousing, all-kids version produced by Ballet Arts Minnesota and the Greater Twin Cities Youth Symphonies.*
- **Nutcracker Fantasy**, *the lyrical version that most Minnesotans grew up seeing, choreographed by the late Loyce Houlton and staged every year by the Minnesota Dance Theater.*
- **The Nutcracker?**, *a twisted take on the classic tale featuring Ken and Barbie, by choreographer Myron Johnson for his Ballet of the Dolls.*
- *Northrop's* **Nutcracker**, *an out-of-town production imported for local audiences to Northrop Auditorium's huge stage. Past shows have included sumptuous productions by Pacific Northwest Ballet, the Joffrey Ballet, and Ballet West.*

through July. Ticket prices vary but average $8 adults, $6 seniors and children ages 3–16, free to children under 2.

GOLF MOUNTAIN
Third floor, North Garden, Mall of America, Bloomington
612/883-8899   **GTC**
This spectacular 18-hole miniature golf operation overlooks Camp Snoopy. Admission: $5 adults, $4 children. Hours vary by season.

HOLIDAZZLE
Nicollet Mall, Minneapolis
612/338-3807   **DMP**
Thousands of families line the sidewalks of Nicollet Mall every night from Thanksgiving to Christmas to take in the spectacle of a dazzling winter parade, complete with a bevy of storybook characters, floats, marching bands, choirs, a grand marshal, and, of course, Santa Claus. Bundle up and have a ball. Carol sing-alongs take place Saturday and Sunday evenings in the IDS Crystal Court before the parade. Admission: Free. Hours: Nov. 24–Dec. 30, daily 6:30 p.m., from 12th Street to 5th Street.

LEGO IMAGINATION CENTER
First floor, South Avenue, Mall of America, Bloomington
612/858-8949   **GTC**
LEGO aficionados of all persuasions will fall head-over-heels in love with this savvy play area. Everywhere you look, there's a LEGO statue, or a LEGO object, each more fanciful than the

GREATER TWIN CITIES

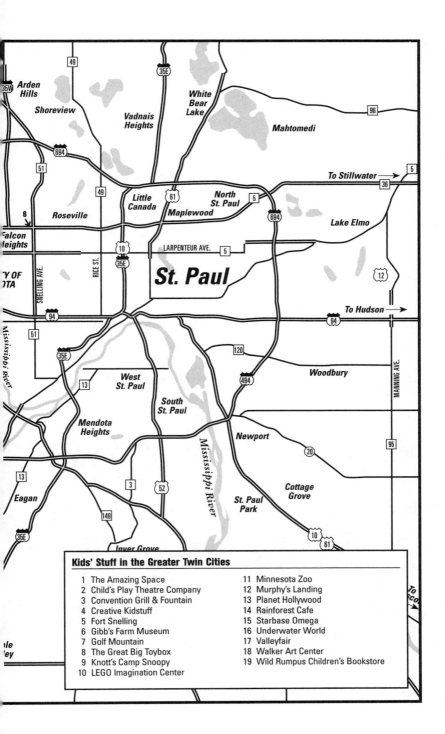

Kids' Stuff in the Greater Twin Cities

1 The Amazing Space
2 Child's Play Theatre Company
3 Convention Grill & Fountain
4 Creative Kidstuff
5 Fort Snelling
6 Gibb's Farm Museum
7 Golf Mountain
8 The Great Big Toybox
9 Knott's Camp Snoopy
10 LEGO Imagination Center

11 Minnesota Zoo
12 Murphy's Landing
13 Planet Hollywood
14 Rainforest Cafe
15 Starbase Omega
16 Underwater World
17 Valleyfair
18 Walker Art Center
19 Wild Rumpus Children's Bookstore

last. There are lots of regularly scheduled LEGO-related events and activities, too, and a full complement of LEGO products in a selection that even Toys 'R' Us can't match. Of course, the full spectrum of LEGO products are available for sale. Admission: Free. Hours: Vary by season.

STARBASE OMEGA
Third floor, South Avenue, Mall of America, Bloomington
612/858-8001   **GTC**
This high-energy and elaborate game of interactive laser-tag is especially popular with kids ages 8 and up. Admission: 20-minute games cost $8.50 single, $12.75 double.

THEME PARKS

KNOTT'S CAMP SNOOPY
Mall of America
612/883-8600   **GTC**
The Mall's biggest entertainment attraction is Knott's Camp Snoopy, a 7-acre indoor amusement park, loaded with more than two-dozen fun rides

that will appeal to kids of all ages. Some of the attractions include a roller coaster, log flume (expect to get a little wet), Ferris wheel, and bumper cars, as well as games, food stalls, shops, and several theaters. During the day, the park can be bright and obnoxious, but at night, the skylights darken and thousands of twinkly lights bring Knott's Camp Snoopy to life. *Peanuts* fans will get a kick out of all the Charlie Brown, Snoopy, and Woodstock touches. Admission: Free. All attractions operate on a point system, with rides varying from one to six points. Points cost 60 cents each, and super-saver packages include 110 points for $50, 60 points for $30, 38 points for $20, and 18 points for $10. Hours: Vary by season.

VALLEYFAIR
1 Valleyfair Dr., Shakopee
612/445-7600   **GTC**
The Upper Midwest's largest theme park boasts 75 scream-inducing rides (including four roller coasters), a refreshing water park, an IMAX theater,

Knott's Camp Snoopy

GMCVA

Come to the Fair

*The two-week **Minnesota State Fair** (1265 Snelling Ave., St. Paul, 612/642-2200 or 612/642-2372 TTY) is the nation's largest, attracting more than 1.3 million people to see everything from agricultural competitions, to stock-car races, to Grandstand concerts, to Midway rides and games, to pie-baking contests. Kids can get their first up-close glimpse of cows, pigs, sheep, and horses in the 4-H animal barns, or take in their small counterparts at the fair's popular petting zoo. Another big attraction is the great fair food: Pronto Pups, cheese curds, walleye-on-a-stick, malts, foot-long hot dogs, cotton candy, and countless other once-a-year delicacies, sold by more than 350 concessionaires. The fair is where you'll see a true cross-section of Minnesota in all its diverse glory. Save yourself a headache (and a few bucks) and park at one of the MCTO's distant lots and take the bus in. Admission: $5 adults, $4 seniors and children ages 5–12, free children under age 4. Hours: 6 a.m. to midnight daily, the last 12 days before Labor Day.*

live entertainment, good food, games, and shops. Kids under age 5 will enjoy Berenstain Bear Country, Half-Pint Park, and Tot Town. The park's 90 acres are lavishly landscaped, and the staff is hyper-friendly. Located about 35 minutes southeast of downtown Minneapolis. Admission: $20.95 adults and children ages 4 and up, $4.95 seniors and children ages 3 and under. Hours: Memorial Day–Labor Day, daily 10–10; May and Sep, open weekends.

STORES KIDS LOVE

CREATIVE KIDSTUFF
4313 Upton Ave. S., Minneapolis
612/927-0653   **MP**

Colorful, creative toys, games, and doodads. Two locations in St. Paul, at 1074 Grand Ave., 612/222-2472; and 10 W. 7th St., 612/225-6606; and, in the Greater Minneapolis area, at 13019 Ridgedale Dr., Minnetonka, 612/540-0022. *(Note: This sight appears on the Greater Twin Cities map, page 114.)*

THE GREAT BIG TOYBOX
7525 France Ave. S., Edina
612/835-2627   **GTC**
A huge selection of educational toys that still manage to be fun.

RED BALLOON BOOKSHOP
891 Grand Ave., St. Paul
612/224-8320   **SP**
A delightful children's bookstore with

The Great Big Toybox

more than 20,000 titles, less than a block from the Victoria Crossing shopping area.

WILD RUMPUS CHILDREN'S BOOKSTORE
2720 W. 43rd St., Minneapolis
612/920-5005 **MP**
Laid out for maximum kid accessibility, this enchanting store is designed to ignite children's interest in reading. *(Note: This sight appears on the Greater Twin Cities map, page 114.)*

RESTAURANTS KIDS LOVE

CONVENTION GRILL & FOUNTAIN
3912 Sunnyside Rd., Edina
612/920-6881 **GTC**
The burgers are the thickest, juiciest, and tastiest in the Twin Cities, the malts are superlative, and the kids' menu will please the finnickiest of eaters. A genuine diner with a family-oriented dining room in the back.

HEARTTHROB CAFE
30 E. 7th St., St. Paul
612/224-2783 **DSP**
The atmosphere is vintage 1950s rock 'n' roll—loud, colorful, slightly obnoxious, but entertaining—and servers glide around on roller skates. The affordable food is burgers, malts, and the like, and it's pretty good. Located in the World Trade Center.

PLANET HOLLYWOOD
Fourth floor, East Broadway, Mall of America, Bloomington
612/854-7827 **GTC**
Kids love the brash surroundings, and everyone gets a kick out of the movieland memorabilia. The food—burgers, pizzas, sandwiches, salads—is well-prepared, and the desserts are huge. No reservations; lunch and dinner daily.

RAINFOREST CAFE
First floor, South Avenue, Mall of America, Bloomington
612/854-7500 **GTC**
The wait may kill you, but kids eat up the fake rainforest decor, live animals, simulated rainstorm (with thunder and lightning, no less), and obligatory gift shop. Food is standard theme-restaurant fare. Shortest lines are during midweek late-afternoons. No reservations; lunch and dinner daily; smoke-free.

Don Wong

7

MUSEUMS AND ART GALLERIES

Minneapolis and St. Paul are serious museum towns, with a number of important collections housed in several world-famous buildings. Minneapolis is home to the Walker Art Center, an internationally renowned contemporary art museum on the southern edge of downtown Minneapolis, as well as the University of Minnesota's acclaimed Frederick R. Weisman Art Museum, housed in a striking new building by architect Frank Gehry on a site overlooking the banks of the Mississippi River. In between, you can explore the encyclopedic collections of European, Asian, and American art at the splendid Minneapolis Institute of Arts.

In St. Paul, uncover the Gopher State's rich past at the Minnesota Historical Society's fascinating new Minnesota History Center. Children can throw themselves into the complexities of nature at the Science Museum of Minnesota, explore why things work at the delightful new Minnesota Children's Museum, or learn about the harsh realities of life on a frontier army post at historic Fort Snelling. Only the museums are shown on the maps in this chapter.

ART MUSEUMS

FREDERICK R. WEISMAN ART MUSEUM
333 E. River Rd., Minneapolis
612/625-9494   **MP**
Frank Gehry's flamboyant building is perhaps the most stunning piece in

the museum's collection and the most talked-about building in the Twin Cities. The "Fred" is the home of the University Art Museum. On the outside, the museum faces the Mississippi River with an undulating and dramatic facade covered in polished aluminum, particularly ravishing at sunset. For all the goofy drama on the

MINNEAPOLIS

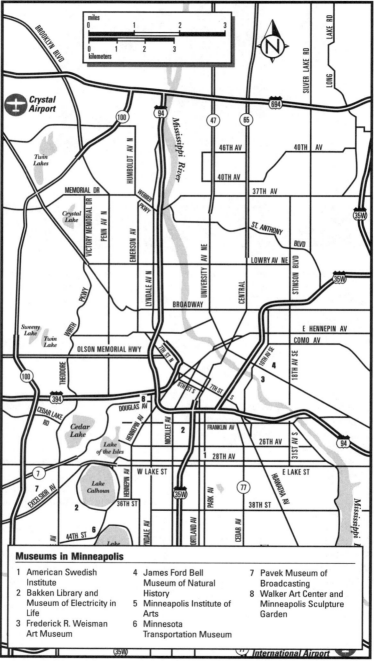

Museums in Minneapolis

1 American Swedish
  Institute
2 Bakken Library and
  Museum of Electricity in
  Life
3 Frederick R. Weisman
  Art Museum

4 James Ford Bell
  Museum of Natural
  History
5 Minneapolis Institute of
  Arts
6 Minnesota
  Transportation Museum

7 Pavek Museum of
  Broadcasting
8 Walker Art Center and
  Minneapolis Sculpture
  Garden

outside, the interior is surprisingly understated, and the modestly scaled and wonderfully lit galleries are so attractive that the *New York Times* called them "possibly the five best rooms for viewing art in the world."

The mostly twentieth-century collection contains the world's largest assemblage of works by Marsden Hartley and Alfred Maurer as well as paintings and prints by Georgia O'Keeffe, Arthur Dove, and Robert Motherwell, among others. The entrance is dominated by Roy Lichtenstein's *World's Fair Mural*. Be sure to take in the river view from the tiny balcony, located one floor above the galleries. And don't miss the Museum Shop, full of affordable baubles and amusing Gehry-related merchandise. Parking is available in a garage under the galleries. Admission: Free. Hours: Tue, Wed, and Fri 10–5; Thur 10–8; Sat and Sun 11–5. Closed Monday.

MINNEAPOLIS INSTITUTE OF ARTS
2400 3rd Ave. S., Minneapolis
612/870-3131
612/870-3132 TDD   MP

With a collection of more than 85,000 objects, the MIA is one of the country's top art museums. Housed in a grand 1915 white marble Beaux Arts building by McKim, Mead and White, the museum's galleries have been undergoing renovations and reinstallations over the past few years, and its permanent collection has never looked better. Unlike many big-city art museums, which have a tendency to overwhelm, the manageable MIA is easily explored in a few hours.

Must-sees include the small but exceptional gallery of French Impressionist paintings, including works by Monet, Degas, Bonnard, and van Gogh; the exquisite collection of carved Oriental jades; *Lucretia*, considered by art historians to be the best Rembrandt in the country; the astounding, muscular *Doryphoros*, one of the finest Roman copies of the well-known but no longer existing Greek statue; and works by old masters such as Titian, El Greco, and Poussin as well as significant works by a laundry list of nineteenth- and twentieth-century American and European artists, including Picasso, Kandinsky, Matisse, Rodin, Rouault, Millet, Stella, and Klee.

But the MIA is chock-full of smaller delights, too; the period rooms are fascinating, the tapestry collection is a wonder, and the newly opened photography and print galleries are appealing showcases for rotating exhibitions culled from the museum's enormous collections. The Minnesota Gallery is constantly introducing the work of new and emerging local artists.

The MIA hosts several major touring shows each year in its large Dayton Hudson Gallery on the second floor. The Studio cafeteria is always a smart choice for a delicious, inexpensive lunch. There's a large but not particularly compelling gift shop just inside the lobby. Admission: Free, although special exhibitions charge $5 for adults, $3.75 for students and seniors, free to children under 12. Hours: Tue, Wed, Fri and Sat 10–5; Thur 10–9; Sun 12–5. Closed Monday. Call 612/870-3200 for 24-hour exhibition information.

MINNESOTA MUSEUM OF AMERICAN ART
75 W. 5th St., St. Paul
612/292-4355   DSP

Financial difficulties have severely curtailed the activities of this

DOWNTOWN ST. PAUL

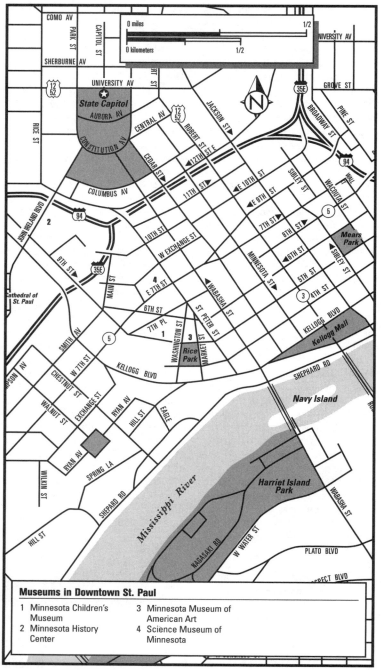

Museums in Downtown St. Paul

1. Minnesota Children's Museum
2. Minnesota History Center
3. Minnesota Museum of American Art
4. Science Museum of Minnesota

museum, which has always lived in the shadow of its Minneapolis cousins. The biggest blow came in 1993, when the museum was forced to abandon its galleries in the jewel-like Jemne Building and decamp to less expensive (but no less thrilling) space in the Landmark Center; the move also limited showing anything but the bare minimum of its fine collection of 10,000 mostly American paintings, drawings, and prints. Admission: Free. Hours: Tue, Wed, Fri and Sat 11–4; Thur 11–7:30; Sun 1–5. Closed Monday.

WALKER ART CENTER AND MINNEAPOLIS SCULPTURE GARDEN
725 Vineland Pl., Minneapolis
612/375-7600
612/375-7585 TDD/TTY   MP

One of the country's most renowned museums of contemporary art, and a center of Twin Cities cultural life. The Walker's nine stark, all-white galleries offer glimpses into the museum's far-flung collection of paintings, sculptures, prints, drawings, and multimedia works, as well as a steady diet of rotating exhibitions. The permanent collection includes important works by a veritable *Who's Who* of contemporary art, including Willem de Kooning, Mark Rothko, Franz Marc, Stuart Davis, Andy Warhol, Joan Mitchell, Roy Lichtenstein, Donald Judd, Sol LeWitt, Chuck Close, and Dan Flavin. The museum is also the repository for Tyler Graphics, and the McKnight Print Room has a peerless collection of contemporary works. In addition, the Walker hosts a schedule of innovative theater, music, dance, film, video, and performance programs as well as classes, workshops, and lectures.

The Walker Book Shop sells a variety of gifts, artist-designed jewelry, toys, museum-related items, and the city's top selection of art books and periodicals. Gallery 8, the museum's cafeteria, offers inexpensive and delicious fare. Spend a few moments in the Information Room for an excellent multimedia introduction to the museum and its current exhibitions. The best day for families to visit is the first Saturday of every month, when the museum schedules free family-oriented events and activities. Admission: $4 adults, $3 seniors and students, and free every Thursday and the first Saturday of each month.

At the Walker

Besides maintaining its permanent collection, which prospered under the stewardship of Milton Friedman for more than three decades and is now overseen by Kathy Halbreich, the Walker Art Center has either originated or lured a number of critically acclaimed exhibitions in recent years, including **Picasso: Selections from the Musee Picasso** *in 1980,* **Tokyo: Form and Spirit** *in 1985,* **Hockney Paints the Stage** *in 1987, and major retrospectives for Jeff Koons (1993), Robert Ryman (1994), and Bruce Naumann (1995).*

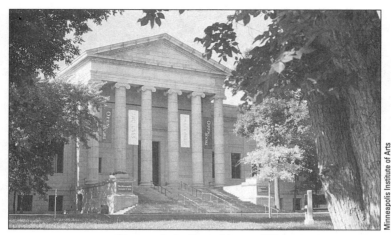

Minneapolis Institute of Arts, p. 121

Hours: Tue, Wed, Fri and Sat 10–5; Thur 10–8; Sun 11–5. Closed Monday. Guided tours every Thursday at 2 and 6 p.m. and every Sunday at 2 p.m. Call 612/375-7577 for 24-hour exhibition information.

The 11-acre **Minneapolis Sculpture Garden** is a wondrous year-round showcase for more than 40 works of art, including major sculptures by George Segal, Isamu Noguchi, Ellsworth Kelly, Richard Serra, Jenny Holzer, Alexander Calder, Henry Moore, Scott Burton, Franz Lipschitz, Mark di Suvero, and others. The garden's entrance is flanked by *Ampersand*, a pair of monumental granite columns by Martin Puryear.

The garden is one of the most popular places in the city and is in constant use, even during the harshest of winter days. The Cowles Conservatory is a perfect gloomy-weather respite, with a changing display of blooming plants as well as a palm court dominated by Frank Gehry's *Standing Glass Fish*. The garden's most famous (and beloved)

symbol is the amusing *Spoonbridge and Cherry*, a 55-foot spoon topped by a 15-foot red Bing cherry, designed by Claes Oldenburg and Coosje van Bruggen. Admission: Free. Hours: Daily 6 a.m. to midnight. Free tours (starting in the Walker's lobby) are available Saturday and Sunday at 1 p.m.

SCIENCE AND HISTORY MUSEUMS

JAMES FORD BELL MUSEUM OF NATURAL HISTORY
10 SE Church St., Minneapolis
612/624-7083 MP

More than 100 species of Minnesota animals and birds are displayed in their native habitats in this museum located on the East Bank of the U of M campus. The kid-scaled Touch and See Room is a favorite. Admission: $3 adults, $2 seniors and children ages 3–16, free to U of M students and children under 3, free every Thursday. Hours: Tue–Fri 9–5, Sat 10–5, Sun 12–5. Closed Monday.

MINNESOTA HISTORY CENTER
345 Kellogg Blvd. W., St. Paul
612/296-6126   DSP

The nation's largest state historical society now has a proper home, and it's a must for visitors and residents alike. The imposing but comfortable building is worth a visit itself. Designed by Hammel, Green and Abrahamson and completed in 1992, the 427,000-square-foot facility admirably frames St. Paul's two most important buildings, the Cathedral of St. Paul and the State Capitol, and yet still manages to stand on its own as a distinctive, almost heroic work of architecture.

The center's permanent exhibitions include the Smithsonian-inspired *Minnesota A to Z*, an ingenious depiction of various aspects of life in Minnesota over the past 150 years. Visitors can also learn how a grain silo operates and how native Minnesotans harvest wild rice. A new exhibition gives a nod to multicultural Minnesota families past and present. Much of the building is devoted to research, and the warehouse areas are as large as three football fields, housing the society's collection of 100,000 objects and 500,000 documents. The center also has a comfortable auditorium, a teeming gift shop, and an excellent cafeteria. Admission: Free. Hours: Tue, Wed, Fri. and Sat 10–5; Thur 10–9; Sun 12–5. Closed Monday.

MINNESOTA TRANSPORTATION MUSEUM
Various sites
612/228-0263

Learn about the history of train, boat, streetcar, and bus travel in Minnesota by visiting this collection of working locomotives, steamships, train depots, roundhouses, trolleys, and motorcoaches. The MTM has five exhibit sites in the Twin Cities area, visited by more than 100,000 people annually. The most popular exhibit is the Como–Harriet Streetcar Line, a rebuilt portion of the once-massive Twin Cities streetcar system, which runs on a 2-mile round-trip course between Lake Harriet and Lake Calhoun. The route is serviced by restored cars dating from 1893, 1908, 1915, and 1947–49. Board at the Linden Hills Station (Queen Avenue and 42nd Street, just west of the Lake Harriet Bandshell) or at the Lakewood Cemetery platform, just south of 36th Street on East Lake Calhoun Parkway. Admission: $1, kids under 4 ride free. Hours: Memorial Day–Labor Day, Mon–Fri every 15 minutes 6:30 p.m. to dusk; Sat 1 p.m. to dusk, Sun 12:30 p.m. to dusk; Sept–Oct weekend hours only.

The museum's other big draw is the *Minnehaha*, a 1906 Lake Minnetonka steamboat, which

Minnesota History Center

SPCVB/Tim Rummelhoff

once used to ferry streetcar passengers all over Lake Minnetonka. Today, the *Minnehaha* plies the lake between the cities of Excelsior and Wayzata. Admission: One-way fare is $5 adults, $4 seniors, $3 children ages 6–16, free to children under 6; round-trip $8 adults, $7 seniors, $5 children ages 6–16, free to children under 6. Hours: May–Sep, Wed–Fri 1–5, Sat and Sun 8–6. Tickets available at the Excelsior dock, located at the end of Excelsior Boulevard near the Ferris wheel; call 612/474-4801 for departures and arrivals.

SCIENCE MUSEUM OF MINNESOTA
30 E. 10th St., St. Paul
612/221-9488 DSP

A fascinating, hands-on center of discovery for kids of all ages. The museum's extensive permanent collections include anthropology, paleontology, biology, and technology exhibits, plus temporary exhibits on everything from holograms, to cyberoptics, to the workings of the human heart. The most popular attraction is the William T. McKnight-3M Omnitheater, which screens a constantly changing repertory of films.

The state's largest reptile (outside of the state Legislature, as some politicos are known to joke) guards the museum's front door, a 40-foot steel iguana by sculptor Nick Swearer. The no-nonsense 1980 facility is beginning to show its age and inadequacies, but the crowds keep pouring in. A new building is slated to rise on a site just below the St. Paul Civic Center and to open in late 1998. Admission: $5 adults, $4 seniors and children ages 4–15, free to children under 3. Hours: Mon–Sat 9:30–9, Sun

10–9. For Omnitheater information, call 612/221-9444.

OTHER MUSEUMS

AMERICAN SWEDISH INSTITUTE
2600 Park Ave. S., Minneapolis
612/871-4907 MP

Get a glimpse into how the other half lived at the turn of the century in this palatial, 33-room French Châteauesque limestone mansion. Four years in the making, the castle was the pride and joy of Swan Turnblad, a Swedish immigrant and self-made millionaire publisher. Upon its completion, he and his wife, Christina, found it too ostentatious for their tastes, so they lived in an apartment across the street, using the house for entertainment purposes only.

After Swan's death, his family founded the American Swedish Institute and donated the house to serve as its museum. Today most of the house is open for exploration, and its ornate interior and lavishly appointed decor truly have to be seen to be believed. The museum also features rotating exhibits on 150 years of the Swedish immigration experience. The building has an excellent gift shop, and in the basement you'll find a bookstore and an informal restaurant. As for the neighborhood, the house was—and remains—the grandest of all the stupendous homes that once lined this section of Park Avenue; unfortunately, the street has seen better days, although a few of the mansions remain (in varying shades of decay) on the four-block stretch between 26th Street and Franklin Avenue. Admission: $3 adults, $2 seniors and children Hours: Tue, Thur–Sat, 12–4, Wed 12–8, Sun. 1–5. Closed Monday.

BAKKEN LIBRARY AND MUSEUM OF ELECTRICITY IN LIFE
3537 Zenith Ave. S., Minneapolis
612/927-6508 **MP**
This eccentric museum houses an extensive collection of rare books, manuscripts, gadgets, and scientific instruments, all relating to the mystery and power of electricity and housed in a beautiful Tudor-style mansion. The library's lush gardens feature more than 200 varieties of medicinal plants. Admission: $3 adults, $2 seniors and children, free to children 8 and under. Hours: Mon–Fri 9–5, by appointment only; Sat 9:30–4:30. Closed Sunday.

MINNESOTA CHILDREN'S MUSEUM
10 W. 7th St., St. Paul
612/225-6001
612/225-6057 TDD **DSP**
This remarkable hands-on institution is a playful adventureland for kids and families, and one of the largest of its kind in the country.

PAVEK MUSEUM OF BROADCASTING
3515 Raleigh Ave. S.,
St. Louis Park
612/926-8198 **GTC**
A modest and slightly eccentric trip back through time, when the wireless was king of mass communications. Founded by amateur radio historian Joseph Pavek, the museum includes a collection of early radio equipment, crystal sets, and other paraphernalia. Admission: $3 adults, $2 seniors and children under 13. Hours: Tue–Fri 10–6, Sat 9–5. Closed Sunday and Monday.

PLANES OF FAME AIR MUSEUM
14771 Pioneer Trail, Eden Prairie
612/941-2633 **GTC**

Get a peek at more than 20 World War II–era fighters and bombers (including a B-17, and a British Spitfire), all restored and maintained in perfect flight condition. Flights are regularly scheduled. Admission: $5 adults, $4 seniors, $2 children ages 7–17, free to children under 6. *(Note: This sight is not shown on the maps in this chapter.)*

ART GALLERIES

BARRY THOMAS FINE ARTS
400 1st Ave. N., Minneapolis
612/338-3656 **DMP**

CIRCA
1637 Hennepin Ave. S.,
Minneapolis
612/332-2386 **DMP**

DOLLY FITERMAN FINE ARTS
100 University Ave. NE,
Minneapolis
612/623-3300 **DMP**

GROVELAND GALLERY
25 Groveland Ter., Minneapolis
612/377-7800 **DMP**

JON OULMAN GALLERY
400 1st Ave. N., Minneapolis
612/333-2386 **DMP**

MONTGOMERY GLASOE FINE ART
300 1st Ave. N., Minneapolis
612/338-6702 **DMP**

NORTHERN CLAY CENTER
2375 University Ave., St. Paul
612/642-1735 **SP**

THOMSON GALLERY
321 2nd Ave. N., Minneapolis
612/338-7734 **DMP**

8

PARKS, GARDENS, AND RECREATION AREAS

The Twin Cities area is truly blessed with some of the most extensive and at-tractive urban parklands in the country. Early city planners in Minneapolis and St. Paul set aside significant amounts of land for public use in the late nine-teenth century, and residents today owe those farsighted city fathers a debt of gratitude for their wisdom in creating an interconnected series of naturally beautiful respites.

Minneapolis in particular has one of the nation's most extensive—and enchanting—park systems. There are 22 lakes within the city limits and al-most all are surrounded by public parklands; many are connected by a 55-mile-long series of "Grand Rounds" parkways that thread their way throughout the city. Although the city turned its back on the Mississippi River for more than a century, it is now reclaiming the St. Anthony Falls area as a recreational destination, and the river gorge from the University of Minnesota to Fort Snelling is one of the most pristine and breathtaking urban waterways in America. In total, the city maintains more than 6,000 acres of parkland at 170 different sites.

St. Paul has a number of delightful parks, too, and the surrounding sub-urban areas are also home to an extensive park system, particularly in Hen-nepin County, whose planners wisely set aside a number of large parklands along its western and southern borders. All parks and gardens in this chapter are shown on the Greater Twin Cities map.

ARNESON ACRES PARK
4711 W. 70 St., Edina
612/920-7229   **GTC**
This unexpected suburban formal garden is just west of the Southdale Shopping Center on 70th Street, east of Highway 100. The park's grounds include a charming gazebo as well as a number of formal blooming beds, all maintained by the Edina Garden Club.

COMO CONSERVATORY
Como Park
1325 Aida Pl., St. Paul
612/489-1740   **SP**
A splendid 1993 renovation has restored this delicate glass inspiration to its original 1915 luster. The building's most dazzling attraction is the soaring Palm Court; the north wing houses tropical plants, and the south wing features a small fern room. Now on the National Register of Historic Places, the conservatory is a lifeline to weather-battered Minnesotans, who flock to its colorful environs for injections of floral color and fragrance year-round. The springtime tulips and daffodils are heaven-sent, and the seemingly endless poinsettia blooms lure crowds each December. The Ordway Japanese Garden is also not to be missed. On weekends during spring and summer months, the conservatory and its surrounding gardens are flooded with bridal parties; many couples are married here, but most come just to be photographed in front of all the blooming bounty. Admission: 50 cents adults, 25 cents seniors and children ages 11 to 16, free to children under age 10. Hours: 10–4 daily from October through May; 10–6 daily from April through September.

COMO PARK
Hamline and West Jessamine Aves., St. Paul
612/266-6400   **SP**
A grand Victorian-era park of great beauty and one of the Twin Cities' most popular outdoor urban destinations. Como's 450 very-active acres are packed with attractions, including a pavilion for concerts, picnics, and bike and paddleboat rentals overlooking pretty Lake Como (612/489-9311); an 18-hole golf course complete with restaurant and pro shop (612/488-9673); a small amusement park with a collection of Midway rides (612/488-4771); an Olympic-size outdoor pool (612/489-2811); a large athletics field; walking and biking trails; and more. Hours: Sunrise to 11 p.m. daily, although hours for attractions may vary.

Cass Gilbert Memorial Park

On the east side of the Capitol, just north of the intersection of Cedar and University Avenues, is tiny Cass Gilbert Memorial Park, which is really nothing more than a lookout, but what a view! The entire Mississippi River Valley yawns below, and it's quite a sight indeed.

COMO ZOO
Como Park
Midway Pkwy. and Kaufman Dr.,
St. Paul
612/488-5571 **SP**
A small and accessible zoo, particularly for parents with young children. Como Zoo was once one of those depressing prisons where animals were kept behind bars. Thankfully, that has all changed (although some of the cages—now empty—remain), but it is still difficult to see animals not native to the climate living in cramped, seminatural habitats, particularly such noble creatures as lions and giraffes. One thing that hasn't changed is the "Sparky the Sea Lion" show, a free entertainment that has delighted kids for decades. Admission: Free. Hours: Vary by season.

EDINBOROUGH PARK
7700 York Ave. S., Edina
612/893-9890 **GTC**
A city park that's entirely indoors, making it a godsend during the sometimes seemingly endless winter months. Managed by the Edina Parks and Recreation Department, Edinborough has a bubbling brook surrounded by paths, trees, and seasonal flowering plants, as well as a skating rink, running track, swimming pool, small health-club facility, and a children's play area. Hours: Sun–Thur, 9–9, Fri–Sat 9–5. Admission: $3, but the kids' play area is free.

HENNEPIN COUNTY REGIONAL PARKS
612/559-9000 **GTC**
Hennepin County operates 13 large parks within its borders as well as in Scott and Carver Counties. Daily parking fee is $4 (or an annual fee of $20). For detailed Hennepin Parks information, call the number above. A few highlights include:

Baker Park Reserve (3800 County Rd. 24, Maple Plain, 612/476-4666) offers swimming and boating on three lakes, including lovely Lake Independence, as well as camp-

Como Park Conservatory, p. 129

Como Park Conservatory

ing, picnicking, golfing, hiking and biking.

Carver Park Reserve (7025 Victoria Dr., Victoria, 612/559-6700) has camping, fishing, and boating on four lakes, hiking and biking trails, and the Lowry Nature Center.

Murphy-Hanrehan Park Reserve (15501 Murphy Lake Rd., Savage, 612/941-7922) has hiking/biking and horseback riding trails.

Hyland Lake Park Reserve (10145 E. Bush Lake Rd., Bloomington, 612/941-4362) has hiking and biking trails, fishing, boating, and the Richardson Nature Center. Just up the street is the **Hyland Hills Ski Area** (8800 Chalet Dr., Bloomington, 612/835-4604), a winter downhill-ski area.

LORING PARK
15th St., Minneapolis   DMP

Loring Park dates back to 1883, when the city bought the land and named it Central Park; it took on its current name in 1890 to honor Charles Loring, the first president of the Minneapolis Park Board. The park's 35 acres (designed by Frederick Law Olmstead, the man behind New York City's Central Park) are among the most active in the city; there always seems to be a basketball game going on, the ponds are teeming with ducks, the paths are full of walkers and bikers, and, in winter, the lake is dominated by skaters. On the park's north side, near the buildings of Minneapolis Community College, is a statue of Ole Bull, a Norwegian violinist who came to Minneapolis in 1856 and is reputed to be the first musician in the city.

Loring Greenway, a well-traveled pedestrian thoroughfare, connects Nicollet Mall with the bucolic acres of Loring Park. The greenway terminates at one of Minneapolis' most amusing curiosities, the Berger Fountain, which is shaped like a giant dandelion.

MEARS PARK
Bounded by Sibley, 5th, Wacouta, and 6th Sts., St. Paul   SP

Named for philanthropist Norman Mears, this lovely little park is downtown St. Paul's other enormously appealing city square. Originally christened Smith Park when it was platted in 1849, the square was the center of the city's burgeoning commercial district for more than 50 years. By the turn of the century, the area was teeming with dry goods wholesalers, shoe manufacturers, and furriers. The district went into a serious decline in the 1960s, and the park took a nose-dive, too. An ill-conceived redesign in 1975 did little to enhance its natural beauty, but a 1992 renovation by the St. Paul Parks and Recreation Division restored the park to its bucolic roots.

MINNEAPOLIS CHAIN OF LAKES
612/661-4800   MP

Four large lakes and a series of connected park areas make up this

GREATER TWIN CITIES

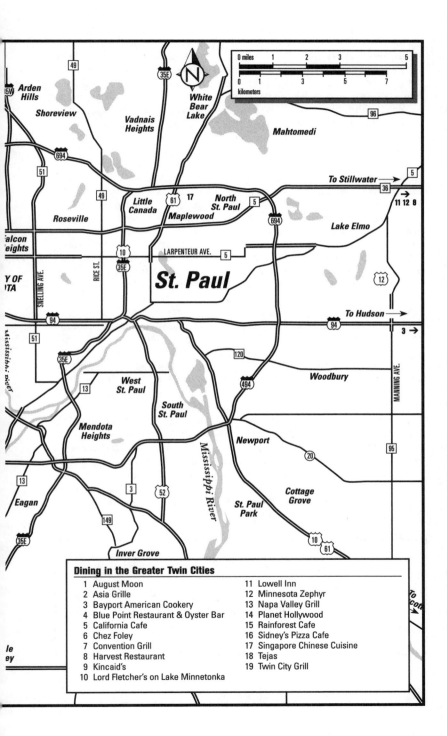

Dining in the Greater Twin Cities

1 August Moon
2 Asia Grille
3 Bayport American Cookery
4 Blue Point Restaurant & Oyster Bar
5 California Cafe
6 Chez Foley
7 Convention Grill
8 Harvest Restaurant
9 Kincaid's
10 Lord Fletcher's on Lake Minnetonka
11 Lowell Inn
12 Minnesota Zephyr
13 Napa Valley Grill
14 Planet Hollywood
15 Rainforest Cafe
16 Sidney's Pizza Cafe
17 Singapore Chinese Cuisine
18 Tejas
19 Twin City Grill

crown jewel of the Minneapolis park system, located on the southern and western fringes of the city. Each has its own distinct personality.

The chain begins at **Cedar Lake**, the cleanest and least urban of the four and also the only lake in Minneapolis with private homes on its shores. Cedar has two public beaches, on its western and southern shores, as well as popular (but technically illegal) clothing-optional "Hidden Beach" on its northeastern shore. Cedar is connected by a shallow channel at its southeastern corner to Lake of the Isles, and the overland connection is made by Dean Parkway.

Lake of the Isles is surrounded by a diverse collection of some of the city's largest, most well-tended homes, and a walk or bike ride around its shores (2.7 miles) is one of the most pleasant strolls in Minneapolis, even during winter months. Isles is really a dredged swamp so swimming is not advised, although the views of downtown and the surrounding neighborhood make it a top choice for canoeists.

Lake of the Isles is connected by channel to **Lake Calhoun**, its southern neighbor and the chain's largest and most urban lake. There are public beaches on the north and east shores, and a popular volleyball area on the lake's southwest corner. Calhoun draws a diverse group of walkers, in-line skaters, and bikers to its 3.1-mile perimeter, and the lake itself attracts windsurfers, canoeists, and kayakers as well as a competitive sailing club when the temperatures permit. Ice-fishing houses dot its frozen waters during the winter. The refectory, located on the northeast corner of the lake, offers refreshments and canoe rentals at low prices.

Just south of Lake Calhoun, about a quarter-mile down William Berry Parkway, is **Lake Harriet**. Named for the wife of Col. Josiah Snelling, Harriet is home to a number of attractions, including the Lake Harriet Bandshell and refectory (northwest corner), Como–Harriet Streetcar Line (northwest corner), paddlewheel boat excursions on the *Queen of the Lakes* (launches take place at the refectory, call 612/370-4962), and Beard's Plaisance, a large sheltered picnic area (southwest corner). Some of the city's most palatial homes line the lake's east parkway. Harriet has two public beaches: one on the east shore, the other on the south shore.

On Harriet's northeastern corner is **Lyndale Park**, a lovely oasis of rolling hills that feature the **Minneapolis Rose Garden**, a meticulously tended and fragrant glen of blooming flowers bordered by two giddy fountains and adjacent to a serene Japanese rock garden.

Walking the Dog

If you're taking your pooch out for a walk, you'll have to put him on a leash (up to 8 feet in Minneapolis, 6 feet in St. Paul). Be sure to bring a bag, since you must dispose of all droppings.

The 5-mile swath of green that is **Minnehaha Parkway** begins on Lake Harriet's southeastern shore and soon connects with Minnehaha Creek as it winds its way across south Minneapolis just below 50th Street all the way east to the Mississippi River. The parkway, a meandering roadway with bicycle and walking paths, lush vegetation, and the gurgling sounds of the creek, is one of the delights of Minneapolis.

At Cedar Avenue, Minnehaha Creek runs into **Lake Nokomis** (to the south) and **Lake Hiawatha** (to the north), two popular and scenic lakes. Nokomis has a busy beach on its northern shore, as well as sailing and canoeing, and Hiawatha has a beach on its east shore. A stroll around the Nokomis' busy perimeter is 2.7 miles.

Biking by the Lake Harriet Bandshell

MINNEAPOLIS SCULPTURE GARDEN
725 Vineland Pl., Minneapolis
612/ 375-7600   MP
This 11-acre garden is an artfully landscaped outdoor extension of the Walker Art Center and is the most-visited attraction in the city of Minneapolis (see Chapter 7, Museums and Art Galleries). Admission: Free. Hours: 6 a.m. to midnight daily. Free tours (starting in the Walker's lobby) are available Saturday and Sunday at 1 p.m.

MINNEHAHA PARK
Hiawatha Ave. at Minnehaha
Pkwy., Minneapolis   GTC
As the creek makes its way toward the Mississippi River, it culminates in Minnehaha Park, one of the city's most-used stretches of parkland. Currently undergoing an extensive $20-million renovation, the park features several large picnic grounds, formal gardens, playing fields, hiking trails, and of course, Minnehaha Falls.

Minnehaha Parkway turns north at the Mississippi River and becomes West River Road, a scenic drive that follows the western bluff of the Mississippi all the way up to the West Bank campus of the University of Minnesota. The views are spectacular, and the roadway is lined with biking and walking trails.

MINNESOTA VALLEY NATIONAL WILDLIFE REFUGE AND RECREATION AREA
3815 E. 80th St., Bloomington
612/335-2323   GTC
This 8,000-acre reserve runs up and down the banks of the Minnesota River from its confluence with the Mississippi at Fort Snelling 35 miles upriver to Jordan. The refuge is crisscrossed by hiking and biking trails, bird-watching promontories, and picnic grounds, and is an amazing stretch of relatively unspoiled river bottoms in the heart of a metropolitan area. The visitors' center (a stone's throw from the Mall of America)

Minnehaha Falls, a dramatic 25-foot cataract, inspires contemporary romantics in the same manner that it led poet William Wadsworth Longfellow to write his epic poem, *The Song of Hiawatha*, even though he himself never saw the falls. A replica of his New England home sits in the park, along with a fanciful, turn-of-the-century commuter rail depot.

offers unparalleled views of the river valley and a number of interpretive exhibits.

MOUNDS PARK
Burns Avenue at Mounds Boulevard, St. Paul
612/226-6400   SP
A 2,000-year-old Indian burial ground is the focus of this 80-acre park, which stretches along the river bluffs and offers superb views of downtown St. Paul and the Mississippi River Valley.

NORMANDALE JAPANESE GARDEN
9400 France Ave. S., Bloomington
612/881-8137   GTC
A serene, 2-acre getaway on the campus of Normandale Community College, the Normandale Japanese Garden is done up in all the requisite Japanese trappings, including delicate bridges, small ponds, exquisite plantings, and lovely vistas.

PEAVEY PLAZA
1111 Nicollet Mall,
Minneapolis   DMP
The sunken public park outside the hall is Peavey Plaza, a remarkable, well-tended inner-city oasis, complete with big shade trees, flowers, a large reflecting pool, splashing water terraces, and quirky tubular stainless-steel fountains. The plaza (designed by M. Paul Friedberg and Associates in 1975) really comes

alive during Sommerfest, the orchestra's annual summer music festival, when every square inch of the place is devoted to food vendors, musicians, and outdoor seating. The reflecting pool gives way to ice skaters during the winter months.

RICE PARK
Bounded by 4th, Market, 5th, and Washington Sts., St. Paul   SP
Any walking tour of downtown St. Paul would naturally begin at Rice Park, undoubtedly one of the prettiest squares in America and the city's oldest public park (1849). Formal but not stuffy, the centerpiece of this grassy knoll is a gurgling fountain, graced with Alonzo Hauser's contemplative sculpture *The Source*. During the annual St. Paul Winter Carnival, the park is the site of a popular ice-sculpture carving contest, and the city festoons the entire square in thousands of twinkling lights, making the whole area a genuine winter wonderland.

THEODORE WIRTH PARK
Theodore Wirth Parkway between I-394 and Golden Valley Rd., Minneapolis   MP
The city's largest park is an urban oasis, filled with scenic vistas and a number of recreational opportunities, and named for the city's most influential parks commissioner. Located on the western edge of the city, the park includes acres of

unspoiled forest and prairie land, as well as an 18-hole golf course, a beach on Wirth Lake, and hiking and biking trails. The fall colors along winding Wirth Parkway can be particularly spectacular.

Tucked inside Wirth Park is the Eloise Butler Wildflower Garden and Bird Sanctuary, the nation's oldest wildflower garden. The Butler garden contains dozens of plants and wildlife native to Minnesota in a rolling terrain marked by woods, wetlands, and bogs. The garden is open 7:30 a.m. to dusk, from April 1 through October 31.

At its northernmost point, Wirth Parkway widens out into Victory Memorial Drive, a dramatic 3-mile promenade of wide lawns and majestic elms, each planted to memorialize the 500 Hennepin County servicemen who perished in World War I. The drive turns east toward the Mississippi River at Grand Army Circle, a shrine to Abraham Lincoln and the servicemen who gave their lives in the Civil War and World War I.

UNIVERSITY OF MINNESOTA LANDSCAPE ARBORETUM
Hwy. 5, Chanhassen
612/443-2460   GTC

This laboratory of 900 exquisitely tended acres is the state's largest public garden and features countless indigenous plant species, as well as a rose garden, a Japanese garden, and more. The spectacular scenery is augmented by lectures, classes, demonstrations, and the Snyder Building, a sturdy stone lodge housing a library, gift shop, and one of the loveliest tea rooms you'll ever run across. Free seasonal 90-minute walking tours of the gardens surrounding the Snyder Building are offered at 10 a.m. Tuesday through Saturday, and motorized tram tours of the arboretum are offered at 11:30 a.m., 1, and 2:30 p.m. Tuesday through Saturday for $1.50. Arboretum admission: $4 adults, $1 children ages 6 to 16, free to children under age 5. Arboretum hours: 8 a.m. to dusk daily.

9

SHOPPING

The Twin Cities is a shopper's mecca, offering retail thrills to satisfy virtually every taste, whim, and pocketbook. From Mall of America, the nation's largest enclosed shopping and entertainment complex, to charming neighborhood shopping areas throughout Minneapolis and St. Paul, the Twin Cities has something for everyone. Only shopping districts and shopping malls are shown on the map in this chapter. If a store is located in a shopping district, the district is indicated in the store's address.

DOWNTOWN MINNEAPOLIS

SHOPPING DOWNTOWN

Nicollet Mall is Minneapolis' main retail drag. Open only to buses and taxicabs, this tree-lined pedestrian haven stretches 12 blocks from Washington Avenue on the north to Grant Street on the south. In between, there's four department stores, four urban multilevel shopping malls, and fine specialty stores, located primarily in the retail spine stretching from 5th to 11th Streets. Downtown shopping can also be found in the **Warehouse District**, which includes an L-shape defined by 1st Avenue and Washington Av-

enue North. Most downtown restaurants and stores participate in the city's "Do the Town" program, which will validate parking in most ramps and lots after 4 p.m. on weekdays and all day Saturday and Sunday with a $20 purchase; look for the green "Do the Town" signs before you park.

CITY CENTER
600 Nicollet Mall, Minneapolis
612/372-1234   DMP
Architecturally graceless (*Star Tribune* columnist Barbara Flanagan called it "that salmon loaf"), this ungainly office, hotel, and shopping complex contains downtown's first enclosed indoor shopping mall. The sunny shopping atrium houses a

large selection of national chain stores plus a popular food court on the third floor. Restaurants include TGIFriday's (612/305-1915); Italianni's (612/305-4848); Nankin Café (612/333-3303), a Minneapolis institution since 1919, complete with campy Cantonese interior decorations; and Goodfellow's (612/332-4800), one of the city's finest restaurants, housed in the meticulously restored art deco interior of the long-gone Forum Cafeteria.

GAVIIDAE COMMON
651 Nicollet Mall, Minneapolis
612/372-1222   DMP
Neiman Marcus anchors the northern end of Gaviidae Common, a pair of shopping complexes straddling two blocks on Nicollet Mall. The five-story mall includes a number of boutiques and shops. Restaurants include D'Amico & Sons, a popular cafeteria-style lunch and dinner spot (first floor, 612/342-2700); Morton's of Chicago, the local branch of the luxe steakhouse (lower level, 612/673-9700); and a Minnesota State Fair–themed food court on the fourth floor. Valet parking in the underground heated ramp; enter on 5th Street.

Across 6th Street stands the other half of Gaviidae (Latin for "loon," the state bird). This attractive shopping center is distinguished by an azure-and-gold barrel-vault skylight (courtesy of architect Cesar Pelli), includes two dozen stores, and is anchored by Saks Fifth Avenue. Valet parking in underground heated ramp; enter on 6th Street.

IDS CRYSTAL COURT
717 Nicollet Mall, Minneapolis
612/376-8000   DMP
One of Minnesota's architectural landmarks, the IDS Center is a full-block complex that includes a 57-story office building (the state's tallest), the Marquette Hotel, and the Crystal Court, one of the country's most joyous indoor public spaces. The heated indoor parking ramp below the Crystal Court is the most centrally located and convenient place to park downtown, particularly in the dead of winter; enter on Marquette Avenue.

Major Department Stores

DAYTON'S
700 Nicollet Mall, Minneapolis
612/375-2200   DMP
When Minnesotans flaunt their much-touted "quality of life," they have Dayton's to thank for at least a part of it. In addition to bolstering the local economy with its retail empire, the company has long been one of the state's most civic-minded benefactors, contributing 5 percent of its pre-tax profits to charity—for a grand total of $350 million over the past half-century.

Gaviidae Common

GMCVA

Dayton's Empire

One of the country's top retail success stories began when George Draper Dayton opened the doors of what eventually became the Dayton Company in 1902. George's descendants expanded the company's holdings with a series of suburban and outstate Dayton's outlets, while creating the Target discount chain, the B. Dalton bookstore business, and a number of shopping malls. A 1969 merger with the J.L. Hudson Company in Detroit created the Dayton Hudson Corporation. In the mid-1980s the corporation (now the nation's fourth-largest retailer) spun off B. Dalton, its shopping center holdings, and a number of department store divisions, but now owns Chicago-based Marshall Field's, Detroit-based Hudson's, and Mervyn's. The civic-minded company also played a major role in the development of the Nicollet Mall in the 1960s.

Minnesotans are genuinely devoted to Dayton's; residents joke that a Dayton's charge card is the equivalent of a driver's license in terms of identification, and when the company was threatened with a hostile takeover in the late 1980s, the state Legislature convened a special session to pass a poison-pill law to thwart the attempt.

The store spans the entire block on Nicollet between 7th and 8th Streets, offering six floors of merchandise. The popular Oak Grill and the Sky Room restaurants are located on the 12th floor, and the in-store 8th-floor auditorium hosts an annual holiday auditorium extravaganza which routinely attracts 400,000 visitors between early November and New Year's. Every March, the Dayton-Bachman Flower Show draws more than 100,000 blizzard-weary Minnesotans to a blooming feast for the eyes and the nose. Dayton's has three don't-miss sales each year: Jubilee in October, Anniversary in February, and Daisy in June. Be sure to visit the Marketplace food and tabletop emporium on the store's lower level, and the tony Oval Room on the 3rd floor.

TRIVIA

There is no sales tax on clothing or groceries in Minnesota.

NEIMAN MARCUS
505 Nicollet Mall,
Minneapolis
612/339-2600 **DMP**
Ever since it opened in 1991, this gracious store and its accommodating sales staff have been the popular new kids in town. The Last Call clearance outlet occupies the entire

fourth floor—a consistent source of jaw-dropping bargains.

SAKS FIFTH AVENUE
655 Nicollet Mall, Minneapolis
612/333-7200 **DMP**
Sedate Saks offers well-edited assortments of men's and children's clothes, plus a wide array of women's designer clothing, accessories, cosmetics, and jewelry. As at Neiman-Marcus, the fourth floor is devoted to marked-down merchandise culled from Saks stores across the country. Called Off Fifth, the prices and selection are often better than at Last Call. Café SFA, on the fourth floor, is one of downtown's best-kept lunch secrets.

SPECIALTY STORES

Antiques

ARCHITECTURAL ANTIQUES
801 Washington Ave. N.
(Warehouse), Minneapolis
612/332-8344 **DMP**
This sprawling store is a treasure trove of every conceivable kind of old lamp, sconce, ornamental pediment, wooden built-in, religious reliquary, and porcelain fixture and doorknob, all salvaged from demolished buildings. The sales staff is smart and resourceful.

Apparel

HUBERT W. WHITE
611 Marquette Ave., Minneapolis
612/339-9200 **DMP**
Hubert W. White is the last of what used to be a thriving downtown men's haberdasher scene. An institution since 1916, this family-owned operation sells a large selection of exclusive men's tailored clothing, sportswear, shoes, and accessories

in clubby surroundings. The store offers excellent service and terrific but infrequent sales.

PARMEE'S
400 1st Ave. N. (Warehouse),
Minneapolis
612/333-0101 **DMP**
This pretty SoHo-esque boutique sells luxe clothing, accessories, and shoes for men and women in a spare loft setting. Splendid sales, excellent service, and labels like Gianni Versace, Giorgio Armani, and Joseph Abboud.

POLO/RALPH LAUREN
Y-Q Building
81 S. 9th St. (Nicollet Mall),
Minneapolis
612/338-7700 **DMP**
The vast Polo/Ralph Lauren store occupies the first floor of the Y-Q Building. Stop in for the clothes, home-related merchandise, and service, but stay for the drop-dead gorgeous ambience.

RAGSTOCK
830 N. 7th St. (Warehouse),
Minneapolis
612/333-8520 **DMP**
The warehouse for the large vintage-clothing store chain.

TEENER'S THEATRICAL DEPARTMENT STORE
729 Hennepin Ave., Minneapolis
612/339-2793 **DMP**
An engrossing crazy-quilt jumble of costumes, makeup, fabric, shoes, and other accoutrements. Knowledgeable service, too.

Arts, Crafts, and Gifts

INDIGO
530 N. 3rd St. (Warehouse),

TIP

The Guthrie Theater Costume Rental Shop (718 Washington Ave. N., Minneapolis, 612/341-3683) rents amazing costumes from the famed Guthrie Theater's voluminous storehouse at reasonable rates.

Minneapolis
612/333-2151   **DMP**
An intoxicating, out-of-the-way haunt devoted to folk arts, textiles, and other exotic must-haves from Africa, Asia, and the Pacific.

METRO MATTER
121 N. 1st St. (Warehouse),
Minneapolis
612/376-0239   **DMP**
Charming Metro Matter offers a wondrous variety of offbeat arts, crafts, and gifts from a wide range of local and national artists and artisans.

RAINBOW ROAD
109 W. Grant St., Minneapolis
612/872-8448   **DMP**
A quirky and entertaining shop filled with greeting cards, clothing, and gifts geared toward the gay and lesbian community.

SISTER FUN
121 N. 4th St. (Warehouse),
Minneapolis
612/672-0263   **DMP**
Famous for its campy collection of retro toys, wacky collectibles, and kitschy paraphernalia, all at bargain-basement prices.

Books, Magazines, and Newsstands

AMAZON BOOKSTORE
1617 Harmon Pl., Minneapolis
612/338-6560   **DMP**

On lovely Loring Park, this 25-year-old store is the source for new and used books, recordings, and other merchandise of interest to women.

BARNES & NOBLE
801 Nicollet Mall, Minneapolis
612/371-4443   **DMP**
Minnesota's largest bookstore. Managed by Andrue Scott, a man with an encyclopedic knowledge of recorded music, the store's music department is the best place in the Twin Cities to find classical, jazz, and musical theater recordings, and you can grab a cup of coffee and a sweet at the store's smart café.

BAXTER'S BOOKS
608 2nd Ave. S., Minneapolis
612/339-4922   **DMP**
This large, inviting bookstore specializes in fiction and books geared toward the neighborhood's businesspeople. Owner Brian Baxter's sister is the actress Meredith (*Family Ties*) Baxter, who occasionally pops in to visit her brother.

BILLY GRAHAM EVANGELICAL BOOKSTORE
1201 Hennepin Ave., Minneapolis
612/338-0500   **DMP**
The world headquarters of the Billy Graham Evangelical Association includes this small bookstore.

JAMES & MARY LAURIE BOOKS
921 Nicollet Mall, Minneapolis

612/338-1114   **DMP**

This bookstore is stocked floor-to-ceiling with rare, used, and out-of-print books, plus a large selection of prints.

LELAND N. LIEN BOOKSELLER
57 S. 9th St., Minneapolis
612/332-7081   **DMP**

A first-rate source for rare, out-of-print, and first-edition titles. The store also has a skilled restoration and conservation department.

SHINDER'S
733 Hennepin Ave., Minneapolis
612/333-3628   **DMP**

This is the flagship store of the state's largest and most comprehensive newsstand chain. A one-stop source for comics, trading cards, and paperbacks, Shinder's also attracts a fascinating cross-section of the city's populace.

Grocers, Markets, and Liquor

MINNEAPOLIS FARMERS' MARKET
Lyndale Ave. N., between
Glenwood Ave. and
Hwy. 55, Minneapolis
612/333-1737   **DMP**

On Thursdays, several dozen Market vendors head downtown and set up shop on Nicollet Mall. Minneapolis' market draws a wider variety of vendors than St. Paul's, but St. Paul's tidy market has a lot more charm.

Shinder's

Competitive prices on farm-fresh produce. Shoppers can also find baked goods, flowers, potted plants, Minnesota honey and wild rice, Hmong arts and crafts, cheese, and prepared meats. Open April through November, daily 6 a.m. to 1 p.m. During the holiday season, Christmas-tree farmers sell their wares through December 25.

Home and Garden

CRATE & BARREL
915 Nicollet Mall, Minneapolis
612/338-4000   **DMP**

A large and affordable selection of dishes, cookware, and household goods in cheery surroundings. Also at Southdale, 612/920-2300.

T I P

Textile do-it-yourselfers should thread their way to Linden Hills Yarns (2720 W. 43rd St., Minneapolis 612/929-1255), the Twin Cities' source for beautiful and unique knitting materials.

GREATER TWIN CITIES

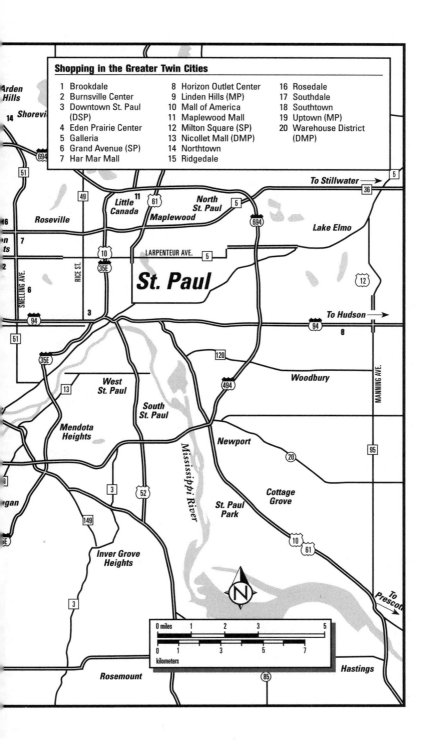

Shopping in the Greater Twin Cities

1 Brookdale
2 Burnsville Center
3 Downtown St. Paul (DSP)
4 Eden Prairie Center
5 Galleria
6 Grand Avenue (SP)
7 Har Mar Mall
8 Horizon Outlet Center
9 Linden Hills (MP)
10 Mall of America
11 Maplewood Mall
12 Milton Square (SP)
13 Nicollet Mall (DMP)
14 Northtown
15 Ridgedale
16 Rosedale
17 Southdale
18 Southtown
19 Uptown (MP)
20 Warehouse District (DMP)

INTERNATIONAL DESIGN CENTER
100 2nd Ave. N. (Warehouse), Minneapolis
612/341-3441 DMP

IDC showcases beautiful furniture, glassware, art, and gifts from Scandinavia on several floors in a sturdy turn-of-the-century warehouse building.

LARKSPUR
514 N. 4th St. (Warehouse), Minneapolis
612/332-2140 DMP

This florist's florist makes the most luxurious blooming arrangements in the Twin Cities. Floral prices are steep, but this alluring shop also sells a wide variety of surprisingly affordable doodads.

Jewelry

J.B. HUDSON
770 Nicollet Mall, Minneapolis
612/338-5950 DMP

This swank, Old-World fine-jewelry emporium also sells expensive china, crystal, and silver, all in ornate, museum-like surroundings.

DOWNTOWN ST. PAUL

SHOPPING DOWNTOWN

Even with the addition of several large shopping complexes, downtown St. Paul's retail climate is partly cloudy, although there is some sunny shopping to be had in the capital city. **Dayton's** (411 Cedar St., St. Paul, 612/292-5222) opened in 1963 and is the remainder of what once was one of a handful of busy department stores; today St. Paul's Dayton's is a more downscale version of its downtown Minneapolis counterpart. **Galtier Plaza** (175 E. 5th St., St. Paul, 612/292-0600) is a well-designed mixed-use development from the late 1980s that incorporates a pair of condominium and apartment towers with a block-long shopping center on three levels. The mall houses a large branch of Lee's Outlet books (second level, 612/225-9118) as well as Galtier Cinema 4 (third level, 612/224-2573), downtown St. Paul's only movie theater. **Town Square** (445 Minnesota St., St. Paul, 612/298-0900) was hailed as the solution to retail flight when it opened in 1980, but this dismal, fortress-style complex of offices, shops, and a hotel has been something of a failure. Many of the storefronts are empty, and a ghost-town atmosphere plagues the place. Town Square's best feature is the inviting indoor garden on the third floor. **World Trade Center** (7th Street and Wabasha Avenue, St. Paul, 612/291-1715) is an attractive suburban-style shopping mall that sits at the base of a rather dour 1987 skyscraper. Its roster includes 40-plus local and national chain stores, but the mall's best store is Maud Borup Candies (second level, 612/293-0530), makers of delicious chocolates since 1907. There's a food court on the third level.

SPECIALTY STORES

Antiques
NAKASHIAN-O'NEIL
23 W. 6th St., St. Paul

St. Paul's Farmers' Market

612/224-5465   **DSP**
This delightfully musty store has been a capital city institution since 1906, specializing in fine antiques and famous for its original selection of holiday decorations.

Apparel

FRANK MURPHY
30 W. 5th St., St. Paul
612/291-8844   **DSP**
Since 1931, this wrought-iron-covered store has been selling women's fashions, from moderately priced to very expensive.

Grocers, Markets, and Liquor

CANDYLAND
435 N. Wabasha St., St. Paul
612/292-1191   **DSP**
Maker of the best caramel corn in the Midwest, bar none, since 1932. Other swell sweets, too.

ST. PAUL FARMERS' MARKET
290 E. 5th St., St. Paul
612/228-8101   **DSP**
Located on the edge of Lowertown, this charming market offers competitive prices on farm-fresh produce, plus baked goods, flowers, potted plants, Minnesota honey and wild rice, Hmong arts and crafts, cheese, and prepared meats. Open April through November, Saturday 6 a.m. to 1 p.m. and Sunday 8 a.m. to 1 p.m.

MINNEAPOLIS

Shopping Areas

The **Uptown neighborhood**, centered on the corner of Hennepin and Lake Streets and close to both Lake Calhoun and Lake of the Isles, bustles with shops, restaurants, bookstores, a popular branch of the Minneapolis Public Library, and several movie theaters. Uptown is anchored by **Calhoun Square** (3001 Hennepin Ave. S., 612/824-1240), a two-level enclosed shopping mall located on the southeastern corner of Hennepin Avenue and Lake Street, and featuring many boutiques and shops. Outside of Calhoun Square, there's a healthy mix of national chain stores scattered throughout the neighborhood as well as a fine selection of local merchants.

Just west of Lake Harriet in south Minneapolis is the small commercial district of **Linden Hills**, which boasts a collection of unique boutiques.

BAY STREET SHOES
(Calhoun Square)
3001 Hennepin Ave. S.,
Minneapolis
612/824-5574   **MP**
Consistently one of the Twin Cities' top shoe stores for both selection and price.

GABRIELA'S
1404 W. Lake St. (Uptown),
Minneapolis
612/822-1512   **MP**
Beautiful vintage party-clothes, jewelry, shoes, and accessories for men and women, as well as the Serious label of naughty vinyl fashions.

IN TOTO
3105 Hennepin Ave. S. (Uptown),
Minneapolis
612/822-2414   **MP**
Located in a handsome old house, In Toto sells fashion-forward men's and women's clothing and accessories by Paul Smith, C.P. Company, Anna Sui, Industria, and Paraboot.

LAVA LOUNGE
2831 Hennepin Ave. S. (Uptown),
Minneapolis
612/871-1211   **MP**
You'll find inexpensive club clothes here, aimed at the crowd that's probably too young to get into any clubs. Lots of merchandise by talented local designers, too.

ST. SABRINA'S PARLOR IN PURGATORY
2751 Hennepin Ave. S. (Uptown),
Minneapolis
612/874-7360   **MP**
The latest in ravewear fills the racks here. The store's Foot Fetish department stocks shoes that are so fashion-forward they're practically in the next solar system. Body jewelry, and an in-house certified body piercer to make it happen.

SCHATZLEIN
413 W. Lake St. (Uptown),
Minneapolis
612/825-2450   **MP**
Country-western wear begins and ends at Schatzlein, which has been outfitting cowpoke-minded Twin Citians since 1907. Huge selection of boots, riding apparel, and hats.

SWANK INC.
407 W. Lake St. (Uptown),
Minneapolis
612/822-2242   **MP**
A carefully selected assortment of vintage 1960s and 1970s fashions at affordable prices.

Arts, Crafts, and Gifts

15 MINUTES
407 W. Lake St. (Uptown),
Minneapolis
612/822-2242   **MP**
If vintage lunchboxes, *Charlie's Angels* glassware, and Smurf key chains turn your crank, stop in at 15 Minutes, which has a dizzying collection of pop-culture collectibles.

JUDITH MCGRANN & FRIENDS
3018 W. 50th St., Minneapolis
612/922-2971   **MP**
Colorful, one-of-a-kind crafts, jew-

elry, gifts, and clothing abound at this appealing store.

PATINA
2404 Hennepin Ave. S. (Uptown), Minneapolis
612/374-4654   **MP**
Browse Patina for clever little objects for the home and office, plus unique toys, books, candles, and picture frames. There's a second location at 5001 Bryant Ave. S., Minneapolis, 612/821-9315.

Books, Magazines, and Newsstands

BORDER'S BOOK STORE
3001 Hennepin Ave. S. (Uptown), Minneapolis
612/825-0336   **MP**
A chain bookstore with an independent atmosphere, Border's is an anchor of the Uptown Minneapolis neighborhood. The store has a knowledgeable sales staff, extensive stock, and a reputation as a pickup joint.

A BROTHER'S TOUCH
2327 Hennepin Ave. S. (Uptown),

Minneapolis
612/377-6279   **MP**
This modest bookstore carries fiction, nonfiction, and magazines for gay and lesbian readers.

DREAMHAVEN BOOKS
912 W. Lake St. (Uptown), Minneapolis
612/823-6161   **MP**
A staggering selection of comic books and science fiction.

ONCE UPON A CRIME
604 W. 26th St., Minneapolis
612/870-3785   **MP**
Mystery and suspense novels line the shelves of this friendly shop, and many authors visit for book-signings.

Grocers, Markets, and Liquor

BROTHERSON'S MEATS
824 W. 36th St., Minneapolis
612/823-7227   **MP**
The best butcher in the Twin Cities, justifiably famous for its smoked hams and bacon.

COASTAL SEAFOODS
2330 Minnehaha Ave.,

Discount Shopping

*Looking for a deal? Visit **Bank's** (615 1st Ave. NE, Minneapolis), a huge dump of a store chock-full of outrageous bargains. The stuff comes from retailers from across the country who have endured some kind of natural or financial disaster, which means that one week there might be men's clothing by Tommy Hilfiger, the next, Schwinn bicycles, Fieldcrest bedding, or baby strollers; be sure to check for smoke damage. Call the hotline (612/379-4321) for weekly merchandise updates.*

Minneapolis
612/724-5911   **MP**
A wide selection of ocean- and lake-fresh fish. Also at 74 Snelling Ave., St. Paul, 612/698-4888.

ST. MARTIN'S GOURMET IMPORTS
617 W. Lake St. (Uptown), Minneapolis
612/823-5981   **MP**
A small and appealing store selling unusual and hard-to-find foodstuffs from around the world.

UNITED NOODLES ORIENTAL FOOD
2015 E. 24th St., Minneapolis
612/721-6677   **MP**
A stretch of Nicollet Avenue in south Minneapolis (from 22nd to 29th Streets) is dotted with a variety of Asian grocery stores, but the best bet is a few miles east at this warehouse-style store, which carries an encyclopedic stock at very low prices.

Home & Garden

ACRES
1426 W. 28th St., Minneapolis
612/872-4122   **MP**
This adorable store brings the pages of the Smith & Hawken catalogue to life, with a wide variety of unique gardening tools, plants, bulbs, seeds, pots, candles, birdhouses, and dishes, including Luna Garcia's simple stoneware.

INGREBRETSON'S
1601 E. Lake St., Minneapolis
612/729-9331   **MP**
A Minneapolis institution that does the Scandinavian import thing better than any other store of its kind in town; there's also an impressive selection of specialty foods.

ROOM SERVICE
1428 W. 31st St.
(Uptown)
Minneapolis
612/823-2640   **MP**
Room Service hawks tons of *objets d'art*, including distinctive glassware, pottery, candles, picture frames, and a small line of attractive contemporary furniture.

STICKS AND STONES
2914 Hennepin Ave. S.
(Uptown)
Minneapolis
612/827-6121   **MP**
Two floors of unique home accessories, lighting, and upholstered furniture, geared toward style-conscious first-home owners.

ST. PAUL

Shopping Areas

Parts of **Grand Avenue**, a streetcar commercial district in the 1920s, were revived beginning in the mid-1970s, and today the area, especially from Dale Street to Fairview Avenue, offers some of the most distinctive shopping in the Twin Cities. **Milton Square** is another area where you'll find a unique selection of shops.

SPECIALTY STORES

Apparel

LULA
1587 Selby Ave.,
St. Paul
612/644-4110   **SP**
Lovely little Lula has a knack for particularly fine "lightly worn" women's wear.

Mall of America, p. 152

Books, Magazines, and Newsstands

THE HUNGRY MIND
1648 Grand Ave.,
St. Paul
612/699-0587 **SP**
Considered by many natives to be the best independent bookstore in the Twin Cities. The library-like stock and bright sales staff are partly responsible for the favorable reputation, but the scholarly setting (adjacent to Macalaster College) and the appealing adjacent restaurant (Table of Contents) have something to do with it, too.

MICAWBER'S BOOKS
2238 Carter Ave.
(Milton Square),
St. Paul
612/646-5506 **SP**
This sweet little bookstore has an extensive children's section and a kids' reading club, and offers free coffee and treats from neighboring Taste of Scandinavia bakery every Sunday (see Chapter 4, Where to Eat).

Home and Garden

COOKS OF CROCUS HILL
877 Grand Ave., St. Paul
612/228-1333 **SP**
Gourmet foods, kitchenware, cookbooks, dishes, and an excellent cooking school, all in a charming renovated house.

COUNTRY PEDDLER
2230 Carter Ave. (Milton Square),
St. Paul
612/646-1756 **SP**
The fine art of quilt-making is celebrated at this store, offering a large stock of fabrics, supplies, and books, plus an extensive schedule of classes.

GREATER TWIN CITIES

In addition to the plethora of shopping malls in Greater Minneapolis—including mega-Mall of America—the upscale shopping area of downtown Edina (France Avenue and 50th Street) is definitely worth a visit.

SHOPPING MALLS

MALL OF AMERICA
Highway 77 at I-494, Bloomington
612/883-8800   GTC

Everything about Mall of America ("the Mall") is b-i-g, so big in fact that locals dubbed it the "mega-mall" long before the first cash register rang up the first sale. The largest shopping and entertainment complex in the United States, this $675-million monster is quickly becoming one of the country's top tourist attractions. The Mall encompasses 4.2 million square feet—enough space for seven Yankee Stadiums. There are nearly 13,000 free parking spots, all located within 300 feet of an entrance, primarily in two huge, seven-story ramps. More than 12,000 people work at the Mall, and nearly 400 shops, restaurants, and entertainment venues call it home.

Since its grand opening in 1992, this mother of all shopping centers has been a resounding success, drawing a constant stream of visitors from around the world as well as legions of credit card–crazy locals. Its effect on surrounding retail areas has not been so upbeat. Several established retail centers have been devastated in one degree or another by the Mall's power-house ability to draw shoppers. Downtown Minneapolis, downtown St. Paul, and the Burnsville and Eden Prairie shopping centers all have boarded-up storefronts to attest to the economic competition that they lost.

Getting to the Mall

From downtown Minneapolis, take I-35W south to Crosstown 62 east to Highway 77 south (Cedar Avenue), approximately 15 minutes. From downtown St. Paul, take I-35E south-east to I-494 west, approximately 15 minutes. From the airport, follow I-494 west, approximately five minutes.

Getting to the Mall is easy via MTCO bus service. A shuttle (routes 4, 7, 42, 54, and 77) runs between the Mall and the Lindbergh Terminal at the Twin Cities International Airport. An express shuttle (route 80) runs between the Mall and the Nicollet Mall in downtown Minneapolis. And a bus goes from the Mall to downtown St. Paul (route 54). Fares are $1.50 during peak hours, $1.25 during nonpeak hours; call 612/373-3333 (612/341-0140 TTY/TTD). All buses drop passengers at the Mall's transit station, just outside the first-floor entrance to East Broadway.

Parking at the Mall

Two eight-story, 6,000-space ramps bookend the Mall's east and west sides. Negotiating them on a busy day can be daunting. The large surface lot across 24th Avenue offers a hassle-free alternative to the ramps on especially mobbed days; it's a quick five-minute walk through the ramp to the East Broadway entrance

Finding Your Way Around

The building itself, although not exactly an architectural triumph, is something of an engineering marvel, primarily in its ability to comfortably host and circulate staggering numbers of visitors. Navigating the Mall is easy. Picture the complex as a giant three-story rectangle, with four department stores, one at each corner, all linked by long corridors with distinct (but hardly distinctive) personalities. **East Broadway** (Sears to Bloomingdale's) is decked out in high-tech stainless steel and blue metal, **South Avenue** (Bloomingdale's to Macy's) sports shades of peach faux art deco, **West Market** (Macy's to Nordstrom) takes on a town-square atmosphere, and **North Garden** (Nordstrom to Sears) is a tiled formal garden. Inside the center of the rectangle is Knott's Camp Snoopy, a seven-acre, four-story amusement attraction. A smaller fourth level houses nightclubs, restaurants, and a 14-screen movie theater complex; a 1.2-million-gallon aquarium is located on the first floor.

Department and Chain Stores

Bloomingdale's (612/883-2500) is the most stylish of the Mall's Big Four, particularly its beautifully merchandised kitchen, tabletop, and bed and bath departments, all on the third floor. **Macy's** (612/888-3333) is more middle-of-the-road, and heavy on its own in-house brands. **Nordstrom** (612/883-2121), the most successful of the Mall's big players, showcases solid clothing and accessories, plus vast shoe departments for men, women, and children; there's also a helpful concierge on the first floor. **Sears'** (612/853-0500) Mall of America branch is one of that giant retailer's most up-to-date ventures.

As for the specialty stores, the Mall is packed with the kinds of chains that lease mall space coast to coast. Several chain discount stores also call the Mall home, including Filene's Basement, Linens 'N Things, Service Merchandise, and Marshall's.

Services

Talk about one-stop shopping. You can plan a warm-weather getaway at the **Florida Vacation Store** and then book your airline ticket next door at **Northwest Airlines** (first floor, East Broadway). Have your teeth

---

Where to Eat

The Mall boasts more than two dozen sit-down restaurants as well as nearly 50 fast-food outlets, located primarily in two gigantic food courts (third floor, North Garden and South Avenue). For descriptions of some of the Mall's restaurant choices, see the Greater Twin Cities zone in Chapter 4, Where to Eat.

TIP

Kids can have a ball at the Mall, choosing between Amazing Space (612/851-0000), Golf Mountain (612/883-8899), LEGO Imagination Center (612/858-8949), Knott's Camp Snoopy (612/883-8600), and Underwater World (888/DIVETIME). For more information on these attractions, see Chapter 6, Kids' Stuff.

cleaned at **Health Partners Dental Clinic** or get a physical at the **Quello Clinic** (third floor, West Market). You can even tie the knot (at prices ranging from $195 to $745)—or renew your vows (from $79 to $295)—at the **Chapel of Love**, which includes a private, 75-seat wedding chapel (second floor, North Garden). Learn about one of the state's largest gaming operations at the **Grand Casino** store (second floor, North Garden). Open a savings account at **First Bank** (third floor, West Market). Work toward your high-school or college degree at the **Metropolitan Learning Alliance** (first floor, East Broadway). Cash a check at **Daddy's Check Cash** (third floor, South Avenue). The **American Association of Retired Persons (AARP)** even staffs a booth here (third floor, West Market).

Specialty Stores

East Broadway
First floor: You'll find Snoopy, Charlie Brown, and the rest of the gang imprinted on gifts, toys, and clothing at **Peanuts** (612/883-8663). Lionel models roar overhead at **The Great Train**

TRIVIA

The Mall of America draws more than 40 million visitors each year.

Store, which stocks every imaginable toy train and railroad-related gizmo (612/851-9988). **Calido Chile Hot and Spicy Traders** is dedicated to the glory of the pepper (612/854-7250).

Second floor: Shoot hoops in the half-court at **Just for Feet**, the world's largest athletic shoe store (612/854-5331). **Babushka** sells imported Russian and Ukranian baubles (612/854-0040). Pick up a hologram or two at **Hologram Land** (612/854-9344).

Third floor: **Marvelous Magnets** sells thousands of refrigerator magnets; they'll send you a free one if you mail them a picture of you and your Amana side-by-side (612/854-2868).

South Avenue
Third floor: Anyone can play a rousing game of interactive laser-tag at **Starbase Omega** ($8.50 single, $12.75 double for 20 minutes, 612/858-8001). One of the Mall's most adventurous clothing stores is **Junkyard**, which sells fashion-forward grunge wear aimed at 12- to 17-year-olds (612/854-6006).

West Market
First floor: **FAO Schwarz** has a large store here, including a fabulous Barbie boutique (612/858-9900). Several dozen carts throng Market Square, also on the first floor. Stop by **Simen Sez**, which celebrates the wonder of the Pez dispenser. **Lake Wobegon USA** is a mini-mart of merchandise

Eight Ways to Avoid Getting Malled

1. *If you really want to see the Mall in all its vulgar, excessive glory, wear comfortable shoes! (Or buy a pair at any of the Mall's 26 shoe stores).*
2. *Arrive early, particularly on weekends. During the interminable winter, the Mall is a major magnet for snow-crazed Minnesotans, and during the hot and humid summer, thousands jam the place to beat the heat.*
3. *Let Bloomie's valet park your car ($5; store's east entrance).*
4. *Check your coat and packages ($1) just inside the Mall from the parking ramp entrances at East Broadway and West Market. Lockers (50 cents) go quickly during the coat-and-boot season.*
5. *Pick up the* Best of the Mall *newspaper at any entrance for event information and money-saving coupons.*
6. *Stop by one of the four Guest Service Centers, located on the first level at each main entrance, for strollers, wheelchairs, lockers, directories, lost-and-found, telephones, foreign language guides, cash machines, shopping bags, and restrooms.*
7. *Ship your booty back home at the CDP Copy Center (third floor, East Broadway, 612/858-9500).*
8. *Rest your weary feet at Bloomingdale's, either in the palatial restrooms or at the inexpensive health-foods counter on the third floor. At Nordstrom, there's an affordable cafeteria on the third floor where you can catch your second wind. Macy's third floor is home to the Mall's least-publicized but tastiest getaway, Wolfgang Puck's Pizzeria.*

from Minnesota's own "A Prairie Home Companion"; the **Pin Place** sells zillions of clever pins. **State Your Name** will put your name on a key chain made from the license plate of any state for four bucks.

Third floor: **Shell Cellar** sells—that's right—shells, by the thousands (612/858-8253). There's a reason why Minnesotans refer to Wisconsin residents as "cheeseheads," and now there's a store devoted to America's Dairyland: **Rybicki Cheese Ltd**. (612/854-3330). Seemingly an acre in size, **Collectibles Showcase** sells every imaginable figurine by such names as Lladro, Pen Delfin, Hummel, G. Armani, Precious Moments Sandicast, and Musgrave (612/854-1553). Cavernous **Oshman's Supersports USA** allows you to test athletic equipment before you buy it (612/854-9444). It's strictly tractors and miniature barnyard animals at fun **Al's Farm Toys** (612/858-9139). **Air Traffic** is the one-stop source for kites (612/858-9599).

North Garden

First floor: **Brainstorms** is dedicated to scientific and medical toys, books, and conversation-starters (612/858-8652). **Charlie's Novelties** sells every imaginable beer-related collectible (612/854-8151).

Second floor: Trekkers will love **Starlog**, a fun sci-fi and comic book store (612/853-9988).

Third floor: Roadside nostalgia from the 1940s, '50s, and '60s is the focus of **Runkel Bros. American Garage** (612/858-9633). You can put your face on the cover of one of hundreds of magazines at **Amazing Pictures** (612/858-8680).

OTHER SHOPPING MALLS

If the Mall of America is too much mall for you to handle, several regional centers can be found in the Twin Cities area. Most of the malls contain a mix of specialty stores and national and local chain stores as well as restaurants and other services.

Brookdale (Highway 100 at Brooklyn Blvd., Brooklyn Center, 612/566-6672)
Burnsville Center (County Road 42 at I-35, Burnsville, 612/435-8182)
Eden Prairie Center (Prairie Center Drive at I-494, Eden Prairie, 612/941-7650)
Har Mar Mall (2100 Snelling Ave. N., Roseville, 612/631-0340)
Maplewood Mall (White Bear Avenue at I-694, Maplewood, 612/770-5020)
Northtown (University Avenue at Highway 10, Blaine, 612/786-9704)
Ridgedale (Plymouth Road at I-394, Minnetonka, 612/541-8464)
Rosedale (Fairview Avenue at Highway 36, Roseville, 612/633-0872)
Southdale (66th Street at France Avenue, Edina, 612/925-7885)
Southtown (Penn Avenue at I-494, Bloomington, 612/375-1077)

SPECIALTY STORES

Apparel

FASHION AVENUE
4936 France Ave. S., Edina
612/929-7917 GTC
Probably the best consignment store in the Twin Cities, with a large selection of clothing. Reasonable prices and excellent service, too.

Arts, Crafts, and Gifts

BLANC DE BLANC
691 Lake St., Wayzata

612/473-8275   **GTC**
An unusual premise for a store: all-white merchandise, aimed at babies, brides, hostesses, and homes. Located in charming downtown Wayzata, which fronts Lake Minnetonka—it's a shopping district that's worth exploring.

GENERAL STORE OF MINNETONKA
14401 Hwy. 7, Minnetonka
612/935-2215   **GTC**
A country store run amok with oodles of stuff you never knew you needed but suddenly cannot live without.

Home and Garden

AMPERSAND
5034 France Ave. S., Edina
612/920-2118   **GTC**
A spacious and expensive store with the latest in dishes, glassware, linens, flatware, stationery, and other related geegaws.

KELLEY & KELLEY NURSERY
2325 Watertown Rd., Long Lake
612/473-7337   **GTC**
It may not have the vast selection of its chain competitors, but K&K more than makes up for it in its unique and utterly beguiling setting, which inspires countless Twin Cities gardeners.

ROOM & BOARD
7010 France Ave. S., Edina
612/927-8834   **GTC**
A standout resource for casual, contemporary furniture and home furnishings.

Grocers, Markets, and Liquor

BYERLY'S
3777 Park Center Dr.,
St. Louis Park
612/929-2100   **GTC**
Only in the Twin Cities would a grocery store be a tourist attraction. This huge complex houses a very popular family restaurant; a cooking school; a

---

Birth of the Mall

America's enclosed suburban shopping mall phenomenon was born in suburban Edina, when Southdale opened its doors on October 8, 1956. It was the nation's first climate-controlled shopping center (designed by Austrian Victor Gruen). Forty years later, Southdale is only one of many regional shopping centers—and, of course, the Mall of America—competing for consumer dollars in the Twin Cities area. It remains the area's most successful mall and actually spawned an entire suburban business district that now includes a hospital campus, office buildings, apartments, and condominiums, an excellent public library, a few parks, and several other shopping areas.

branch of Wood's Chocolate Shop; a coffee bar; an unexpected Gift Gallery selling everything from $10 baubles to $5,000 statues; full-service deli, meat, and seafood departments; a bank; a terrific bakery; a 24-hour pharmacy; a liquor store; a photo lab; a Chinese take-out restaurant; and a post office. The store is decked out with crystal chandeliers, original art, and carpeted isles. Byerly's has a home economist on staff, and is open 24 hours for those who prefer to pick up their groceries in the wee hours of the morning. There are eight other Byerly's locations throughout the Twin Cities.

Discount Shopping

OPITZ OUTLET
4320 Excelsior Blvd.,
St. Louis Park
612/922-2435 GTC
Opitz carries an ever-changing melange of deeply discounted men's, women's, and children's clothing; household goods, and other assorted merchandise. The store hotline (612/922-9088) provides an updated list of sale merchandise.

ROOM & BOARD OUTLET
4650 Olson Hwy.,
Golden Valley
612/529-6089 GTC
The contemporary furniture and home furnishings mecca has an outlet store with a good selection of beds, chairs, tables, sofas, and lamps. Open only on Saturday and Sunday.

Factory Outlet Shopping

HORIZON OUTLET CENTER
I-94 at County Rd. 19 (Exit #251),
Woodbury
612/735-9060 GTC
More than 40 outlet stores, including such names as American Tourister, Book Warehouse, Casual Corner, Eddie Bauer, Fanny Farmer, Fieldcrest/Canon, Hush Puppies, Levi's, Naturalizer, Petite Sophisticate, Sara Lee Bakery, Speigel,

Byerly's—a grocery store attraction

Zac Mangel

Upscale Shopping

Just across 69th Street from Southdale is the **Galleria** (France Avenue at 69th Street, Edina, 612/925-9534), an upscale shopping mall anchored by **Gabbert's,** a rambling furniture, home accessories, and design studio showplace. This understated mall also includes a number of novel specialty stores, including **Polly Berg** (exquisite lingerie and bedding), **Main Street Kids** (adorable and often expensive kids' clothes), **T.R. Christian** (china and crystal), **Cedric's** (men's and women's European clothing and furs), **Stroud's** (linens), **Oilili** (colorful women's and children's clothing from the Netherlands), a huge two-story **Barnes & Noble** bookstore, and nearly 60 other high-end shops. There are several popular restaurants here, too, including **Sydney's Pizza Café**, the **Good Earth**, and **Ciatti's**.

Sunglass Hut, and Winona Knits. The mall is 15 minutes from downtown St. Paul. Open Monday through Saturday 11 a.m. to 9 p.m., Sunday 11 a.m. to 6 p.m.

MEDFORD OUTLET CENTER
I-35 at Exit #48, Medford
507/455-4111

Forty factory-direct stores, including G.H. Bass, Liz Claiborne, Jordache, Guess?, Mikasa, Rocky Mountain Chocolates, Champion, and Geoffrey Beene. Located one hour south of the Twin Cities. Open Monday through Saturday 10 a.m. to 9 p.m., Sunday 11 a.m. to 6 p.m.

TANGER FACTORY OUTLET MALL
I-35 at Hwy. 95, North Branch
800/727-6885

Thirty-two designer and manufacturer outlet stores featuring savings of 25 to 65 percent off retail prices. A 45-minute drive north of the Twin Cities, the mall is open Monday through Saturday 10 a.m. to 9 p.m., Sunday 11 a.m. to 7 p.m.

Minnesota Office of Tourism

10

SPORTS AND RECREATION

Blame it on the weather. Rather than fight its extremes, Minnesotans embrace them, hurling themselves into the outdoors with an abandon that few other regions can match. Whether it's taking advantage of every precious moment of warm summer weather, or reveling in the cold, crisp air of winter, Twin Citians are a sports-minded people, passionate about their sports teams and dedicated to a wide variety of indoor and outdoor recreation. Whatever your recreational passion—spectator or participant—you'll find it in the Twin Cities. Only the professional sports venues are shown on the maps in this chapter.

BEACHES

The Greater Twin Cities area has a number of lifeguarded beaches in addition to those listed below. Call 612/661-4875 for more information.

BAKER PARK RESERVE
2301 County Rd. 19, Maple Plain
612/559-9000   GTC
Lifeguard service, showers, and changing rooms. Open 11 a.m. to 8 p.m. daily June through August. Parking fee is $4.

BRYANT LAKE REGIONAL PARK
6400 Rowland Rd., Eden Prairie
612/559-9000   GTC

Lifeguard service, showers, and changing rooms. Open 11 a.m. to 8 p.m. daily June through August. Parking fee is $4.

CEDAR LAKE
2100 and 3300 Cedar Lake Pkwy.,
Minneapolis   MP
Open daily noon to 8 p.m. June through August.

CLEARY LAKE
REGIONAL PARK
18106 Texas Ave., Prior Lake
612/559-9000   GTC
Lifeguard service, showers, and 8 p.m. daily June through August. Parking fee is $4.

TIP

Rent in-line skates for $6/hour or $12/day at Rolling Soles (1700 W. Lake St., Minneapolis, 612/823-5711), about two blocks from the skater-filled paths surrounding Lake Calhoun.

ELM CREEK PARK RESERVE
13080 Territorial Rd., Maple Grove
612/559-9000 GTC
Lifeguard service, showers, and changing rooms. Open 11 a.m. to 8 p.m. daily June through August. Parking fee is $4.

FISH LAKE REGIONAL PARK
14500 Bass Lake Rd., Maple Grove
612/559-9000 GTC
Lifeguard service, showers, and changing rooms. Open 11 a.m. to 8 p.m. daily June through August. Parking fee is $4.

FRENCH REGIONAL PARK
12605 County Rd. 9, Plymouth
612/559-9000 GTC
Lifeguard service, showers, and changing rooms. Open 11 a.m. to 8 p.m. daily June through August. Parking fee is $4.

LAKE CALHOUN
Lake Calhoun Pkwy., Minneapolis
MP
Beaches are open daily noon to 8 p.m. June through August.

LAKE HARRIET
North Lake Harriet Parkway at Rosewood Rd. and 4740 E. Lake Harriet Pkwy., Minneapolis MP
Open daily noon to 8 p.m. June through August.

LAKE HIAWATHA
28th Ave. S. and E. 45th St., Minneapolis MP

Open daily noon to 8 p.m. June through August.

LAKE JOHANNA
3500 Lake Johanna Blvd., Arden Hills
612/777-1707 GTC
A lifeguarded beach open noon to 6 p.m. daily June through August.

LAKE NOKOMIS
4955 and 5001 E. Nokomis Pkwy., Minneapolis MP
Open daily noon to 8 p.m. June through August.

LAKE OWASSO
370 N. Owasso Blvd., Shoreview
612/777-1707 GTC
A lifeguarded beach open noon to 6 p.m. daily June through August.

LAKE PHALEN
Just off Wheelock Pkwy., St. Paul
612/776-9833 SP
This lifeguarded public beach is open noon to 7 p.m. June through August.

LAKE REBECCA PARK RESERVE
9831 County Rd. 50, Rockford
612/559-9000 GTC
Lifeguards, showers, and changing rooms. Open 11 a.m. to 8 p.m. daily June through August. Parking fee is $4.

LONG LAKE
1500 Old Hwy. 8, New Brighton
612/777-1707 GTC

Hennepin Parks

One of the 10,000 lakes

A lifeguarded beach open noon to 6 p.m. daily June through August.

THEODORE WIRTH LAKE
**3200 Glenwood Ave. N.,
Minneapolis   MP**
Open daily noon to 8 p.m. June through August.

WHITE BEAR LAKE
**1300 Lake Ave., White Bear Lake
612/777-1707   GTC**
A lifeguarded beach open noon to 6 p.m. daily June through August.

BICYCLING

Bike Rentals

THE ALTERNATIVE BICYCLE SHOP
**2408 Hennepin Ave. S.,
Minneapolis
612/374-3635   MP**
Pedal the Minneapolis Chain of Lakes on a tandem bike, available for rent here for $6/hour, $20/day.

BENNETT'S CYCLE
**3540 Dakota Ave., St. Louis Park
612/922-0311   GMP**
Mountain bikes rent here for $29.99/day.

CALHOUN CYCLE
**1622 W. Lake St., Minneapolis
612/827-8231   MP**
Tandem bicycles rent for $8/hour or $32/day; mountain bikes are $24/day.

CAMPUS BIKES
**213 Oak St. SE, Minneapolis
612/331-3442   MP**
Mountain bikes rent here for $18/day.

COMO LAKESIDE PAVILION
**Como Park, St. Paul
612/488-4297   SP**
Tandems rent for $6/hour.

Bike Trails

CITY OF MINNEAPOLIS
612/661-4800   MP
The City of Lakes boasts nearly 50 miles of interconnected paved bike trails along its Grand Rounds system of parkways, which includes Victory Memorial Drive and Theodore Wirth Parkway on the city's north side, the Chain of Lakes and Minnehaha Parkway on the south side, and the East River Road on the edge of the Mississippi River. The paths are also very popular with in-line skaters, and all have adjacent walking trails, too.

NATIONAL SPORTS CENTER
**1700 105th Ave. NE, Blaine
612/785-5600   GTC**
This velodrome is the nation's only all-weather wood cycling track, and its bleachers can accommodate more than 2,000 fans.

Airborne Adventure

For $125 per person, **Apple Express Hot Air Balloon Co.** *(612/430-2800),* **Balloon Adventures** *(612/474-1662),* **Stillwater Balloons** *(612/439-1800), or* **Scenic Adventures Hot Air Balloon Flights** *(612/432-7009) will send you up, up, and away for a hot-air balloon adventure over the Twin Cities.*

If free-falling out of an airplane is your idea of fun, there are two places—both about an hour from the Twin Cities—where you can make it happen: **Freefall Fantasy** *in Cologne (612/466-5545) and* **Skydive Hutchinson** *in Hutchinson (612/433-3633).*

BOWLING

There are 45 bowling alleys in the Twin Cities area to choose from. The two below are standouts.

BRYANT-LAKE BOWL
810 W. Lake St., Minneapolis
612/825-3737　　　　　　**MP**
Only eight lanes, but the crowd is young, hip, and friendly, the food is far beyond anything you'd expect at a bowling alley, and the beer and wine selection is tops in its class. Bowling costs $1.50/line, and shoe rental is free.

STARDUST BOWLING LANES
2520 26th Ave. S., Minneapolis
612/721-6211　　　　　　**MP**
Thirty lanes, a huge game room, cocktail lounge, and late-night (2 a.m.) hours. Bowling costs $2/line before 5 p.m., $2.50/line after 5 p.m.

CANOEING

HENNEPIN COUNTY PARK RESERVES
612/559-9000　　　　　　**GTC**
Daily canoe rental is available at most park reserves, including Hyland, Lake Rebecca, Clearly Lake, Fish Lake, and French.

LAKE CALHOUN REFECTORY
W. Lake St. and E. Lake Calhoun Pkwy.,
612/370-4964　　　　　　**MP**
Canoes are available for rent, and canoeists can paddle via channels

With Padelford Boats (612/227-1100), you can navigate the Mississippi River from both St. Paul (Harriet Island) and Minneapolis (Boom Island) on the *Jonathan Padelford, Harriet Bishop Anson Northrup, Betsy Northrup,* or *Josiah Snelling.* It can be a relaxing way to see the towns and enjoy a warm summer's day. Hours: Memorial Day to Labor Day, daily noon and 2 p.m.

GREATER TWIN CITIES

Mounds View
Spring Lake Park
Brooklyn Park
252
10
94
Maple Grove
Brooklyn Center
694
94
65
New Brighton
Plymouth
New Hope
Crystal
Columbia Heights
Robbinsdale
Minneapolis
Golden Valley
280
494
UNIVERSITY MINNESOTA
Wayzata
12
394
55
3
2
LAKE ST.
St. Louis Park
101
7
Minnetonka
Hopkins
100
35W
77
To Excelsior
Edina
62
169
Mpls St. Paul International Airport
To Chanhassen
494
Richfield
CEDAR AVE.
Eden Prairie
Mall of America
Minnesota River
35W
Bloomington
4
Shakopee
Savage
13
N
13
Burnsville
77
0 miles 1 2 3 5
42
0 1 3 5 7
kilometers
35
Lakeville
1

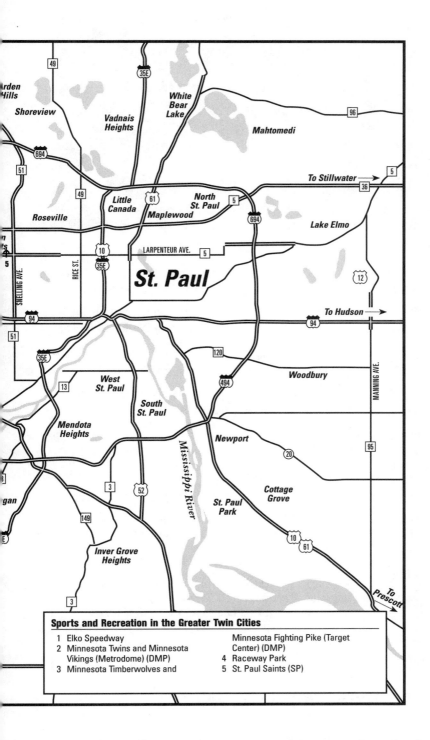

Sports and Recreation in the Greater Twin Cities

1 Elko Speedway
2 Minnesota Twins and Minnesota Vikings (Metrodome) (DMP)
3 Minnesota Timberwolves and Minnesota Fighting Pike (Target Center) (DMP)
4 Raceway Park
5 St. Paul Saints (SP)

Canoeing on Lake of the Isles

from Calhoun to both Lake of the Isles and Cedar Lake.

GOLF

The Twin Cities area has 50 18-hole and 28 nine-hole public golf courses and a large roster of private clubs, too. The most challenging and appealing public clubs are listed below.

EDINBURGH USA
8700 Edinbrook Crossing,
Brooklyn Park
612/424-9444   **GTC**
An 18-hole, par-72 course.

MEADOWBROOK GOLF CLUB
201 Meadowbrook Rd., Hopkins

612/929-2077   **GTC**
An 18-hole, par-72 course.

THEODORE WIRTH GOLF CLUB
1301 Theodore Wirth Pkwy.,
Minneapolis
612/521-9731   **MP**
An 18-hole, par-72 course.

UNIVERSITY OF MINNESOTA
GOLF COURSE
2275 W. Larpenteur Ave., St. Paul
612/627-4000   **SP**
An 18-hole, par-71 course.

HEALTH CLUBS

Twin Citians have been bitten by the fitness bug, and local entrepreneurs

Cruise the waters of Lake Minnetonka with one of several charter companies. Al and Alma's (612/472-3098) will do the driving for you and your party; Rockvam Boat Yards (612/471-9515) rents a wide range of pontoon or fishing boats for your own use, and can supply you with motors, maps, sunblock, and even lemonade and ice cream.

have responded in kind with a staggering number of well-equipped health clubs. Several offer aerobics classes and facilities.

BALLET ARTS MINNESOTA
528 Hennepin Ave., Minneapolis
612/340-1071   DMP
Disciples of the Pilates Method will feel at home here.

BALLY TOTAL FITNESS
3970 Sibley Memorial Dr., Eagan
612/452-0044   GTC
Eight locations in the Twin Cities; the Eagan spot has especially extensive facilities.

THE FIRM
1300 Nicollet Mall, Minneapolis
612/377-7141   MP
Nobody does a better aerobic workout than the thigh-busting professionals at this studio. With a wide variety of daily classes for all fitness levels, The Firm also offers spinning, an intense, instructor-led, stationary bicycle workout.

JABZ
5812 W. 36th St., St. Louis Park
612/925-0323   GTC
Kickboxing fans will get a charge out of this take-no-prisoners fitness center.

LIFE TIME FITNESS
3550 Vicksberg Ln. N., Plymouth
612/509-0909   GTC
The upstart of the health-club bunch,

with seven other locations and three more on the drawing boards.

NORTHWEST RACQUET, SWIM AND HEALTH CLUBS
600 1st Ave. N., Minneapolis
612/673-1200   DM
Thirteen locations across the metropolitan area; the flagship club, located under the Target Center, is definitely worth a visit for its amazing array of facilities.

THE SWEATSHOP FITNESS TRAINING CENTER
171 Snelling Ave. N., St. Paul
612/646-8418   SP
Offers aerobics classes as well as a fully equipped gym.

YMCA
30 S. 9th St., Minneapolis
612/371-8900   DMP

YMCA
476 N. Robert St., St. Paul
612/292-4100   DSP
Both Ys have modern, spacious facilities in both downtown Minneapolis and downtown St. Paul, as well as a number of suburban locations.

HORSEBACK RIDING

A handful of stables in the outlying areas of the Twin Cities offer saddle rentals and extensive trails, all for about $15 per hour.

Minnesota Office of Tourism

Outdoor skating

BRASS RING STABLES
9105 Norris Rd., Elk River
612/441-7987   GTC

DIAMOND T RANCH
4889 Pilot Knob Rd., Eagan
612/454-1464   GTC

EAGLE CREEK STABLES
7301 Eagle Creek Blvd., Shakopee
612/445-7222   GTC

KINNI VALLEY RIDING STABLES
1181 30th Ave., River Falls, WI
715/425-6184

ICE SKATING

Indoor Skating

There are several dozen ice arenas in communities throughout the Twin Cities metro area. A few of the most noteworthy are below.

BLOOMINGTON COMMUNITY ICE GARDEN
3600 W. 98th St., Bloomington

612/948-8842   GTC
A huge facility with three indoor rinks.

BRAEMAR ARENA
7501 Hwy. 169, Edina
612/484-0268   GTC

BURNSVILLE ICE CENTER
251 Civic Center Pkwy., Burnsville
612/895-4650   GTC

EDEN PRAIRIE COMMUNITY CENTER
16700 Valley View Rd.,
Eden Prairie
612/949-8470   GTC

MINNETONKA ICE ARENA
3401 Williston Rd., Minnetonka
612/939-8310   GTC

ROSEVILLE ICE ARENA AND JOHN ROSE MINNESOTA OVAL
1200 Woodhill Rd., Roseville
612/484-0268   GTC
Both indoor and outdoor rinks, plus a regulation outdoor speed-skating oval used by in-line skaters during summer.

Outdoor Skating

During winter, neighborhoods across the Twin Cities are dotted with outdoor skating rinks. St. Paul has more than 30 every winter (call 612/777-1707), and more than 50 rinks are flooded across Minneapolis neighborhoods (call 612/661-4875).

LAKE COMO
Hamline and W. Jessamine Ave.
St. Paul
612/266-6400   SP
For genuine winter-wonderland recreational skating, check out the rinks near the pavilion here. Beautiful urban scenery, big expanses of ice, and a warming house.

Nordic Skiing

Cross-county skiers will love the ever-expanding miles of groomed trails that sprout up all over the Twin Cities after the snow flies. Various city, county, and state park boards manage different trails. In Minneapolis, call 612/522-4584; in St. Paul, call 612/266-6445; in Hennepin County, call 612/559-6778; in Ramsey County, call 777-1707; for state parks, call 612/296-6157.

LAKE OF THE ISLES
26th St. and E. Lake of the Isles
Parkway, Minneapolis   MP
The northernmost finger of the lake offers superb skating. Lovely urban scenery, large expanse of ice, and a warming house.

ROSEVILLE ICE ARENA AND
JOHN ROSE MINNESOTA OVAL
1200 Woodhill Rd., Roseville
612/484-0268   GTC
See description page 168.

ROLLER SKATING

CHEAP SKATE
3075 Coon Rapids Blvd.,
Coon Rapids
612/427-8980   GTC

ROLLER GARDEN SKATE CENTER
5622 W. Lake St.,
St. Louis Park
612/929-5518   GTC

SKATELAND SKATE CENTER
7308 Lakeland Ave. N.,
Brooklyn Park
612/425-5858   GTC

SKATEVILLE FAMILY ROLLER
SKATING
201 River Ridge Circle,

Burnsville
612/890-0988   GTC

SKIING

While the runs don't exactly recall the Rockies, there are a number of well-groomed downhill ski areas within an hour's drive of the Twin Cities, all with snowmaking capabilities, nighttime lighting, chalet facilities, and more. Most are open mid-November through late March.

AFTON ALPS
County Rd. 20, Afton
612/436-5245   GTC
About 15 minutes east of downtown St. Paul, Afton has 18 chairlifts, 37 runs, four chalets, a school, and rentals. Open daily 9 a.m. to 10 p.m.

BUCK HILL
15400 Buck Hill Rd., Burnsville
612/435-7174   GTC
About 20 minutes south of downtown Minneapolis, this ski area has ten runs and four chairlifts.

WELCH VILLAGE
Hwy. 61 and County Rd. 7, Welch
612/222-7079
About an hour south of the Twin Cities, Welch has 35 runs and a

T I P

The Minnesota Ski Council is a good source for information on ski schools, race leagues, clinics, equipment swap meets, and more; call 612/673-0828.

snowboard park. Open 9 a.m. to 10 p.m. daily.

WILD MOUNTAIN
37350 Wild Mountain Rd., Taylors Falls
612/257-3550
About an hour north of the Twin Cities, this area has 23 runs (with great views of the St. Croix River valley), four chairlifts, a ski school, and late-night (until 3 a.m.) skiing every Friday.

TENNIS

NICOLLET TENNIS CENTER
4005 Nicollet Ave., Minneapolis
612/825-6844   **MP**
Eleven indoor courts, open to the public for $14/hour per court.

NORTHWEST RACQUET, SWIM AND TENNIS CLUB
5525 Cedar Lake Rd., St. Louis Park, St. Paul
612/546-5474   **MP**
This club has a lock on the most extensive indoor and outdoor tennis facilities in the Twin Cities; call for facility information.

REGENCY ATHLETIC CLUB AND SPA
1300 Nicollet Mall, Minneapolis
612/343-3131   **DMP**
The Regency Athletic Club and Spa

offers four four-season hard courts atop a parking ramp overlooking downtown Minneapolis.

SPECTATOR SPORTS

Auto Racing

ELKO SPEEDWAY
26350 France Ave., Elko
612/461-3395   **GTC**
Catch the excitement of bombers, NASCAR late-models, sportsmen, and thunder cars racing on a high-banked asphalt oval. Admission: $10 adults, $4 children ages 5–12, free to children under 5. Opens at 7 p.m. Saturday and holidays May through August.

RACEWAY PARK
1 Checkered Flag Blvd., Shakopee
612/445-2257   **GTC**
A quarter-mile asphalt track for late models, short-trackers, hobby stocks, and figure-eight races. Admission: $9 adults, $4 children ages 5–12, free to children 5 and under. Opens at 7 p.m. Sunday and Wednesday from June to August.

Greyhound Racing

ST. CROIX MEADOWS
Hudson, Wisconsin
715/386-6800
Watch greyhound racing from an enclosed, air-conditioned clubhouse. The dogs run in a May-to-August

St. Paul Saints

season, and simulcast racing is also available. Admission: $1, free to children 12 and under. Hours: Open daily at 11 a.m.; racing begins Wed at 3 p.m., Thur and Fri at 7 p.m., Sat and Sun at 1 p.m. Closed Monday. Located 20 minutes from St. Paul in Hudson, Wisconsin, just south of I-94.

Horse Racing

CANTERBURY PARK
1100 Canterbury Rd., Shakopee
612/445-7223 GTC
After a few years' hiatus, the excitement of horse racing returns to Minnesota at this handsome, well-equipped facility. Horses hit the track in a season that runs from late May to mid-August, and the park's tele-racing center is open year-

round. Hours: Thur–Sat first post at 6:30 p.m., Sun and holiday first post at 2 p.m. Admission: $3 adults, free to children 17 and under; seniors free on Sunday.

PROFESSIONAL SPORTS

Baseball

MINNESOTA TWINS
Chicago Ave. and 5th St.
Metrodome, Minneapolis
612/375-1366 DMP
The two-time World Series champions (1987 and 1991) play in the American League West Division at the cheerless Hubert H. Humphrey Metrodome, a 1982 multiuse domed stadium that seats 55,000 for baseball

T I P

Blaine Soccer Complex has the largest concentration of soccer fields in the state—55 outdoor fields plus an indoor facility (1700 105th Ave. NE, Blaine, 612/785-5600).

and 62,000 for football. The stadium's white Teflon roof is the largest air-supported dome in the world, and has only deflated once, when it was knocked flat during a particularly wicked blizzard in the winter of 1985.

The Twins came to Minnesota in 1961, and the team has had its share of legendary players, including Rod Carew, Harmon Killebrew, Tony Oliva, Kirby Puckett, Frank Viola, and Kent Hrbek. Team favorites aside, watching baseball here can be a bit of a downer, especially on a sunny summer's day, when many fans long for the old, open-air days at Metropolitan Stadium in Bloomington. In terms of sightlines, the Dome clearly favors football, and unless you can get a seat in the lower decks on the first- and third-base lines, it almost makes more sense to stay home and watch the game on television.

Outside the Dome, the city has tried to bring some pre- and post-game life to the area with the addition of Metrodome Plaza at Chicago Avenue and 5th Street. While the design is as second-rate as the Dome itself, the pedestrian-friendly space has managed to draw crowds for food, music, and games, making the Metrodome experience a little less sterile. Surface parking is easy to come by, or it's just as quick to park downtown and take a shuttle bus down 4th Street. The team operates a Twins Pro Shop near the Rosedale Shopping Center (2401 Fairview Ave., Roseville, 612/635-0777).

ST. PAUL SAINTS
1771 Energy Park Dr., St. Paul
612/644-6659 SP
Outdoor baseball returned to the Twin Cities in 1993, and it's been a hit from day one. The Saints, part of the Northern League, play minor-league

baseball with major-league attitude. Part of the draw is the zany mood (one of the team's owners is actor Bill Murray, who makes an occasional appearance); the friendly, family-oriented atmosphere; and the enthusiastic crowd. The team also nabs a big-name player every now and then (Darryl Strawberry, Jack Morris), and St. Paul's cheerful, 6,000-seat stadium brings the field action right up to the bleachers. Tickets, unfortunately, are a scarce commodity.

Basketball

MINNESOTA TIMBERWOLVES
600 1st Ave. N., Target Center,
Minneapolis
612/337-3865 DMP
Since this NBA expansion team hit the court in 1989, its win-loss record has pretty much stunk (in its first year, the team lost 60 games, a new and rather embarrassing NBA record), but going to a 'Wolves game can be fun, partly because of the high-level energy of the fans and because of the relative luxury of Target Center, a 16,000-seat arena in the heart of downtown Minneapolis. The arena is connected by skyway to several thousand parking spots in three huge city-owned ramps that line 2nd Avenue North, and is within walking distance of several dozen bars, restaurants, and clubs for pre- and post-game revelries.

Football

MINNESOTA FIGHTING PIKE
600 1st Ave. N., Target Center,
Minneapolis
612/339-4900 DMP
Arena football made its debut in the Twin Cities in 1996, and fans all agree that it's a gas. The fast-action game

Intercollegiate Sports

The University of Minnesota's Golden Gophers play a full roster of Big Ten intercollegiate sports, and many teams attract an extremely loyal following, which puts ticket availability at a premium (call 612/624-8080). The teams with the most fervent followings include **men's basketball**, *which play at the recently renovated Williams Arena (1925 University Ave. SE);* **men's hockey** *at Mariucci Arena (1901 4th St. SE);* **football** *at the Metrodome; and* **women's basketball** *at Williams Arena.*

racks up big points (matches average more than 80 points per game) on a field that's just 50 yards long. The Pike play amid a party atmosphere, and the season is short enough (June through July) to keep everyone interested.

MINNESOTA VIKINGS
Chicago Ave. and 5th St.,
Metrodome, Minneapolis
612/333-8828 DMP
Under the stewardship of former head coach Bud Grant, the Vikes traveled to the Super Bowl four times in the 1970s; unfortunately, they never took the trophy home, but the fans remain as loyal as ever. Now under the watchful eye of coach Dennis Green, the Vikings still manage to pack the Metrodome (getting a ticket is easier than it was during the team's glory days at Metropolitan Stadium), and the stadium works much better when a football is being thrown across its artificial turf. This 1961 expansion team has had its share of NFL stars, including Fran Tarkenton, Ed Marinaro, Chuck Foreman, Alan Page, Ahmad Rashad, and Carl Eller.

Hockey

MINNESOTA ARCTIC BLAST
601 2nd Ave. S.
Minneapolis
612/376-7825 DMP
One of 18 American and Canadian teams playing roller hockey during the summer months. The action can be a fast and furious warm-weather fix for hockey nuts.

Soccer

MINNESOTA THUNDER
1700 105th Ave., NE,
Blaine
612/893-1442

T I P

Fishing is a popular pastime in the Land of 10,000 Lakes, but a license is required for anglers over age 16. Call 612/296-4506 for details.

Michal Daniel

11

PERFORMING ARTS

Few cities boast as wide a range and quality of performing arts as the Twin Cities. Local boosters will often point to the statistic that the area contains more theater companies per capita than any other American city outside of New York. Minneapolis and St. Paul are blessed with a rich theater scene, and the sophisticated theatergoing audience flocks to both major institutions (including the Guthrie Theater and the Children's Theatre Company) and to exciting new local stars like Theatre de la Jeune Lune and the Jungle Theatre. The Twin Cities is also the only major metropolitan area in the country that supports two orchestras (outstanding ones at that), and the local dance and music scene is varied and talented. Minneapolis and St. Paul are also a prime destination for a plethora of touring Broadway shows, nationally renowned music acts, and internationally respected dance companies, all of whom appear at a wide variety of performing arts venues across both cities. Only the major performing arts venues are shown on the maps in this chapter.

THEATER

CHANHASSEN DINNER THEATRES
501 W. 78th St., Chanhassen
612/934-1525 or 800/362-3515   GTC
One of the nation's largest theatrical operations, this sprawling complex houses four stages under one roof, including its 600-seat main stage, which produces one lavish musical comedy after another. Other stages

include the 231-seat Fireside Theatre, the 120-seat Playhouse, and the 118-seat Club Theatre.

CHILD'S PLAY THEATRE CO.
1719 Main St., Hopkins
612/931-2290   GTC
A theater company devoted to works geared toward—and performed by—kids. The repertory is heavy on fairy tales and children's classics, but includes a smattering

DOWNTOWN MINNEAPOLIS

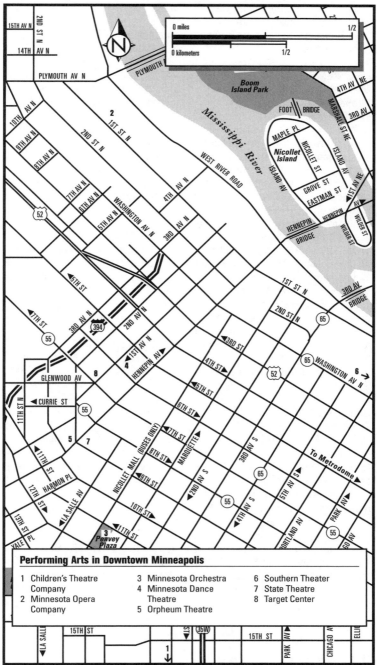

Performing Arts in Downtown Minneapolis

1 Children's Theatre
   Company
2 Minnesota Opera
   Company
3 Minnesota Orchestra
4 Minnesota Dance
   Theatre
5 Orpheum Theatre
6 Southern Theater
7 State Theatre
8 Target Center

of new works, too. The very affordable performances take place at the Eisenhower Community Center (1001 Hwy. 7), just outside downtown Hopkins. Season runs October through June.

CHILDREN'S THEATRE COMPANY
**2400 3rd Ave. S.,
Minneapolis
612/874-0400   DMP**
A Minnesota institution since 1965, and a thrilling way to introduce young imaginations to the world of the theater. From its beautiful 746-seat facility on the Minneapolis Institute of Arts campus in south Minneapolis, CTC's hyper-talented company of children and young-at-heart adults produces winning adaptations of classic children's works (including *The Story of Babar, Strega Nona, The Hobbit, Linnea in Monet's Garden, A Wrinkle in Time, The 500 Hats of Bartholomew Cubbins*, and dozens more), as well as new plays. CTC has a truly amazing technical department. Its production of *How the Grinch Stole Christmas* has quickly become an annual holiday tradition.

GREAT AMERICAN HISTORY THEATRE
**30 E. 10th St., St. Paul
612/292-4323   DSP**
For nearly 20 years this adventurous company has produced new plays (and revived or adapted classics) that explore varying facets of history. Most of the Great American History Theatre's productions are staged in the Crawford-Livingston Theatre in downtown St. Paul. The thrust-style stage is a cozier version of the Guthrie Theater, and was originally intended to be that theater's second stage.

GUTHRIE THEATER
**725 Vineland Pl., Minneapolis
612/377-2224   MP**
One of the nation's leading repertory theaters, the Guthrie started the regional theater explosion when Sir Tyrone Guthrie opened his new 1,400-seat house in 1963. Since that time, the Guthrie (now under the leadership of artistic director Joe Dowling, formerly of Dublin's Abbey and Gaeity Theaters) has been challenging and enriching audiences with a broad repertory of classical and contemporary works, and remains one of the most influential cultural institutions in the state. Season runs June through March.

HEY CITY STAGE
**824 Hennepin Ave., Minneapolis
612/333-9202   DMP**
This new downtown addition has been home to the long-running hit *Tony 'n' Tina's Wedding* since its doors opened in 1995.

ILLUSION THEATRE
**528 Hennepin Ave., Minneapolis
612/339-4944   DMP**
For more than 20 years, this company has concentrated on presenting new plays that address contemporary social, political, and personal issues. Illusion's summertime Fresh Ink series showcases a wide and always interesting variety of works-in-progress. Most performances take place at Illusion's Hawthorne Theater, located on the eighth floor of Hennepin Center for the Arts.

IN THE HEART OF THE BEAST PUPPET AND MASK THEATRE
**1500 E. Lake St., Minneapolis
612/721-2535   MP**
The home of wild and wonderful puppet theater. At a Heart of the

Beast show you may encounter 10-foot puppets, outrageous masks, and everything in between. It's all highly original and completely enthralling. Performances take place in the theater's home, a former neighborhood movie house that was rescued from a sad life as a porn theater.

JUNGLE THEATRE
**709 W. Lake St.,
Minneapolis
612/822-7063** MP
Acclaimed productions of American classics are the hallmark of this critics' darling, performed in a tiny theater; the close confines only add to the intensity of the goings-on.

LAKESHORE PLAYERS
**4820 Stewart Ave.,
White Bear Lake
612/429-5674** GTC
Lakeshore Players is a well-respected community theater company that produces entertaining versions of musical comedies,

American classics, and works for children.

MIXED BLOOD THEATER
**1501 S. 4th St., Minneapolis
612/338-6131** DMP
High-energy, thoughtful Equity productions of new works by American playwrights in an intimate theater housed in an old firehouse.

OLD LOG THEATRE
**5175 Meadville St., Greenwood
612/474-5951** GTC
The Twin Cities' oldest professional theater produces a steady roster of crowd-pleasing comedies and dramas in its comfortable theater near the shores of Lake Minnetonka.

OUTWARD SPIRAL THEATER COMPANY
**2531 Johnson St. NE, Minneapolis
612/789-7622** MP
The Twin Cities' only theater company dedicated to producing works for gay, lesbian, bisexual, and transgender audiences.

Old Log Theatre

Old Log Theatre

August Wilson

*Playwright August Wilson (*Seven Guitars, Joe Turner's Come and Gone, Ma Rainey's Black Bottom*) lived in St. Paul for a time during the 1980s, in a big house on Holly Avenue in the city's Cathedral Hill neighborhood, not far from the Penumbra Theatre. Wilson was a regular at Sweeney's Saloon (96 N. Dale St., St. Paul, 612/221-9157), where he would sit at the bar, nurse a drink, chain-smoke, and write.*

PARK SQUARE THEATRE
408 St. Peter St., St. Paul
612/291-7005   **DSP**

A typical Park Square season includes a brash mix of Shakespeare, Molière, Tom Stoppard, and Lanford Wilson, all wonderfully produced and marvelously acted in the compact Seventh Place Theatre. The season runs from January through August.

PENUMBRA THEATRE
270 Kent St., St. Paul
612/224-3180   **SP**

Led by Lou Bellamy, this troupe is Minnesota's only professional com-

Guthrie Theater production, p. 176

Michal Daniel

pany presenting plays by African American playwrights. Penumbra has a rich history with Pulitzer Prize–winning playwright August Wilson. A critically acclaimed musical adaptation of Langston Hughes' *Black Nativity*, the theater's holiday show, is a December tradition.

PLYMOUTH PLAYHOUSE
2705 Annapolis Ln. N., Plymouth
612/553-1600   **GTC**

A professional company specializing in small-scale musicals and comedies.

RED EYE COLLABORATIVE
15 W. 14th St., Minneapolis
612/870-0309   **DMP**

A laboratory for experimental works by new and emerging theater artists.

TEATRO LATINO DE MINNESOTA
3501 Chicago Ave. S.,
Minneapolis
612/432-2314   **MP**

Theater that enlivens and shares the Latino experience, featuring original works by Latino playwrights.

THEATRE DE LA JEUNE LUNE
105 N. 1st St., Minneapolis
612/333-6200   **DMP**

Dynamic productions with a decidedly French flair. This adventurous company, which has a fanatical following, started in Paris in 1978 and used to spend half a year in the City of Light and the other half in the City of Lakes, eventually settling down here. Its handsome 500-seat theater is located in a renovated 1889 warehouse.

THEATRE IN THE ROUND PLAYERS
245 Cedar Ave., Minneapolis
612/333-3010 **DMP**
This dedicated community theater has been producing comedies, dramas, and classics for more than 40 years. Its arena-style stage is one of the anchors of the Seven Corners area, near the U of M's West Bank campus.

CLASSICAL MUSIC AND OPERA

AMERICAN COMPOSERS FORUM
332 Minnesota St., St. Paul
612/228-1407 **DSP**
A nationwide organization that promotes the musical development of composers through commissions, performances, and recordings.

DALE WARLAND SINGERS
120 N. 4th St., Minneapolis
612/339-9707 **DMP**
A touring choir of superb vocal musicians, with an extensive annual concert series led by conductor Dale Warland.

EX MACHINA
230 Crestway Ln.,
West St. Paul
455-8086 **GTC**
The Twin Cities' self-described "antique music company" presents vividly produced and beautifully

performed operas (most of them slightly obscure) from the Baroque period.

MINNEAPOLIS COMMUNITY COLLEGE GOSPEL CHOIR
1501 Hennepin Ave., Minneapolis
612/288-0990 **DMP**
Scorching music-making from a constantly touring group of singers.

MINNESOTA CHORALE
528 Hennepin Ave., Minneapolis
612/333-4866 **DMP**
A 150-voice choir that often performs with the Minnesota Orchestra and the St. Paul Chamber Orchestra.

MINNESOTA OPERA COMPANY
620 N. 1st St., Minneapolis
612/333-2700 **DMP**
This ambitious company got its start as Center Opera in the late 1960s, as an operatic offshoot of the Walker Art Center. For its first 15 years it produced almost entirely new works, premiering—and in most cases commissioning—works by renowned composers from around the world, including Dominick Argento, Conrad Susa, Yale Marshall, Harrison Birtwistle, Werner Egk, William Mayer, Hiram Titus, and Eric Stokes. The company shifted focus when it moved into the Ordway Music Theatre in the mid-1980s, turning to a more classically oriented repertory. Recent seasons have included productions of *Macbeth, Madame Butterfly*, and *Pelleas et Melisande*, and tickets are tough to come by.

MINNESOTA ORCHESTRA
1111 Nicollet Mall, Minneapolis
612/371-5656 **MP**
One of the country's finest orchestras, the Minnesota Orchestra has been making great music since 1904.

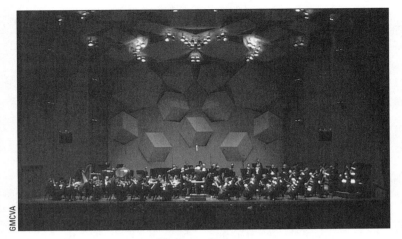

Minnesota Orchestra

Under the direction of the youthful and spirited Eiji Oue, the orchestra has been guided by some of the most influential conductors of the 20th century, including Edo de Waart, Sir Neville Marriner, Stanislaw Skrowaczewski, Antol Dorati, Dimitri Mitropoulos, and Eugene Ormandy. The orchestra's regular season runs September through May, with concerts at Orchestra Hall on Wednesday evening, Friday morning, and Friday evening; the Friday concert is broadcast live on Minnesota Public Radio station KSJN, 99.5 FM. Sommerfest, the vibrant and wildly popular summer festival of Viennese music, has been luring crowds and stars to Orchestra Hall for more than 20 years and is the nation's only inner-city summer music festival staged by a major orchestra.

PLYMOUTH MUSIC SERIES OF MINNESOTA
1900 Nicollet Ave. S., Minneapolis
612/870-0943   DMP
There is never a dull moment with this much-recorded vocal and or-chestral ensemble. PMS focuses on little-known works in the classical repertory as well as new works—most of which are specifically commissioned by the series, led by the indefatigable and Grammy Award–winning conductor Philip Brunelle.

ST. PAUL CHAMBER ORCHESTRA
75 W. 5th St., St. Paul
612/292-3248   DSP
The nation's only full-time chamber orchestra is also one of the Twin Cities' most cherished cultural institutions. Now under the musical direction of Hugh Wolff, this remarkable 32-member ensemble offers a nine-month season of concerts in different Twin Cities venues, tours constantly, and records often. Wolff follows in the footsteps of Dennis Russell Davies and Pinchas Zucherman; Christopher Hogwood is the SPCO's principal guest conductor, and Bobby McFerrin is the orchestra's musical advisor and a frequent guest conductor. The SPCO also attracts a heady list of international

DOWNTOWN ST. PAUL

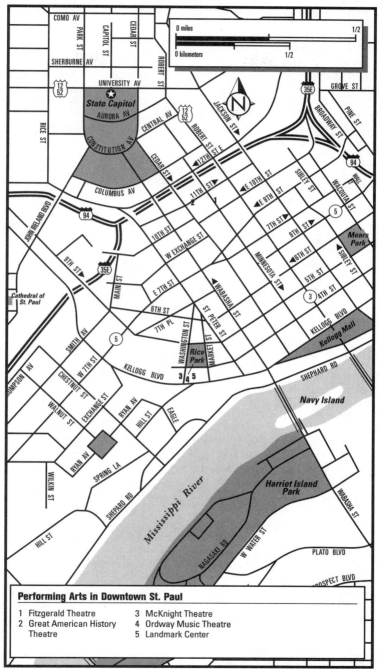

Performing Arts in Downtown St. Paul

1 Fitzgerald Theatre
2 Great American History Theatre
3 McKnight Theatre
4 Ordway Music Theatre
5 Landmark Center

guest artists and conductors, and commissions new works, particularly from composer-in-residence Aaron Jay Kernis.

SCHUBERT CLUB
75 W. 5th St., St. Paul
612/292-3267   **DSP**
This producing organization brings internationally renowned musical artists to the stage of the Ordway Music Theatre and sponsors an extensive series of recitals and chamber concerts. The club also operates a fascinating (and free) antique musical instruments museum, located in the basement of Landmark Center.

TWIN CITIES GAY MEN'S CHORUS
528 Hennepin Ave., Minneapolis
612/891-9130   **DMP**
This all-male ensemble produces four major concerts each year for a wide and enthusiastic audience.

DANCE

BALLET OF THE DOLLS
1629 Hennepin Ave. S., Minneapolis
612/333-2792   **DMP**
For over ten years, the Dolls have been presenting outlandish theater-dance works from the seemingly bottomless imagination of choreographer/director Myron Johnson, brought to life by one of the Twin Cities' most talented ensembles. Season runs September through May.

ETHNIC DANCE THEATRE
2337 Central Ave. NE, Minneapolis
612/782-3970   **MP**
The company sets its sights on the dance traditions of cultures around the world, and its regularly scheduled concerts are ablaze with color and movement.

JAMES SEWELL BALLET
620 N. 1st St., Minneapolis
612/672-0480   **DMP**
A gifted chamber-sized ballet troupe showcasing the choreography of James Sewell, a former principal dancer with Feld Ballet/NY.

JAZZDANCE by Danny Buraczeski
528 Hennepin Ave., Minneapolis
612/824-4851   **DMP**
Another immensely talented company, inspired by Danny Buraczeski, one of the nation's leading jazz choreographers.

MARGOLIS/BROWN COMPANY
115 Washington Ave. N., Minneapolis
612/339-4709   **DMP**
Theater-dance works with an edge, in a newly transplanted company.

MINNESOTA DANCE THEATRE
528 Hennepin Ave., Minneapolis
612/338-0627   **DMP**
The company of the late, great Loyce Houlton, MDT was once the leading ballet company in the Upper Midwest but fell upon hard times in the late 1980s. It is now enjoying a modest comeback under the direction of Houlton's daughter, Lise, a former principal dancer with American Ballet Theatre.

NANCY HAUSER DANCE CO.
1940 Hennepin Ave. S., Minneapolis
612/871-9077   **MP**
The company and school of pioneering modern-dance icon Nancy Hauser continues to teach and

perform her particular brand of movement.

ZENON DANCE CO.
528 Hennepin Ave., Minneapolis
612/338-1101 DMP
The Twin Cities' leading modern-dance company, with a decade-long history and a large repertory of works by choreographers from around the world.

ZORONGO FLAMENCO DANCE THEATRE
528 Hennepin Ave.,
Minneapolis
612/377-0701 DMP
Hot-hot-hot dance theater with a definite Latin flavor, featuring flamenco musicians and dancers from around the world.

CONCERT VENUES

CEDAR CULTURAL CENTER
416 Cedar Ave., Minneapolis
612/228-2674 MP
A former movie house, the Cedar is a little rough around the edges, and is now used for a wide variety of folk, rock, jazz, and blues concerts.

FITZGERALD THEATRE
10 E. Exchange St., St. Paul
612/290-1221 DSP
The beloved home of Garrison Keillor's "A Prairie Home Companion" (heard on 225 radio stations every Saturday evening) is a prize of a theater. It opened in 1910 as the Schubert Theater, and by the time it received an extensive renovation in 1986, it was going by World Theater; the theater received its third and current name in 1994 to honor author and local son F. Scott Fitzgerald. The small house (with great acoustics)

squeezes just over 900 seats on the main level and two balconies, none very far from the stage.

LAKE HARRIET BANDSHELL
West Lake Harriet Pkwy. at
William Berry Pkwy.,
Minneapolis
612/661-4800 MP
An enchanting open-air facility on the shores of Lake Harriet, the fourth such bandshell on this site since 1888. An eclectic mix of music (jazz, rock, folk, and classical), free admission, and usually beautiful skies lure the crowds from Memorial Day to Labor Day; many picnic or stroll around the lake (a 3-mile walk) before the music starts. Most concerts begin at 7:30 p.m. Monday through Saturday and at 5:30 p.m. on Sunday. The Minneapolis Parks Pops Orchestra, a Lake Harriet tradition for more than half a century, plays light classical, opera, and Broadway favorites every Saturday and Sunday from late June through late July.

MCKNIGHT THEATRE
345 Washington St., St. Paul
612/224-4222 DSP
This small house seats 300 people in a theater that mimics its next-door neighbor, the Ordway. Noteworthy for its fine sightlines, clear acoustics, and comfortable chairs.

NORTHROP AUDITORIUM
84 Church St. SE, Minneapolis
612/624-2345 MP
The largest theater in the state as well as the largest auditorium on a college campus in the country. This big old barn, dating from 1929, seats 4,800 and since 1977 has produced a glittering annual dance series featuring internationally renowned dance companies. Recent guests have

MINNEAPOLIS

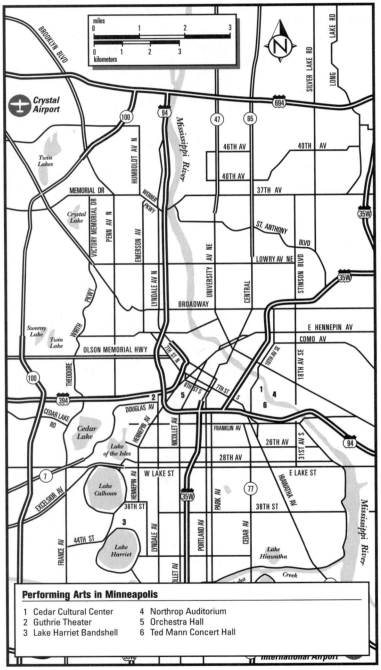

Performing Arts in Minneapolis

1 Cedar Cultural Center
2 Guthrie Theater
3 Lake Harriet Bandshell
4 Northrop Auditorium
5 Orchestra Hall
6 Ted Mann Concert Hall

Ordway Music Theater

included American Ballet Theatre, Mark Morris Dance Troupe, San Francisco Ballet, Frankfurt Ballet, Miami City Ballet, Paul Taylor Dance Company, Urban Bush Women, Mazowsze, Alvin Ailey American Dance Theater, Joffrey Ballet of Chicago, Feld Ballet/NY, Sankai Juku, and Bale Folclorico da Bahia.

Northrop hosted a two-week spring engagement of the Metropolitan Opera for more than 50 years, and the hall was home to the Minneapolis Symphony for more four decades, until Orchestra Hall opened in 1974. Northrop's acoustics are marginal at best. When a reporter asked Minneapolis Symphony music director Eugene Ormandy in the mid-1930s how he thought the auditorium's acoustics could be improved, he replied, "dynamite." The most coveted seats are in the lower balcony, or in the center of the main floor after about the tenth row. Parking is available in a heated underground ramp (enter on Pleasant Street), and although the majority of the crowds use the cam-

pus ramps behind University Avenue, a closer (and less crowded) alternative is the Coffman Union ramp (enter on East River Road).

ORCHESTRA HALL
1111 Nicollet Mall, Minneapolis
612/371-5656   MP
An acoustical marvel. Built specifically to meet the needs of the Minnesota Orchestra, the hall's permanent musical shell is a departure from the traditional proscenium arch. In less skilled hands, such a choice might limit the auditorium's practicality, but it has only enhanced the quality of this superb, 2,400-seat concert hall. The auditorium itself is especially attractive, with its animated ceiling of large plaster cubes and warm rose and periwinkle tones.

ORDWAY MUSIC THEATER
345 Washington St., St. Paul
612/224-4222   DSP
The crown jewel of downtown St. Paul is a center of cultural life in the capital city. This elegant horseshoe-shaped opera house is the principal

home of the St. Paul Chamber Orchestra, Minnesota Opera, and the Schubert Club. It also manages to squeeze in a heady schedule of touring productions as well as its own internationally flavored dance and music series, Planet Ordway. The theater seats 2,000 for classical music and 1,800 for opera; the best seats are the upper reaches of the orchestra, the center mezzanine, and the center balconies. Steer clear of the boxes; although they afford lots of leg room, the sightlines can be iffy.

ORPHEUM THEATRE
910 Hennepin Ave., Minneapolis
612/339-7007 DMP
Once one of the largest stops on the nation's vaudeville circuit, the Orpheum was restored in 1994 to its glory days to the tune of $10.5 million, and this 2,700-seat palace now features a constant stream of Broadway musicals, concerts, and events.

O'SHAUGHNESSY AUDITORIUM
2004 Randolph Ave., St. Paul
612/690-6700 SP
An intimate 650-seat theater (with excellent sightlines, due in part to the hall's continental seating arrangement) that can be converted to a larger 1,800-seat hall simply by raising the ceiling and opening up the 1,150-seat balcony. Located on the pretty campus of the College of St. Catherine, O'Shaughnessy produces an exciting fall and spring series that showcases the talents of the Twin Cities' top dance companies.

ST. PAUL CIVIC CENTER
143 W. 4th St., St. Paul
612/224-7403 DSP
A dirge, but improving, thanks to a recent $50-million renovation. The bare-bones, 18,000-seat arena is lit-

tle better than an enormous oil tank, although the influx of cash promises to lighten things up. With its clear sightlines and reasonably close-in stage, the Civic Center's 5,000-seat Roy Wilkins Auditorium is probably the best place to see a rock concert in the Twin Cities, although lamentably few are fortunate enough to get booked into this well-designed space.

SOUTHERN THEATER
1420 Washington Ave. S.,
Minneapolis
612/340-1725 DMP
A flexible and intimate performance space in Seven Corners near the U of M's West Bank campus, the Southern is the favorite of a wide variety of theater and dance companies, musicians, and cabaret artists.

STATE THEATRE
805 Hennepin Ave., Minneapolis
612/339-7007 DMP
A restored 1921 vaudeville house of infectious charm and wit, now all dressed up for touring Broadway shows, concerts, lectures, and meetings after an $8.8-million renovation in 1991. Seats 2,176.

TARGET CENTER
600 1st Ave. N., Minneapolis
612/673-0900
612/673-1688 TDD DMP
A major venue for touring rock concerts. For an arena, the acoustics aren't bad, and because of its cramped downtown location, most of the modern center's 18,200 extra-wide seats offer fairly decent sightlines. Several thousand parking spots (connected by skyway) are within walking distance, and the neighborhood is full of restaurants, bars, and clubs for pre- and post-concert fun.

TED MANN CONCERT HALL
2128 S. 4th St., Minneapolis
612/626-1892   **MP**

The concert hall and opera house of the University of Minnesota on the school's West Bank campus opened in 1994 and was named for its primary benefactor, the movie theater mogul. The auditorium, although spartan, has excellent acoustics and wonderful sightlines, and works particularly well for choral concerts. The lobby has a panoramic view of the Mississippi River.

BUYING TICKETS

EVENT USA
800/745-7328

Ticket broker specializing in sporting events, concerts, and theater. Expect to pay more (prices vary) than the ticket price, plus a handling fee.

TICKET EXCHANGE
800/800-9811

Ticket broker with a wide range of sporting events, concerts, and theater. Expect to pay more (prices vary) than the ticket price, plus a handling fee.

TICKETMASTER
612/989-5151

Ticket agent with a huge selection of concerts, sporting events, theater, attractions, and special events. Expect to pay a surcharge of $2 to $5 per ticket and a handling fee of $1 to $1.50 per order.

TICKET WORKS
612/870-1099

Ticket agent with a selection of special events, theater, concert, attractions, and sporting events. Expect to pay a surcharge of $1 to $2 per ticket, with no handling fee.

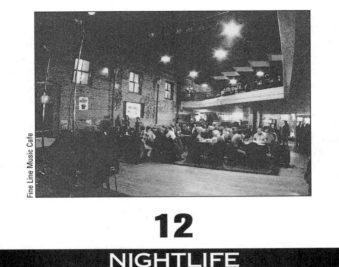

Fine Line Music Cafe

12

NIGHTLIFE

While it may lack the buzz of a Chicago, New York, or Los Angeles, the Twin Cities' nightlife scene isn't without its assets. Jazz and blues are big here, and there are a number of clubs that not only put the spotlight on local artists but also manage to lure in the best talent in the country, particularly joints such as First Avenue and the Fine Line Music Café. The local music scene has produced a number of nationally prominent acts, including the Replacements, Hüsker Dü, Lipps Inc., and The Artist Formerly Known as Prince.

Much of the Twin Cities' nightlife is concentrated in downtown Minneapolis, although clubs, bars, and music venues of note are scattered throughout the metropolitan area. Out-of-state visitors may be surprised to learn that things end early in puritanical Minnesota; bars must stop serving liquor at 1 a.m., and although they can remain open—and dry—until 3 a.m. under certain circumstances, few do. One pleasant surprise is that Twin Citians loathe paying a cover charge, so very few establishments collect dollars at the door. When they do, the fee rarely exceeds $10 and is usually under $5. Listings in the Greater Twin Cities area are not shown on the maps in this chapter.

DANCE CLUBS

CLUB METRO
733 Pierce Butler Route, St. Paul
612/489-0002 SP
The top lesbian bar in the Twin Cities features two huge dance floors, a game room, and a number of smaller venues for conversation, all set in a

former indoor-volleyball sports bar. The crowds are especially large on Friday and Saturday evenings. No cover.

FIRST AVENUE
701 First Ave. N., Minneapolis
612/332-1775 DMP
The city's biggest nightclub is famous

DOWNTOWN MINNEAPOLIS

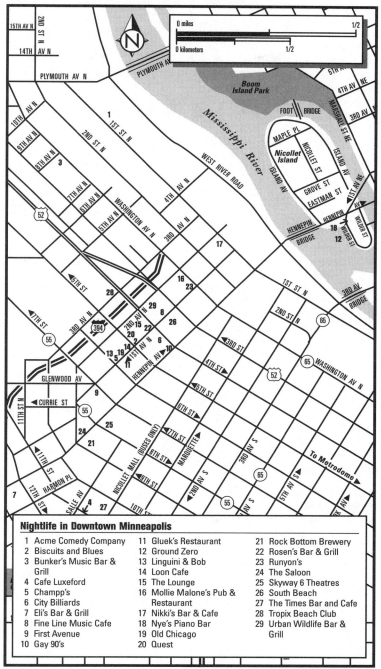

Nightlife in Downtown Minneapolis

1 Acme Comedy Company
2 Biscuits and Blues
3 Bunker's Music Bar & Grill
4 Cafe Luxeford
5 Champp's
6 City Billiards
7 Eli's Bar & Grill
8 Fine Line Music Cafe
9 First Avenue
10 Gay 90's

11 Gluek's Restaurant
12 Ground Zero
13 Linguini & Bob
14 Loon Cafe
15 The Lounge
16 Mollie Malone's Pub & Restaurant
17 Nikki's Bar & Cafe
18 Nye's Piano Bar
19 Old Chicago
20 Quest

21 Rock Bottom Brewery
22 Rosen's Bar & Grill
23 Runyon's
24 The Saloon
25 Skyway 6 Theatres
26 South Beach
27 The Times Bar and Cafe
28 Tropix Beach Club
29 Urban Wildlife Bar & Grill

for its role in *Purple Rain*, the movie that put The Artist Formerly Known as Prince (and the Minneapolis Sound) on the map. Today the Avenue still books the very best on the contemporary music touring circuit, and practically everyone in the business has played here at one point or another in their career. Housed in a former Greyhound bus station, the place is big enough to please even the most persnickety of club kids, and on weekend nights the massive crowds can be a little daunting. Inside the Avenue is Seventh Street Entry, the claustrophobic place to hear the cream of the up-and-coming local and national music scene. Cover varies.

GAY 90'S
408 Hennepin Ave., Minneapolis
612/333-7755   **DMP**

More of a shopping mall than a nightclub, the state's largest gay bar literally offers something for everyone, including a large straight following who come for the excellent dance music and the extremely popular (and free) drag show at the La Femme Show Lounge on the second floor. The 90's has nine different bars, including two discos, plus male strippers, a supper club, a coffee shop, game room, and a leather bar. Friday and Saturday nights are almost obnoxiously packed. No cover.

GROUND ZERO
15 N.E. Fourth St., Minneapolis
612/378-5115   **DMP**

Just across the Mississippi River from downtown Minneapolis, this large club offers a different musical theme every night, including its infamous Bondage A Go-Go, a leather-and-latex evening every Thursday. Cover varies.

O'GARA'S GARAGE
164 N. Snelling Ave., St. Paul
612/644-3333   **SP**

Local blues, rock, jazz, and progressive music nightly at this venue next door to O'Gara's, a restaurant and bar popular with college students and twentysomethings. No cover.

QUEST
110 N. Fifth St., Minneapolis
612/338-3383   **DMP**

This high-style club was formerly Glam Slam, a sometimes-hangout for The Artist Formerly Known as Prince, and it's still a great place to dance to the latest live and recorded music as well as a prime spot in which to see and be seen. Cover varies.

THE SALOON
830 Hennepin Ave., Minneapolis
612/332-0835   **DMP**

A younger gay crowd congregates at the Saloon. They come for the good-looking clientele as well as what many consider to be the best DJs in town. No cover.

SOUTH BEACH
325 First Ave. N., Minneapolis
612/204-0790   **DMP**

A club with attitude (surly bouncers-slash-doormen, a strictly enforced dress code in the land of 10,000 Dockers) and a south Florida theme. There are several bars, a dance floor, and a fairly ambitious restaurant, all under one roof. The motif changes nightly and includes everything from salsa to disco. Cover varies.

TROPIX BEACH CLUB
400 Third Ave. N., Minneapolis
612/333-1006   **DMP**

If you're young, uninhibited, and looking for a no-holds-barred night on the town, then consider Tropix, which packs in a rowdy, post-collegiate crowd for heavy drinking, dancing, and pickups. Cover varies.

MUSIC CLUBS

Jazz

CAFE LUXEFORD
1101 LaSalle Ave., Minneapolis
612/332-6800 **DMP**
Great live jazz in a charming setting in a small café just inside the lobby of the Hotel Luxeford, a half-block from Orchestra Hall in downtown Minneapolis. Good food, too. No cover.

THE DAKOTA BAR & GRILL
1021 E. Bandana Blvd., St. Paul
612/642-1442 **SP**
The Twin Cities' premiere jazz club, with a heady combination of local and national acts, set in a renovated railroad switching house. Sunday nights—a roundtable of local acts, hosted by pianist Dan Chouinard—are a particular treat. Excellent food, too.

THE TIMES BAR AND CAFE
1036 Nicollet Mall, Minneapolis
612/333-2762 **DMP**
Dark, clubby, and grown-up, this Nicollet Mall fixture (kitty-corner from Orchestra Hall) features live music every night, interesting food and welcoming surroundings. No cover charge.

Blues

BISCUITS AND BLUES
430 First Ave. N., Minneapolis
612/333-2583 **DMP**
This California chain is the latest entry in the Twin Cities blues explosion. Located at a prime Warehouse

The Saloon

District corner, the club offers decent Southern cooking and a far-flung variety of blues acts in a sprawling, two-level venue. Cover varies.

BLUES SALOON
601 Western Ave., St. Paul
612/228-9959 **SP**
Local and national blues acts in a crowded, snug setting every Thursday through Monday night. The Blues Saloon Maniacs Open Jam takes the stage every Monday night. Cover varies.

BUNKER'S MUSIC BAR & GRILL
761 Washington Ave. N.,
Minneapolis
612/338-8188 **DMP**
Live blues, R&B, and funk are the hallmarks of this cramped and always-crowded hangout, located off the Warehouse District beaten path about seven blocks north of First Avenue on Washington Avenue. Cover varies.

FAMOUS DAVE'S BLUES & BBQ
3001 Hennepin Ave. S.,

ST. PAUL

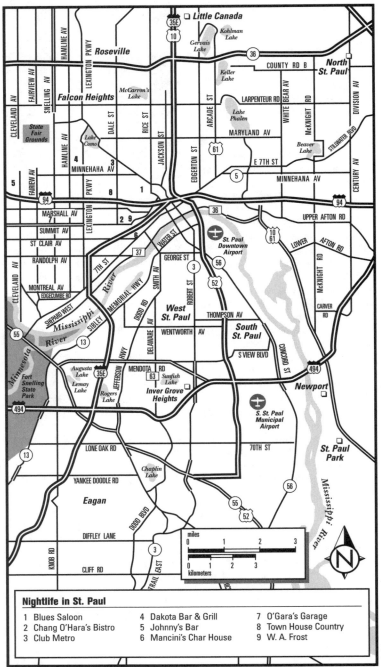

Nightlife in St. Paul

1 Blues Saloon
2 Chang O'Hara's Bistro
3 Club Metro
4 Dakota Bar & Grill
5 Johnny's Bar
6 Mancini's Char House
7 O'Gara's Garage
8 Town House Country
9 W. A. Frost

Wine Bars

A number of wine bars have sprouted up across the Twin Cities in the past few years. Here's a quick guide to the most pleasant options: **Bobino** *(222 E. Hennepin Ave., Minneapolis, 612/623-3301);* **Bev's Wine Bar** *(250 N. Third St., Minneapolis, 612/337-0102);* **Edith's** *(452 Selby Ave., St. Paul, 612/221-1061);* **Giorgio's Wine Bar** *(1601 W. Lake St., Minneapolis, 612/822-7071);* **Jitters Café** *(1026 Nicollet Mall, Minneapolis, 612/338-8511);* **Lucia's Wine Bar** *(1432 W. 32 St., Minneapolis, 612/823-7125); and the* **New French Bar** *(128 N. Fourth St., Minneapolis, 612/338-3790);* **The Vintage** *(579 Selby Ave., St. Paul, 612/222-7000).*

Minneapolis
612/822-9900   **MP**
The Famous Dave's franchise blew into Uptown's Calhoun Square in the fall of 1996, with crowd-pleasing results. The barbecue is just as good as at Dave's other outlets, but this huge operation (designed to resemble a 1930s-era El station in downtown Chicago) also offers a full bar and the Blues All-Stars, a kicking 11-player house band. Lots of fun and no cover.

Other Clubs

THE CABOOZE
917 Cedar Ave., Minneapolis
612/338-6425   **MP**
One of the Twin Cities' top live music venues, with a nightly double bill of rock, blues, progressive, or reggae. A big dance floor, too, and a devoted crowd. Cover varies.

FINE LINE MUSIC CAFÉ
318 First Ave. N., Minneapolis
612/338-8100   **DMP**
A fabulous room for the engaging blend of local and national folk, rock, blues, jazz, and gospel acts that gets booked into this concert hall/restaurant-and-bar hybrid. The Fine Line's sightlines—and acoustics—are excellent, and while the food's nothing special, it's not bad, either. The Sunday gospel brunch is not to be missed. Cover varies.

RIVERVIEW SUPPER CLUB
2319 N. West River Rd.,
Minneapolis
612/521-7676   **MP**
National and local jazz, blues, and funk artists bring this spendy and predominantly African-American club alive seven nights a week. Cover varies.

Country and Western

MEDINA ENTERTAINMENT
CENTER
500 Hwy. 55, Medina
612/478-6661   **GTC**

Located about 30 minutes west of downtown Minneapolis, this enormous facility (which started life as a ballroom) books a surprisingly large number of national country acts, but its second stage is also home to big band, swing, rock, and oldies. There's also a bowling alley and a restaurant. Cover varies.

TOWN HOUSE COUNTRY
1415 W. University Ave., St. Paul
612/646-7087   SP
One of the Twin Cities' oldest gay bars has been a country-western mecca for more than a decade, providing a combination of live and recorded music. The club's North Star Lounge features cabaret acts, including local piano-lounge legend Lori Dokken. Cover varies.

PUBS AND BARS

AMERICA'S ORIGINAL SPORTS BAR
Fourth Floor, East Broadway, Mall of America

612/854-5483   GTC
What better location for what has to be the country's largest sports bar than at the nation's largest shopping mall? This gargantuan good-time has something for everyone, including billiards, video games, a basketball half-court, live music and dancing, countless video monitors, and more bars than you thought possible. Huge crowds. Cover varies.

BRYANT LAKE BOWL
810 W. Lake St., Minneapolis
612/825-3737   MP
An unlikely south Minneapolis hot spot, this neighborhood bowling alley was reinvented in the early 1990s into a hip hangout for young and old alike. Great people-watching, excellent beer and wine selections, good (and cheap) food, and bowling, too. The adjacent cabaret offers a steady—and eclectic—diet of comedy, music, performance, and movies at low, low prices. No cover.

CHAMPP'S
100 N. Sixth St., Minneapolis

The Cabooze, p. 193

The Cabooze

612/335-5050   **DMP**

A huge sports bar in Butler Square, with the standard sports bar menu. The big draw here is the huge bar fronting on First Avenue, as well as the celebrated summertime bar, which is wedged into an adjacent alley and packs the revelers in by the hundreds during the warm-weather months. Other locations include downtown St. Paul, Richfield, Minnetonka, Burnsville, New Brighton, and Maplewood. No cover.

CHANG O'HARA'S BISTRO
498 Selby Ave., St. Paul
612/290-2338   **SP**

Jazz, blues, and Latin are the musical draws in this renovated fire station, which has a snug bar, a spacious dining room, and a charming and secluded garden. No cover.

CITY BILLIARDS
25 N. 4th St., Minneapolis
612/338-2255   **DMP**

Eight-ball never looked so good as in this upscale billiards hall, which also serves a light lunch, dinner, and late-night menu as well as a full bar. No cover.

ELI'S BAR & GRILL
1225 Hennepin Ave., Minneapolis
612/332-9997   **DMP**

Downtown's best kept food-and-drink secret, this long and narrow boîte—housed on the first floor of a nineteenth-century apartment house—provides surprisingly inventive lunch and dinner fare. Genuinely friendly atmosphere and a great bar, too. No cover.

FIGLIO
3001 Hennepin Ave. S.,
Minneapolis
612/822-1688   **MP**

The Calhoun Square restaurant is also known for its large and rather dark bar, which packs in a young and diverse crowd, particularly on weekend nights.

FREIGHT HOUSE
305 S. Water St., Stillwater
612/439-5718   **GTC**

Of all the bars and clubs in pretty Stillwater, this one draws the largest crowds. Inside you'll find a restaurant, several bars, an outdoor deck, and a large nightclub with a big dance floor. No cover.

GLUEK'S RESTAURANT
16 N. 6th St., Minneapolis
612/338-6621   **DMP**

The only place in town to get a tall, cold mug of Gluek's beer on tap, this quasi-German beer hall also serves a vaguely Teutonic menu. The crowd is young, loud, and fun-loving. No cover.

IVORIES
605 N. Hwy. 169, Plymouth
612/591-6188   **GTC**

The piano bar to end all piano bars, its restaurant serves lunch, dinner, and a champagne Sunday brunch. No cover.

JOHNNY'S BAR
2251 W. University Ave., St. Paul
612/645-4116   **SP**

Don't let the dreary exterior fool you. A center for this emerging area of artists and artisans, Johnny's offers up a huge selection of beers and a friendly, congenial atmosphere. No cover.

LINGUINI & BOB
100 N. Sixth St., Minneapolis
612/332-1600   **DMP**

The handsome bar of this D'Amico brothers Butler Square restaurant screams "Pottery Barn," and it's a comfortable place to enjoy a glass of wine or a drink before setting out for some of the Warehouse District's more animated watering holes. The bar in D'Amico Cucina (L&B's very expensive downstairs sibling, 612/338-2401) is also an alternative getaway from the Warehouse District/Target Center hubbub.

LOON CAFE
500 1st. Ave. N., Minneapolis
612/332-8342 **DMP**
The city's first downtown sports bar still packs 'em in before, during, and after Metrodome and Target Center games. The throngs come for the clubby atmosphere and stay for the three-alarm chili, burgers, and other delights. Get a seat in one of the tables near the big picture windows and watch the world go by on First Avenue and Fifth Street. No cover.

LORD FLETCHER'S ON THE LAKE
3746 Sunset Dr., Spring Park
612/471-8513 **GTC**
The center of action on Lake Minnetonka in the summer months. Fletcher's labyrinthian dock leads up to an even larger deck, which is mobbed on lazy summer afternoons. The restaurant itself is divided into three separate sections and is considerably more formal than its outdoor counterparts. No cover.

THE LORING BAR
1624 Harmon Pl., Minneapolis
612/332-1617 **MP**
One of the most interesting places in town for a glass of wine or beer, nibbly things, conversation, and peerless people-watching. The big windows offer priceless views of Loring Park, the furniture recalls upscale garage sales, and the lighting is romantically dim. Live nightly music. No cover.

THE LOUNGE
411 Second Ave. N., Minneapolis
612/333-8800 **DMP**
Another quiet respite from the loud downtown bar scene, this collection of small rooms is furnished with plush, comfy sofas and chairs designed to encourage conversation and mingling. There's food, too, and the crowd is mid-30s and up, prosperous, heterosexual, and on-the-make. No cover.

LYLE'S BAR & RESTAURANT
2021 Hennepin Ave., Minneapolis
612/870-8183 **MP**
A south Minneapolis landmark for decades, this dark and smoky neighborhood hangout draws a diverse crowd for drinks, chatter, a game room, and terrific hamburgers. No cover.

MANCINI'S CHAR HOUSE
531 W. Seventh St., St. Paul
612/224-7345 **SP**
Really more of a steakhouse than a bar, this see-it-to-believe-it blend of Las Vegas show lounge and northern Minnesota supper club has a large bar that draws one of the Twin Cities' most unlikely cross-sections of people. The live music at Mancini's includes an inevitable polka band or two.

MOLLIE MALONE'S PUB & RESTAURANT
119 Washington Ave. N., Minneapolis
612/333-1675 **DMP**
Although not as Irish as its name might imply, Miss Malone's is a quiet hangout (particularly the cozy art deco bar up front, which has some of

William's Uptown Pub & Peanut Bar, p. 200

the most flattering lighting in the Twin Cities), and the kitchen does great things with standard American fare. No cover.

NIKKI'S BAR AND CAFE
107 Third Ave. N., Minneapolis
612/340-9098   **DMP**
Piano and vocals in a cluttered setting. The restaurant prepares pastas and pizzas quite well, and the large outdoor garden is a frequent summertime destination. No cover.

NYE'S PIANO BAR
112 Hennepin Ave. E.,
Minneapolis
612/379-2021   **DMP**
Lovely Lou Hanson holds court at her organ six nights a week (as she has for nearly a quarter-century) at this sing-along bar that draws one of the richest cross-sections of patrons in the Twin Cities. No cover.

OLD CHICAGO
508 First Ave. N., Minneapolis
612/338-8686   **DMP**
Another entry in the sports-bar wars,

this chain draws the crowds for its burger-pasta-pizza routine, zillions of varieties of beer, and large span of billiard tables. Other locations include Uptown Minneapolis and Eagan. No cover.

THE ROCK BOTTOM BREWERY
825 Hennepin Ave.,
Minneapolis
612/332-2739   **DMP**
The city's most ambitious brew pub, and the suds aren't bad. An outlet of a Colorado-based chain, the atmosphere is rather cookie-cutterish, and the food won't win any awards, but that doesn't keep a young, good-looking (a less kind person might use the word "yuppie") crowd from mobbing the place. No cover.

ROSEN'S BAR & GRILL
430 First Ave. N.,
Minneapolis
612/338-1926   **DMP**
A popular sports bar owned by Mark Rosen, sports anchor for the local CBS television affiliate, this place is known for its big, friendly crowds,

Bargain and Drive-In Theaters

*At the **bargain theaters**, seats cost a buck or two, and the films aren't new but haven't yet jumped to video. The pick of the litter includes the six-screen **Apple Valley Theatres** (7200 W. 147th St., Apple Valley, 612/432-1199), the **Boulevard Theatre** (5315 Lyndale Ave. S., Minneapolis, 612/823-7471), and the **Excelsior Dock 1, 2 and 3** (26 Water St., Excelsior, 612/474-6275).*

*And although they are definitely a dying breed, a few drive-ins remain on the outskirts of the Twin Cities area, including the **65-Hi** (10100 Central Ave. NE, Blaine, 612/780-3063, about 25 minutes north of downtown Minneapolis), the **Cottage View** (9338 SE East Point Douglas Rd., Cottage Grove, 612/458-5965, about 20 minutes southeast of downtown St. Paul), and the **Vali-Hi** (11260 Hudson Blvd., Lake Elmo, 612/436-7464, about 20 minutes east of downtown St. Paul).*

decent food, and short distance (two blocks) to Target Center. No cover.

RUNYON'S
107 Washington Ave. N., Minneapolis
612/332-7158   DMP
Still a draw for the post-college, first-job crowd after more than a decade, Runyon's still makes a wicked buffalo chicken wing, and the long, narrow bar and attractive surroundings are all designed to make meeting strangers easy. No cover.

SHERLOCK'S HOME
11000 Rd Circle Dr., Minnetonka
612/931-0203   GTC
The Twin Cities' first brew pub cranks out a number of excellent beers, and the food is also pretty good. The atmosphere is that of an English pub,

which should come as no mystery, given its name. No cover.

URBAN WILDLIFE BAR & GRILL
331 2nd Ave. N., Minneapolis
612/339-4665   DMP
By day, this corner bar serves up a mean hamburger and fries to the local neighborhood office workers. By night, the Lowlife is often packed cheek-to-cheek with straight, good-looking, and predominantly single twentysomethings. No cover.

W.A. FROST
374 Selby Ave., St. Paul
612/224-5715   SP
A soaring ceiling, huge windows, and tons of wood make W.A. Frost, a former nineteenth-century apothecary institution, one of the most comfortable and alluring places in

MINNEAPOLIS

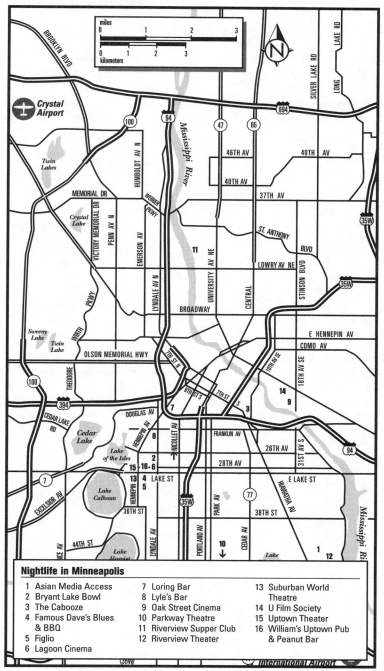

Nightlife in Minneapolis

1 Asian Media Access
2 Bryant Lake Bowl
3 The Cabooze
4 Famous Dave's Blues
    & BBQ
5 Figlio
6 Lagoon Cinema

7 Loring Bar
8 Lyle's Bar
9 Oak Street Cinema
10 Parkway Theatre
11 Riverview Supper Club
12 Riverview Theater

13 Suburban World
    Theatre
14 U Film Society
15 Uptown Theater
16 William's Uptown Pub
    & Peanut Bar

which to enjoy a quiet conversation and a drink or two.

WILLIAM'S UPTOWN PUB & PEANUT BAR
2911 Hennepin Ave., Minneapolis
612/823-6271 **MP**
The restaurant on the ground floor has been an Uptown fixture for years, but it's the downstairs peanut bar—and its countless beers by the bottle—that still draws a fairly young crowd.

COMEDY CLUBS

ACME COMEDY COMPANY
708 N. First St., Minneapolis
612/338-6393 **DMP**
In the 1980s, when stand-up comedy was king, it seemed that there was a club popping up on every available corner. Acme is one of the few remaining comedy rooms in the Twin Cities from that era, and with good reason: it books an entertaining mix of local and national acts, and offers a series of dinner packages with Sticks, the restaurant next door. $10 cover.

KNUCKLEHEADS
Fourth floor, East Broadway, Mall of America
612/854-5233 **GTC**
The premiere Twin Cities comedy club draws from a national roster

of comedians, and the spacious surroundings and animated crowds make for a fun night out.

MOVIE HOUSES OF NOTE

There are more than 300 screens in 59 theaters to choose from in the seven-county metropolitan area, but unfortunately, very few exceptionally large screens exist in the area, and the majority are located in characterless suburban shoebox multiplexes. There are, however, a number of distinctive and comfortable places to enjoy a good movie or two.

ASIAN MEDIA ACCESS
3028 Oregon Ave. S., Minneapolis
612/349-2549 **MP**
A nonprofit that imports a heady roster of the latest in Asian cinema, as well as little-known films and classics. Most screenings take place at the delightful Riverview Theater.

THE CINEMA CAFE
1925 Burnsville Pkwy., Burnsville
612/894-8810 **GTC**
2749 Winnetka Ave. N., New Hope
612/546-2336 **GTC**
These two suburban operations combine dining with moviegoing. All seats are $2.50, most movies are rated G, there's beer and wine, and while the food isn't exactly haute cuisine, it's not bad, either.

Luck Be a Lady Tonight

*Native American-owned casinos are a booming business in Minnesota, and a number of showy facilities are located within two hours' drive of the Twin Cities. **Mystic Lake Casino** (2400 Mystic Lake Blvd., Prior Lake, 612/445-9000 or 800/262-7700) is the state's largest and most lavish casino, conveniently located one-half hour south of downtown Minneapolis. Other gaming options include: **Grand Casino Hinckley** (I-35 at Highway 48, Hinckley, 800/472-6321); **Grand Casino Mille Lacs** (Highway 169 North, Onamia, 800/626-5825); and **Treasure Island Casino** (5734 Sturgeon Lake Rd., Welch, 800/222-7077).*

GENERAL CINEMA MALL OF AMERICA 14
Upper East Side, Mall of America, Bloomington
612/546-5700   GTC
Among multiplexes, the biggest screens, cleanest facilities, and best film picks belong to this huge complex. Runners-up include the deluxe **Centennial Lakes Cinema 8** (7311 France Ave. S., Edina, 612/546-5700, just a few blocks south of Southdale) and the attractive **St. Anthony Main 5** (201 SE Main St., Minneapolis, 612/331-4723).

LAGOON CINEMA
1320 Lagoon Ave., Minneapolis
612/825-6006   MP
After a week's run on the big screen at the Uptown, most flicks move down the street to the Goldwyn/Landmark's Lagoon Cinema, a comfortable and popular new five-screen multiplex devoted to small, art-house movies. Both theaters offer a money-saving discount card, five admissions for $25.

OAK STREET CINEMA
309 Oak St. SE, Minneapolis
612/331-3134   MP
The Twin Cities' sole revival house. Located near the U of M, this enterprising operation screens an astonishing range of films, and the marquee often changes daily.

PARKWAY THEATRE
4814 Chicago Ave. S., Minneapolis
612/822-3030   MP
A bit of a dump, this low-key neighborhood theater features a quirky selection of titles, cheap popcorn, and low-low admission prices.

RIVERVIEW THEATER
3800 42nd Ave. S., Minneapolis
612/729-7369   MP
The Riv hasn't changed one iota since it opened in 1948—the space-age lobby predates *The Jetsons* (be sure to check out the bathrooms), and the big auditorium and its wide screen remain intact. Movies are generally a few months old, and all

seats are $1.75; the bargains continue at the refreshment counter.

ROSEVILLE 4 THEATRES
1211 Larpenteur Ave. W., Roseville
612/488-4242   **GTC**
If a comfortable seat is all that matters, then park it at this small multiplex. All seats are not only plush but a mere $2 per ticket.

SKYWAY 6 THEATRES
711 Hennepin Ave., Minneapolis
612/333-6100   **DMP**
The main auditorium here has a huge screen and shows Hollywood's biggest blockbusters. Unfortunately, this tired multiplex cries out for a good hosing down, at the very least.

SUBURBAN WORLD THEATRE
3022 Hennepin Ave. S., Minneapolis
612/825-6688   **MP**
If you like a little atmosphere with your popcorn, catch a show at the Sub World. The ceiling twinkles with stars, and the interior is done up like a Moorish palace. Good sightlines, too, particularly from the loges.

U FILM SOCIETY
10 Church St. SE, Minneapolis
612/627-4430   **MP**
At the University of Minnesota, U Film is for serious film aficionados. The fiefdom of director Al Milgrom for more than a quarter-century, U Film shows every kind of foreign, little-known, and fascinating film and hosts both the annual Rivertown Film Festival and the Twin Cities Gay, Lesbian, Bisexual and Transgender Film Festival. Screenings take place in a somewhat uncomfortable lecture hall in Nicholson Hall (10 Pleasant St. SE) or at U Film's main venue in the roomy and recently renovated auditorium of the James Ford Bell Museum of Natural History.

UPTOWN THEATER
2906 Hennepin Ave. S., Minneapolis
612/825-6006   **MP**
The Twin Cities' best large single-screen theater. An anchor of the Uptown neighborhood, this 1930s treasure has a large auditorium (complete with cozy balcony perfect for necking) and serves up a steady diet of indie films.

13

DAY TRIPS FROM THE TWIN CITIES

DAY TRIP: Duluth

Distance from the Twin Cities: *150 miles, 3-hour drive*
The city on the lake is also Minnesota's window to the world. The St. Lawrence Seaway made Duluth's harbor (the largest freshwater—and furthest inland—harbor in the world) a destination for ocean vessels, and big boats line up at its docks from April until October. For a self-guided orientation to this vertiginous city, take a spin on **Skyline Parkway**, a winding hilltop drive that offers breathtaking views of the lake, harbor, and surrounding areas.

Nearly 100,000 people call this rugged city home, and a visit here can be a pleasant diversion in any season. The city's **Spirit Mountain** recreational area (218/628-2891) offers great Alpine and Nordic skiing in the winter, and camping and hiking in the summer, just ten minutes from downtown Duluth. When the weather's warm, everyone heads down to the lakefront, much of which has been redesigned for recreational uses.

Learn about the history of Lake Superior shipping at the fascinating **Canal Park Marine Museum** (Canal Park, Duluth, 218/727-2497); to find out when to expect a big ship, call the **Boatwatcher's Hotline** at 218/722-6489. No visit to Duluth is complete without a pilgrimage to the **Aerial Bridge**, which spans the canal that cuts Minnesota Point in two and opens up the city's harbor to the lake. The 1905 landmark is only one of two of its kind in the world, and it's a treat to watch the 300-foot roadway fly up the bridge's two towers, making their 50-foot journey in less than 15 seconds.

Another highlight is the *William A. Irvin*. This 600-foot U.S. Steel ore

TWIN CITIES REGION

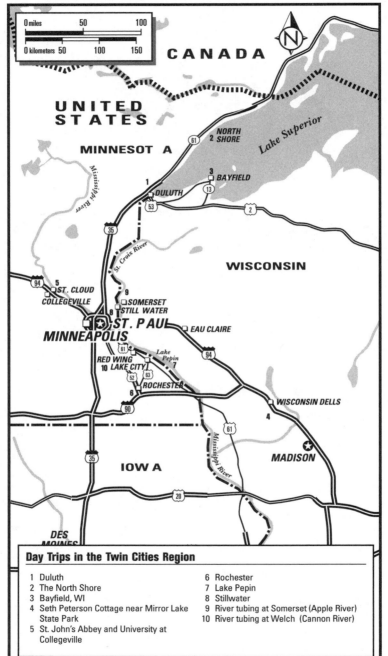

Day Trips in the Twin Cities Region

1 Duluth
2 The North Shore
3 Bayfield, WI
4 Seth Peterson Cottage near Mirror Lake State Park
5 St. John's Abbey and University at Collegeville
6 Rochester
7 Lake Pepin
8 Stillwater
9 River tubing at Somerset (Apple River)
10 River tubing at Welch (Cannon River)

carrier sailed the Great Lakes from 1938 to 1978 and is now open for 60-minute guided tours from May through October at its mooring just opposite the **Duluth Entertainment Center** near Canal Park (admission: $6 adults, $5 seniors and students, $3.50 children ages 3–12, free to children under 3; call 218/722-7876). You can also get a whirl around the harbor with **Vista Fleet's** fun and fascinating sightseeing tours, which last 1.75 hours and run from May through October. The dock is located next to the Irvin (admission: $8.50 adults, $4 children ages 3–11, free to children under 3; call 218/722-6218).

The **Canal Park** area, where Minnesota Point juts out from the shoreline, offers stunning views of the harbor, the lake, and the city itself, and its renovated warehouses offer lots of shopping and restaurant options. The big player is **Grandma's Saloon and Grill** (522 S. Lake Ave., 218/727-4192), a sprawling joint that is constantly mobbed; it hosts the state's largest marathon every June. From Canal Park, take a quick stroll up the Lake Walk to **Fitger's Brewery** (600 E. Superior St.), which was transformed in the 1980s into a festival shopping center, complete with interesting shops, a brew pub bearing the Fitger's name (218/726-1392), and the very fine Fitger's Inn.

Another Duluth attraction is **The Depot** (506 W. Michigan Ave., 218/727-8025), a lovingly restored 1892 railroad station that is now home to arts organizations and a popular train museum. And be sure to visit **Glensheen** (3300 London Rd., Duluth, 218/724-8864), a 39-room mansion of lush Jacobean splendor. Built on the shores of Lake Superior in 1908 for the Congdon family, this opulent home is now owned by the University of Minnesota and is open to the public for tours. If you're staying overnight, book a room at **Fitger's Inn** (218/722-8826) and ask for a lake view; the **Mansion** (3600 London Rd., 218/724-0739), a bed and breakfast housed in another Congdon-built mansion, next door to Glensheen; or at the city's largest hotel, the **Radisson Duluth** (505 W. Superior St., 218/727-8981), a round curiosity just down the street from the city's fine 1920s enclave of government buildings.

Getting There from the Twin Cities: *Take I-35 north.*

DAY TRIP: The North Shore

Distance from the Twin Cities: *150 to 300 miles, 3-hour to 6-hour drive*
The Lake Superior coastline stretches for 150 exceedingly scenic miles to the U.S.–Canadian border, and the sightseeing and recreational opportunities are boundless. The vistas are unlike anything else in Minnesota: craggy cliffs, deep forests, low-lying mountain ranges, and pounding waves. Highway 61 journeys all the way north from Duluth to Grand Portage, the North Shore's final Minnesota town.

The best scenery begins north of **Two Harbors**, a small town about 45 minutes north of Duluth. Twelve miles up the coast from Two Harbors is **Gooseberry Falls State Park** (218/834-3855), one of Minnesota's most-visited state parks, which offers stunning scenery, hiking, picnicking, and camping (call 800/246-CAMP to reserve one of the park's 70 sites).

Eight miles to the north, the Minnesota Historical Society operates **Split Rock Lighthouse** (218/226-6372), a turn-of-the-century landmark perched atop a sheer 100-foot cliff with awesome views of the lake. Admission: $4 adults, $3 seniors, $2 children ages 6–16, free to children under 6. Hours: May–Oct, daily 9–5.

Lutsen (about an hour north of Duluth, 218/663-7212) attracts hordes of wintertime weekenders to its challenging lake-view ski slopes and its gorgeous 1949 wood-timbered lodge and cabins. Although Lutsen's condos are comfortable, they are completely charmless; request a room in the lodge. If you can't get in at Lutsen, try **Bluefin Bay** in Tofte (218/663-7296), about ten minutes to the south. The facilities are modern, and many of the condos open directly onto the lake.

Continue north on Highway 61 to **Grand Marais**, one of the oldest fur-trading settlements on the lake. Fifteen miles past the city on the shores of Lake Superior is **Naniboujou Lodge**, a splendiferous 1929 hunting club that has to be seen to be believed. The main hall is a whirlwind of color, the handiwork of Canadian artist Antoine Gouffee. Shaped like an upside-down canoe, every surface of the entire room is awash in stylized abstractions of Cree characters, done up in vivid greens, reds, yellows, and blues; the kaleidoscope makes it the most endearing dining room in the state. The lodge is open May through October and some weekends in winter; some rooms ($65 to $75 per night) have fireplaces, all have private baths.

Thirty-five miles north of Grand Marais is **Grand Portage** and the site of the **Grand Portage National Monument** (218/387-2788), a late-seventeenth-century fort and fur trading post that's definitely worth a visit.

Northeastern Minnesota is also home to several major national recreational areas, including the pristine **Boundary Waters Canoe Area, Voyageurs National Park**, and **Superior National Forest**, all of which contain hundreds of thousands of acres of virgin forest, several thousand crystal-clear lakes and wilderness lands of unspoiled beauty. The town of **Ely** is a major stopping point for all three and is most accessible from Duluth by taking Highway 61 northeast just past Silver Bay, then continuing northwest away from the lake on Highway 1.

Getting There from the Twin Cities: *Take I-35 north to Duluth, then Highway 61.*

Split Rock Lighthouse

Phyllis Kedl/Unicorn Stock Photos

Lake Superior

Minnesota Office of Tourism

DAY TRIP: Bayfield, Wisconsin

Distance from the Twin Cities: *250 miles, 5-hour drive*
The southern coast of Lake Superior is nothing like its rocky, wave-pounded sibling to the north. From the bustling ports of Duluth and its sister city of Superior, Wisconsin, the southern shore's long stretches of calm, sandy beaches eventually lead to the Apostle Islands and the hill-hugging town of Bayfield, which is about 90 minutes east of Duluth/Superior and about a five-hour drive from the Twin Cities.

Bayfield was founded in 1856 and thrived until the turn of the century as a fishing, lumber, and mining center. Much of the brownstone used in New York City and Chicago was mined near Bayfield, and the town boomed until the material went out of fashion.

The town's numerous shops and galleries are quaint without veering too far into cloying, and there are a few restaurants worth checking out, too. Grab a tasty lunch—and save room for the peanut butter–chocolate pie—at **Maggie's** (257 Manypenny Ave., 715/779-5641). Step back into the 1940s for genuine roadhouse fare at **Gruenke's** (17 N. First St., 715/779-5480). Or if you really feel like putting on the dog, have supper or book a room at the **Old Rittenhouse Inn** (301 Rittenhouse Ave., 715/779-5111), a massive and wildly overdecorated Victorian mansion blessed with magical views of the Apostle Islands. Each room has a private bath and a fireplace, and rates run $99 to $199, including breakfast.

During the warm months, you can rent sailboats or kayaks from **Bayfield's Marina**, or catch the auto ferry for the 20-minute journey to picturesque **Madeline Island**, the largest of the Apostle Islands and home to **La Pointe**, which was founded in 1667, making it one of the oldest European settlements in the Midwest. The island is a relaxing, quiet, and beautiful getaway (the fall colors in late September and early October are particularly stunning), and there are a number of lodging possibilities. Pamper yourself at lovely **Woods Manor**, a seven-room B&B with fabulous views of the lake and Bayfield; rates run $109 to $189 per night, including breakfast; call 715/779-3102 or 800/822-6315. The **Inn on Madeline Island** offers lakeside condominiums just off the La Pointe marina and an 18-hole golf course, as well as a fine restaurant; call 715/747-6315.

If tenting it is more your speed, try the well-managed campground at scenic **Big Bay State Park**, about 6 miles outside La Pointe (715/779-3346). Or if you prefer a little privacy, more than a dozen cottages and homes scattered across the island are available for rent through the Inn on Madeline Island; call 715/747-6315.

Getting There from the Twin Cities: *Take I-35 north to Duluth, Highway 2 south to Superior, Highway 13 east to Bayfield.*

DAY TRIP: Seth Peterson Cottage

Distance from the Twin Cities: *250 miles, 5-hour drive*
Frank Lloyd Wright aficionados—or those with a romantic streak a mile long—should consider booking an overnight stay in one of the master architect's undiscovered treasures. The Seth Peterson Cottage, a Wright prize from the late 1950s, is about five hours southeast of the Twin Cities. The cottage's one drawback is that it is located dangerously close to what has to be one of the most hideous tourist traps in the United States, the **Wisconsin Dells**.

Happily, the nightmare that is the Dells will fly out of your head the minute you approach this intimate and appealing house, which has been available for overnight stays since a nonprofit group purchased it in 1992 and invested more than $300,000 into a much-needed restoration.

Laid out to take advantage of its superb site, high above the woods of **Mirror Lake State Park** on a secluded ridge overlooking pristine Mirror Lake, the 900-square-foot cottage is designed within an inch of its life, so much so that Wright's son-in-law described it as having "more architecture per square inch than any other Taliesin-designed structure."

The tiny house, a summer retreat for Mr. Peterson, is packed with details that exemplify a late-career Wright at the peak of his form: outside, a beautifully detailed sandstone-and-wood exterior that's sheltered by deep overhangs and punctured by panoramic picture windows; inside, soaring ceilings, smooth flagstone floors, a huge stone fireplace, and cozy rooms flooded with natural light. Both the kitchen and bath have been discreetly modernized, and the coffee table is well-stocked with plenty of Wright reading material.

Although it technically sleeps four, thanks to a queen-size hide-a-bed in the living room, it's a good idea to rent à deux—not only because the cottage is an exceedingly romantic spot, but also because access to the sole bathroom is through the bedroom, putting privacy at a premium.

Nabbing a reservation can be exasperatingly difficult: weekends are often booked a year in advance, and even a plain old Tuesday can be spoken for three or four months ahead of time. Rents run $225 per night or $995 per week. Call the Sand County Service Company at 608/254-6551 or write P.O. Box 409, Lake Delton, Wisconsin 53940. If you can't book an overnight stay, the cottage is open to the public for tours on the second Sunday of every month from 2 to 5 p.m., admission $2.

If you get a little peckish on the drive down, stop for a slice of pie at the **Norske Nook** in Osseo, Wisconsin (about 90 minutes east of St. Paul on I-94). The Nook (207 W. 7th St., Osseo 715/597-3069) bakes up at least two dozen varieties daily, and pie this good rarely comes out of a commercial kitchen.

Getting There from the Twin Cities: *Take I-94 south and east to the Wisconsin Dells, and follow the signs to Mirror Lake State Park.*

DAY TRIP: St. John's Abbey And University

Distance from the Twin Cities: *80 miles, 1.5-hour drive*
The small town of Collegeville is home to the world's largest Benedictine monastery, as well as some eye-popping architecture. Architect Marcel Breuer crafted a truly amazing assemblage of buildings at this men's college and preparatory school during the late 1950s and early 1960s, and a quick visit up to the campus (particularly during the autumn months, when the picturesque countryside is ablaze with color) should be on the itinerary of any Breuer fan.

Breuer devised a 100-year plan for the school (the original handsome brick buildings were centered around a European quadrangle) and designed its remarkable science hall and library, plus four dormitories. The most thrilling place on campus is Breuer's monumental 2,000-seat **Abbey Church**. Probably the most dramatic building in Minnesota, this 1954 poured-concrete masterpiece is simplicity itself: a huge, placid sanctuary of sloping walls, blunt geometric forms, and cleverly placed windows, all of which work to make it appear as if the massive concrete ceiling is being supported by glass; a baptistery, flooded with light from an immense stained-glass window; and an adjacent bell tower, an overpowering sculptural slab that looms over the church and dominates the entire campus. Mass in this otherworldly place is a transcendent experience.

The **Hill Monastic Manuscript Library** (320/363-3514) is a world-famous scholarly center with an astounding collection of early Christian manuscripts. On a lighter note, the monks bake a classic loaf of cracked-wheat bread, and you shouldn't leave campus without stocking up. Call 320/363-2011 for details.

Getting There from the Twin Cities: *Take I-94 north to Collegeville, about 10 miles past St. Cloud.*

DAY TRIP: Rochester

Distance from the Twin Cities: *90 miles, 1.75-hour drive*

Life in this company town centers around the world-famous **Mayo Clinic**. Dr. William Mayo and his sons Will and Charlie helped start the fledgling St. Mary's Hospital in 1889, and their revolutionary surgical techniques drew patients and other physicians from around the country.

Mayo Medical Center

In 1914, they founded their unique group practice and named it the Mayo Clinic. Unlike other medical practices of the time, the Mayo pioneered a scheme to offer a wide variety of specialists for promoting total patient care, a widely copied wellness management model that the clinic continues to use to this day.

Today the clinic is one of the world's most renowned healthcare institutions, as well as the home of a prestigious medical school and a giant research unit, and has more than 800 physicians and 7,000 other medical personnel. Free tours of the clinic are available Monday through Friday at 10 a.m. in the Judd Auditorium (200 1st St. SW, 507/284-9258); reservations recommended for groups of ten or more.

Get a glimpse at how the Mayos lived at **Mayowood** (3720 Mayowood Rd. SW), their palatial 1891 mansion. The huge, 57-room house, located on 3,000 acres with commanding views of the Zumbro River valley, is now owned by the Olmstead County Historical Society and is open to the public for an interesting one-hour tour. Admission: $8 adults, $5 children ages 15 and under. Hours: Varies, call 507/287-8691.

Another magnificent doctor's-house tour is the **Plummer House** (1091 Plummer Ln.), a 1924 Tudor now owned by the Rochester Parks and Recreation Department. The house is most noteworthy for its carefully manicured 11-acre gardens, which are open to the public daily from sunrise to sunset. Dr. Henry Plummer played a significant role in the development of the Mayo Clinic, joining the Mayo's staff in 1901. Admission: $2 adults, $1 children. Hours vary; call 507/281-6160.

The Plummer name is also attached to the Clinic's most beloved building, at **2nd Street SW and 2nd Avenue SW**, a 1928 wedding cake of a tower, topped with an open belfry housing the Rochester Carillon; its collection of 56 bells (with a range of four and one-half octaves) makes it the largest of its kind in North America. Recitals are regularly scheduled; call 507/284-2511 for details. Look for an image of Dr. Plummer—clutching a handful of drawings—that's carved into the corner of this richly detailed building.

The hotel of choice in Rochester is the mighty **Kahler Hotel** (20 2nd Ave. SW, Rochester, 507/282-2581), a 1920s-era grand dame with over 700 rooms and suites located across the street from the Mayo Clinic.

Getting There from the Twin Cities: *Take Highway 52 south.*

DAY TRIP: Lake Pepin

Distance from the Twin Cities: *50 miles, 1-hour drive*
One of the Mississippi River's most beguiling charms is Lake Pepin. The landscape changes from rolling hills to dramatic cliffs, and the Father of Waters widens—at some points, up to a mile—for some of the state's most beautiful scenery.

Besides all of this natural beauty, and all its attendant recreational opportunities, there is also plenty to see and explore in the Lake Pepin region.

Start at **Red Wing**, which is upstream from the lake and one of the state's great river towns. The town itself has an enchanting collection of brick commercial buildings, churches, a fine courthouse, several public squares, and a levee that still attracts major boating traffic, including periodic visits from the *Delta Queen*, a luxury paddlewheel passenger boat. The restored **Sheldon Theatre**, a 1904 beauty and the nation's first municipal theater, was fully restored in the late 1980s and now lures an impressive draw of musical and theatrical talent.

There are lots of antiques stores here, as well as a number of pottery outlets, including the famous **Red Wing Pottery** company (612/388-3562). The city's top hotel is the **St. James** (406 Main St., Red Wing, 612/338-2846); ask for a room in the old section. Tour the **Cannon Valley Trail**, a 19-mile hiking and paved biking trail following the scenic Cannon River from Red Wing to **Cannon Falls** (call 507/263-3954). You can rent a bike at **Ripley's Rental** in Red Wing (612/388-5984) or at the **Welch General Store** (612/388-7494) in tiny Welch, about midway along the Cannon Valley Trail.

Cross the Mississippi at Red Wing and proceed south on the Wisconsin side of the river; the Minnesota side, Highway 61, is a plain four-lane highway, while the Wisconsin alternative, Highway 35, winds and curves its way over hills on the top of the bluffs. Proceed south to the delightful town of **Stockholm**. There are several antique stores, art galleries, and shops in this small town, as well as two excellent restaurants, the **Star Café** (715/442-2023) and the **Jenny Lind Café & Bakery** (715/442-2358).

Or, if you feel like a more memorable meal, consider lunch or dinner at the **Harbor View Café**, on the banks of the river in **Pepin** (715/442-3893, open Thursday through Monday, May to October; no credit cards), about

---

Aveda Spa and Retreat

This soothing, rejuvenating center of wellness and beauty is the brainchild of Horst Rechelbacher, the mastermind behind the popular Aveda products line. It's a fabulous place for lunch or dinner or for a day or a week of pampered self-indulgence. Daily packages start at $156, and weekly rates hover around $1,500. The spa is located at 1015 Cascade N., Osceola, Wisconsin, 715/294-4465, about 70 miles northeast of the Twin Cities in the St. Croix River valley.

---

15 minutes south of Stockholm. This ambitious and inviting restaurant draws a regular clientele from devoted foodies all around the region. Tiny little Pepin (Laura Ingalls Wilder is probably its most famous resident) also has a number of galleries, antique stores, a professional summer theater company, and a handful of charming bed and breakfasts.

Continue south to **Nelson** and go back across the river at **Wabasha**, where you'll encounter more small-town delights, including antiques, a bustling marina, and several B&Bs; have an ice-cream cone at **The Cooler** (257 W. Main St., 612/565-2585), located in the old city hall.

Go back upriver to **Lake City**, appropriately named because of its strategic location on Lake Pepin. Lake City is crawling with boating, swimming, and other lake-related recreational opportunities, and is just downriver from **Frontenac State Park** (612/345-3401). This pretty park offers panoramic river views, as well as camping, hiking, picnicking, and fishing.

Getting There from the Twin Cities: *Take Highway 61 south to Red Wing, cross the river to Wisconsin Highway 35, and head south to Wabasha; cross the river again at Wabasha and head north to Lake City.*

DAY TRIP: Stillwater

Distance from the Twin Cities: *15 miles, 20-minute drive*

Minnesota's oldest city is also one of its most idyllic. Picturesque Stillwater has been hugging this stretch of the St. Croix River for almost 150 years, and its well-preserved nineteenth-century downtown area is a haven for locals and out-of-towners, who come for the great shopping, the wonderful array of restaurants, and the largest concentration of bed and breakfasts in the state (see Chapter 3, Where to Stay). Stillwater can be mobbed on the weekends, and the best time to enjoy its quiet, sophisticated pleasures is on a much less frenetic weekday.

Antiques are big business in Stillwater. **The Mill Antiques** (410 N. Main

St., 612/430-1818) has 200 dealers on its three levels. Ditto the **Isaac Staples Sawmill Complex** (410 N. Main St., 430-1816). Others worth peeking into include **American Gothic Antiques** (236 S. Main St., 612/439-7709), **Main Street Antiques** (118 N. Main St., 612/430-3110), **Midtown Antique Mall** (214 S. Main St., 612/430-0808), and **More Antiques** (312 N. Main St., 612/439-1110).

Stillwater is also a haven for those who love a good book. **St. Croix Antiquarian Booksellers** (232 S. Main St., 612/ 430-0732) puts 25 sellers under one roof; you'll find 30 vendors at the **Stillwater Book Center** (229 N. Main St., 612/430-8183);

Kayaking at Welch Mill

and philosophy and theology are the specialties of **Loome Theological Booksellers** (320 N. 4th St., 612/430-1092).

The town is also the gateway to the recreational possibilities of the St. Croix River, and its docks are packed in the warm-weather months with an amazing array of pleasure craft. The river itself is federally protected, and much of its sylvan beauty remains intact.

Getting There from the Twin Cities: *Take Highway 36 east from St. Paul.*

DAY TRIP: River Tubing Areas

Distance from the Twin Cities: *Welch, 50 miles, 1-hour drive; Somerset, Wisconsin, 50 miles, 1-hour drive*
There's no better way to relax on a humid summer's day than to float down a river on an inner tube, and there are two places—both about an hour's drive from the Twin Cities—that are designed for just such a sun-soaked folly.

At **Welch Mill Canoeing and Tubing** (14818 264th Street Path, Welch, 612/388-9857 or 800/657-6760), $5 gets you a large tube, a 15-minute shuttle trip upriver, and a quiet and exceedingly scenic four-hour aquatic sojourn down the **Cannon River**. The river runs through a county park, which means the surroundings are wooded and unspoiled, and the rolling topography and clean, waist-deep river (complete with gentle rapids) are a treat when taken in from the vantage point of a big old inner tube. Pack a picnic lunch (rent an additional inner tube for your cooler) and a ton of sunblock, and make it a day for the whole family. The mill also rents canoes at very reasonable rates. Weekends and holidays are naturally the most popular days on the river, but on most weekdays it can feel as if you have the entire valley to yourself. Welch is located about 1 hour southeast of the Twin Cities, about ten minutes west of Red Wing. Hours: Mon–Fri 10–dusk, Sat and Sun 8–dusk.

Tubing connoisseurs prefer the Cannon to the goings-on at the much more well-established operations of the **Float-Rite Park** in Somerset, Wisconsin (Highway 1, Somerset, 715/247-3453 or 800/826-7096). There's a lot more happening here, including miniature golf, volleyball courts, a video arcade, a campground, and more, but it all translates into more crowds, more noise, more litter, and much less relaxation. What's worse, the decidedly unspectacular **Apple River** lacks the natural beauty of the Cannon, and it's much shallower, which means that unwanted scrapes are a lot more common. Tube rates are higher, too: $8 on the weekends and holidays, $7 during the week.

Getting There from the Twin Cities: *Take Highway 52 south 25 miles to Highway 50, head east for 15 miles to County Road 7, and then 2 miles to Welch; take Highway 36 east, cross the St. Croix River at Stillwater, then take Highway 64 northeast 25 miles to Somerset, Wisconsin.*

APPENDIX: CITY·SMART BASICS

IMPORTANT PHONE NUMBERS

EMERGENCY

Police, 911
Fire, 911
Ambulance, 911

MAJOR HOSPITALS

CHILDREN'S HEALTH CARE MINNEAPOLIS
612/813-6100

CHILDREN'S HEALTH CARE ST. PAUL
612/220-6000

FAIRVIEW SOUTHDALE HOSPITAL
612/924-5000

FAIRVIEW-RIVERSIDE MEDICAL CENTER
612/672-6000

HENNEPIN COUNTY MEDICAL CENTER
612/347-2121

NORTH MEMORIAL MEDICAL CENTER
612/520-5100

ST. PAUL-RAMSEY MEDICAL CENTER
612/221-3456

UNITED HOSPITAL
612/220-8000

UNIVERSITY HOSPITAL AND CLINIC
612/626-3000

EMERGENCY CENTERS

ALCOHOL AND DRUG INTERVENTION AND REFERRAL
612/879-3501

CRISIS INTERVENTION CENTER
612/347-3161
TTY, 612/347-5711

FIRST CALL FOR HELP (UNITED WAY)
612/335-5000

POISON CENTER
612/347-3141
TTY, 612/337-7474

SUICIDE PREVENTION
612/347-2222

VISITOR INFORMATION

MINNEAPOLIS CONVENTION AND VISITORS ASSOCIATION
612/661-4700

ST. PAUL CONVENTION AND VISITORS BUREAU
612/297-6985

BLOOMINGTON CONVENTION AND VISITORS BUREAU
612/858-8500

MINNESOTA OFFICE OF TOURISM
800/657-3700

CITY TOURS

CAPITAL CITY TROLLEYS
612/223-5600

MEDICINE LAKE/GREY LINES
612/469-5020
METRO CONNECTIONS
612/333-8687

RIVER CITY TROLLEYS
612/673-5123

CAR RENTAL

AVIS
800/831-2847
Three Twin Cities locations

BUDGET
612/727-2600
Seven Twin Cities locations

ENTERPRISE RENT-A-CAR
800/325-8007
Seventeen Twin Cities locations

HERTZ
800/654-3131
Two Twin Cities locations

NATIONAL CAR RENTAL
800/227-7368
Three Twin Cities locations

RENT-A-WRECK
612/474-6554
Two western suburban locations

THRIFTY CAR RENTAL
800/367-2277
Nine Twin Cities locations

CITY MEDIA

NEWSPAPERS: DAILIES

FINANCE AND COMMERCE
615 S. 7th St., Minneapolis
612/333-4244   DMP

Legal notices and a smattering of financial and investment news.

ST. PAUL PIONEER PRESS
345 Cedar St., St. Paul
612-222-5011   DSP
The underdog in Twin Cities journalism tries harder, and often succeeds. The paper's columnists (Karen Lamphear and Nick Coleman) are more readable than their Minneapolis counterparts, and critics Jim Walsh (popular music), Larry Millett (architecture), and Chris Hewitt (movies) are tops in their fields. Monday through Saturday is a quarter, and Sunday is a buck.

STAR TRIBUNE
425 Portland Ave., Minneapolis
612/673-4000   DMP
One of the only daily papers in America to eschew its city's name, the Strib is the result of a 1980s merger between the morning *Minneapolis Tribune* and the evening *Minneapolis Star*. The Sunday edition ($1.50) is read by more than 700,000 Minnesotans, and the Monday through Saturday versions (35 cents) have a circulation of 400,000.

NEWSPAPERS: ALTERNATIVE WEEKLIES

CITY PAGES
401 N. Third St., Minneapolis
612/375-1015   DMP
The *Reader*'s fierce competitor, with news, arts, and an extensive nightlife guide, including many useful pages of bar and nightclub ads. Wednesday. Free.

TWIN CITIES READER
10 S. 5th St., Minneapolis
612/321-7300   DMP

Covering the news, arts, and entertainment scenes for more than 20 years. A thorough events guide. Every Wednesday. Free.

SPECIALIZED PUBLICATIONS

EMPLOYMENT WEEKLY
10 S. 5th St., Minneapolis
612/321-7300 DMP
A job-hunter's resource, published each Wednesday by the *Twin Cities Reader*.

FAMILY TIMES
P.O. Box 16422, St. Louis Park
612/922-6186 GTC
Family-oriented news and entertainment, published mid-month ten times per year.

focusPOINT
401 N. 3rd St., Minneapolis
612/288-9008 DMP
Weekly local and national news and opinion for gays, lesbians, bisexuals, and transgenders, published every Wednesday. Free.

LAVENDER MAGAZINE
2344 Nicollet Ave. S., Minneapolis
612/871-2237 MP
News, politics, and arts and entertainment for gays, lesbians, bisexuals, and transgenders, published every other Friday.

MINNEAPOLIS ST. PAUL CITYBUSINESS
527 Marquette Ave., Minneapolis
612/288-2100 DMP
In-depth business and financial news, every Friday. Newsstands.

MINNESOTA JOURNAL OF LAW AND POLITICS
527 Marquette Ave., Minneapolis
612/335-8808 DMP

Irreverent and occasionally thoughtful monthly magazine that dissects local politics and the Twin Cities legal industry. Newsstands.

MINNESOTA SPORTSPAGE
514 Nicollet Mall, Minneapolis
612/359-3395 MP
Every facet of sports, both amateur and professional, throughout the state of Minnesota. Weekly. Free.

MINNESOTA WOMEN'S PRESS
771 Raymond Ave., St. Paul
612/646-6938 SP
A newspaper covering the diversity of women's experiences, published every other Wednesday. Free.

Q MONTHLY
10 S. 5th St., Minneapolis
612/321-7300 DMP
News, features, profiles, and arts and entertainment publication for gays, lesbians, and bisexuals, published on the first of the month by the *Twin Cities Reader*. Free.

SKYWAY NEWS
15 S. 5th St., Minneapolis
612/375-9222 DMP
A weekly newspaper covering both the downtown areas of Minneapolis and St. Paul. Tuesdays. Free.

SOUTHWEST JOURNAL
4948 Washburn Ave. S., Minneapolis
612/922-6263 MP
The Twin Cities is home to a bevy of community-based newspapers, and this is the most comprehensive, well-written one of the bunch, covering the upscale south Minneapolis neighborhoods surrounding the busy Chain of Lakes. Every other Wednesday. Free.

INFO FOR ALL:

American Jewish World
Asian American Pages
Computer User
Insight News
Minneapolis Spokesman
Minnesota Parent
St. Paul Recorder

MAGAZINES

Architecture Minnesota
Catholic Digest
Colors
Corporate Report Minnesota
Minnesota History
Minnesota Monthly
Mpls/St. Paul
Twin Cities Business Monthly

RADIO STATIONS

KBCW 1470 AM/Country
KBEM 88.5 FM/Jazz
KCFE 105.7 FM/Contemporary rock
KDWA 1460 AM/'50s and '60s
   country
KDWB 101.3 FM/Contemporary
   rock
KEEY 102.1 FM/Country
KEGE 93.7 FM/Modern rock
KFAI 90.3 FM/Community-based
   alternative
KFAN 1130 AM/Sports, talk
KKCM 1530 AM/Christian music
KLBB 1400 AM/'40s, '50s, '60s
KMJZ 950 AM, 104.1 FM/Jazz
KMOJ 89.9 FM/Soul, jazz, reggae,
   blues
KMZZ 980 AM/Hard rock
KNOF 95.3 FM/Religious
KNOW 91.1 FM/Minnesota Public
   Radio news/talk
KQQL 107.9 FM/Oldies
KQRS 92.5 FM, 1440 AM/Rock
KSJN 99.5 FM/Minnesota Public
Radio/classical music

KSTP 1500 AM/News and talk
KSTP 94.5 FM/Contemporary pop
KTCJ 690 AM/Progressive rock
KTCZ 97.1 FM/Progressive rock
KTIS 900 AM, 98.5 FM/Religious
KUOM 770 AM/University of
   Minnesota alternative
KYCR 1570 AM/Religious
   programming
WBOB 100.3 FM/Country
WCAL 89.3 FM/Public classical
WCCO 830 AM/News, general
   interest, "The Good Neighbor"
WCTS 1030 AM/Religious news and
   music
WIMN 1220 AM/Nostalgia
WIXK 1590 AM, 107.1 FM/Country
WLKX 95.9 FM/Country
WLTE 102.9 FM/Contemporary pop
WMIN 740 AM/'40s, '50s, '60s
WMNN 1330 AM/News and
   information
WREV 105.1 FM/Alternative rock
WWTC 1280 AM/Children's, Radio
   AAHS

TV STATIONS

ABC: KSTP Channel 5
CBS: WCCO Channel 4
FOX: WFTC Channel 29
NBC: KARE Channel 11
PBS: KTCA Channel 2 and KTCI
   Channel 17
WBS: KMSP Channel 9
INDEPENDENT: KLGT Channel 23
AND KXLI Channel 41

BABYSITTING & CHILD CARE

CLUB KID
7585 France Ave. S., Edina
612/831-1055   **GTC**

KID'S PLAY
5611 Xerxes Ave. N., Brooklyn
Center
612/566-2114   **GTC**

KID'S QUEST
Eden Prairie Center, Eden Prairie
612/941-1007   **GTC**

SICK CHILD CARE
550 Osborne Rd., Fridley
612/780-6600   **GTC**

BANKING

FIRST BANK MINNEAPOLIS
601 2nd Ave. S., Minneapolis
612/973-4004   **DMP**

FIRST BANK ST. PAUL
332 Minnesota St., St. Paul
612/973-1111   **DSP**

FIRSTAR BANK
386 N. Wabasha, St. Paul
612/293-9000   **DSP**

NORWEST BANK
6th and Marquette, Minneapolis
612/667-9378   **DMP**

TCF BANK
801 Marquette Ave., Minneapolis
612/823-2265   **DMP**

DISABLED ACCESS INFORMATION

ACCESS PROJECT
1300 Mendota Heights Rd.,
Mendota Heights
612-405-2482   **GTC**

COURAGE CENTER
3915 Golden Valley Rd.,
Golden Valley
612/520-0520   **GTC**

MULTICULTURAL RESOURCES

CENTRO CULTURAL CHICANO
2025 Nicollet Ave. S., Minneapolis
612/874-1412   **MP**

GAY AND LESBIAN HELPLINE
310 E. 38th St., Minneapolis
612/822-8661   **MP**

GERMANIC AMERICAN INSTITUTE
301 Summit Ave., St. Paul
612/222-7027   **SP**

MINNEAPOLIS AMERICAN INDIAN CENTER
1530 E. Franklin Ave., Minneapolis
612/871-4555   **MP**

SONS OF NORWAY INTERNATIONAL
1455 W. Lake St., Minneapolis
612/827-3611   **MP**

VIETNAMESE CULTURAL ASSOCIATION OF MINNESOTA
2985 Northview St., Roseville
612/297-5451   **GTC**

POST OFFICES

Post offices are located in nearly every Twin Cities metropolitan area community. The two main branches are in downtown Minneapolis and downtown St. Paul, and a 24-hour station is located at Minneapolis/ St. Paul International Airport, just outside the Charles A. Lindbergh Terminal.

AIRPORT AIR MAIL CENTER
5000 Green Ln.
St. Paul, MN 55111

DOWNTOWN MINNEAPOLIS
100 S. 1st St.
Minneapolis, MN 55401

DOWNTOWN ST. PAUL
180 E. Kellogg Blvd.
St. Paul, MN 55101

PUBLIC HOLIDAYS

Martin Luther King Jr. Day
Presidents' Day
Memorial Day
Independence Day
Labor Day
Columbus Day
Veterans Day
Thanksgiving Day
Christmas Day

TIME AND WEATHER

MINNESOTA HIGHWAY CONDITIONS
612/296-3076

ROUND-THE-CLOCK WEATHER UPDATES
612/375-0830

INDEX

Other Books from John Muir Publications

Rick Steves' Books

Asia Through the Back Door, 400 pp., $17.95
Europe 101: History and Art for the Traveler, 352 pp., $17.95
Mona Winks: Self-Guided Tours of Europe's Top Museums, 432 pp., $18.95
Rick Steves' Baltics & Russia, 160 pp., $9.95
Rick Steves' Europe, 576 pp., $18.95
Rick Steves' France, Belgium & the Netherlands, 304 pp., $15.95
Rick Steves' Germany, Austria & Switzerland, 272 pp., $14.95
Rick Steves' Great Britain & Ireland, 320 pp., $15.95
Rick Steves' Italy, 224 pp., $13.95
Rick Steves' Scandinavia, 192 pp., $13.95
Rick Steves' Spain & Portugal, 240 pp., $13.95
Rick Steves' Europe Through the Back Door, 512 pp., $19.95
Rick Steves' French Phrase Book, 192 pp., $5.95
Rick Steves' German Phrase Book, 192 pp., $5.95
Rick Steves' Italian Phrase Book, 192 pp., $5.95
Rick Steves' Spanish & Portuguese Phrase Book, 336 pp., $7.95
Rick Steves' French/German/Italian Phrase Book, 320 pp., $7.95

A Natural Destination Series

Belize: A Natural Destination, 344 pp., $16.95
Costa Rica: A Natural Destination, 416 pp., $18.95
Guatemala: A Natural Destination, 360 pp., $16.95

City·Smart™ Guidebook Series

City·Smart Guidebook: Cleveland, 208 pp., $14.95
City·Smart Guidebook: Denver, 256 pp., $14.95
City·Smart Guidebook: Minneapolis/St. Paul, 232 pp., $14.95
City·Smart Guidebook: Nashville, 256 pp., $14.95
City·Smart Guidebook: Portland, 232 pp., $14.95
City·Smart Guidebook: Tampa/St. Petersburg, 256 pp., $14.95

Travel+Smart™ Trip Planners

American Southwest Travel+Smart Trip Planner, 256 pp., $14.95
Colorado Travel+Smart Trip Planner, 248 pp., $14.95
Eastern Canada Travel+Smart Trip Planner, 272 pp., $15.95
Florida Gulf Coast Travel+Smart Trip Planner, 232 pp., $14.95
Hawaii Travel+Smart Trip Planner, 256 pp., $14.95
Kentucky/Tennessee Travel+Smart Trip Planner, 248 pp., $14.95
Minnesota/Wisconsin Travel+Smart Trip Planner, 240 pp., $14.95
New England Travel+Smart Trip Planner, 256 pp., $14.95
Northern California Travel+Smart Trip Planner, 272 pp., $15.95
Pacific Northwest Travel+Smart Trip Planner, 240 pp., $14.95

Other Terrific Travel Titles

The 100 Best Small Art Towns in America, 256 pp., $15.95
The Big Book of Adventure Travel, 384 pp., $17.95

Indian America: A Traveler's Companion, 480 pp., $18.95
The People's Guide to Mexico, 608 pp., $19.95
Ranch Vacations: The Complete Guide to Guest and Resort, Fly-Fishing, and Cross-Country Skiing Ranches, 632 pp., $22.95
Understanding Europeans, 272 pp., $14.95
Undiscovered Islands of the Caribbean, 336 pp., $16.95
Watch It Made in the U.S.A.: A Visitor's Guide to the Companies that Make Your Favorite Products, 328 pp., $16.95
The World Awaits, 280 pp., $16.95
The Birder's Guide to Bed and Breakfasts: U.S. and Canada, 416 pp., $17.95

Automotive Titles

The Greaseless Guide to Car Care, 272 pp., $19.95
How to Keep Your Subaru Alive, 480 pp., $21.95
How to Keep Your Toyota Pickup Alive, 392 pp., $21.95
How to Keep Your VW Alive, 464 pp., $25

Ordering Information

Please check your local bookstore for our books, or call **1-800-888-7504** to order direct and to receive a complete catalog. A shipping charge will be added to your order total.

Send all inquiries to:
John Muir Publications
P.O. Box 613
Santa Fe, NM 87504